The Good Life

The Good Life

The Moral Individual in an Antimoral World

Cheryl Mendelson

BLOOMSBURY

LONDON · BERLIN · NEW YORK · SYDNEY

First published in Great Britain 2012

Copyright © 2012 by Cheryl Mendelson

Bloomsbury Publishing Plc
50 Bedford Square
London WC1B 3DP

www.bloomsbury.com

Bloomsbury Publishing, London, New York, Berlin and Sydney

A CIP catalogue record for this book is available from the British Library

ISBN 9781408833674

10 9 8 7 6 5 4 3 2 1

Typeset by Westchester Book Group
Printed in Great Britain by Clays Ltd, St Ives Plc

For Edward

CONTENTS

Introduction

THIS IS A book about the *moral mentality*, a distinctive
mind-set that underlies key elements of Western culture
and much of modern world culture. It concentrates on aspects
of this mentality that, I believe, particularly need attention
today and shows how they fit into a larger picture that I have
drawn here only in outline. The subject could fill a much longer book, in fact whole shelves of books, but a short one works
best to present the big picture that it strives for.

Its subject is a dauntingly difficult one. The very word *moral*
has multiple ambiguities, and its several meanings open out
into vast complexes of thought, feeling, and action. It can be
legitimately approached from scores of different angles and
levels, yet because it is highly charged, unfamiliar approaches
often inspire fury, condescension, or offense. Morality inter-
weaves reason, knowledge, instinct, intuition, and emotion in
an intricate network of personal, historical, and cultural patterns. Books and essays about morality thus often seem guilty
of overemphases and underemphases. The nature of moral
concern itself acts as an obstacle to adequate descriptions of it
outside those in novels and poems. Moral concern ordinarily

functions as a dimension or a valence of thought, not as its focus. Thus any head-on approach to the subject tends to sound slightly false or "off" simply because it forces us to center attention on things that properly form part of the receding background of consciousness.

But perhaps the biggest problem for any contemporary writer about morality is that decades of contention about "values" have resulted in such a thorough politicization of the subject that the term itself suggests a variety of unpleasant political sub-texts. How this has happened, and why it must be undone, is a central theme of this book. But given that the political Right has now falsely claimed morality as its turf, the reader might find it useful at the outset to know that I have always favored labor unions, strong regulation of business and finance, universal healthcare, abortion rights, sexual and racial equality, and gay rights, and that I oppose the death penalty and most military adventures; however, in matters of private and family life, some of my views lean in directions that tend, often misleadingly, to be labeled conservative.

This book is written for people who have the moral mentality, and it describes things they are already familiar with: how they themselves think, feel, and act; the increasingly strong antagonism to morality, or antimoralism, in our culture; the false moral pretensions of ideologues who are actually pseudomoral and antimoral. It is a book about the obvious addressed to the convinced. But when denials of the obvious are loud enough, a book like this has its place.

The book is not neutral. It presents a sketch of some of the things that morality is in both its personal and social dimensions, but it does so for moral purposes. Thus it offers a morally charged description of phenomena that historians, sociologists, biologists, anthropologists, psychologists, neurologists, and other experts, all in their own ways, attempt to describe factually and noncommittally. This book, that is, tries to isolate some characteristics, strengths, and vulnerabilities of moral thinking and acting that matter now *morally*.

The subject matter will raise in readers' minds the questions of who on earth could be qualified to write such a book and why it got written. These are legitimate questions, and the only possible answers are not reassuring. As a work of moral observation, this book is necessarily an amateur work for the reason that there is no such thing as a moral expert—no holy men or women, no seers, no scientists, scholars, or philosophers who by virtue of their professions know the right answers. No academic training exists that produces wisdom or goodness in its students; the best moral judges are certified by no boards and pass no qualifying exams. Knowledge and intelligence are sometimes vital to good moral judgment, but if the question is moral, the boundaries of the answer are always going to be wide, fluid, and human, not narrow or technical. Morally speaking, once we are adults, we are rarely justified in setting aside the responsibility to judge for ourselves and relying instead on what some trained or blessed individual tells us is right. The people we rely on for advice when we are troubled and uncertain are merely other people like ourselves on whom circumstance, upbringing, moral effort, or experience may have bestowed insight—insight that they may or may not be able to put to use in their own lives. Moral judgment always addresses the question "What should I do?" but sometimes good judgment fails to lead to good action.

This is a work of moral reflection—an essay, not an empirical study—but it is not a book of moral advice except in an
attenuated sense. To write it, I had to overcome a sense of my
own limits, moral and otherwise, and I managed to do so only
because wiser people than I persuaded me that many readers
would find the ideas in it helpful and encouraging. Its themes
have been a lifelong preoccupation, inspired by events that rendered its questions a matter of urgent interest and provided unusual personal and academic opportunities to grapple with them.
I will give a nutshell account of these events here because moral
reflection draws upon the whole person in ways that mathematics, physics, or carpentry do not, and readers are entitled to
ask who is talking.

THE ROOTS OF this book extend back to three dislocations in my
life, one in adolescence, another in my first professional career
as an academic, and another in my second professional career as
a lawyer. I spent my childhood on a small farm in the Appala-
chian southwest corner of Pennsylvania. The closest big town,
Morgantown, West Virginia, was about thirty miles south. This
was a world of hills, coal-mining towns, and farms, with an odd
mixture of people, some of them early-twentieth-century immigrants who came to work the mines and some men like my
father, descendants of the first settlers in the region, "borderlanders," as historians call them now, from southern Scotland
and northern Ireland and England who arrived in the 1760s.
These people took part in some of the fiercest, cruelest fighting of
the American Indian Wars and were hot-blooded Revolutionar-
ies. When the Revolutionary War ended, they launched the
Whiskey Rebellion. Later, they were eager participants in each

of the nation's wars. They were always wholehearted fighters, with contempt for Quakerish pacifism. Yet, like the Quakers, they had the special psychology that I call the moral mentality, with the special moral capacity for self-reflection and self-criticism.

Many people in my childhood world spent their lives in what amounted to a moral quest. This was not something they talked about or, I imagine, consciously thought of, and it rarely assumed any heroic form. Nonetheless, they attempted to shape their lives by strongly felt moral imperatives, even if they avoided churches and even if they were not models of sober respectability. Envy, drunkenness, lust, dishonesty, and general crankiness were often more visible than uprightness. Even so, their lives had a moral substrate that gave them a characteristic outlook and led them to regard wealth, fame, and power as illegitimate, though tempting, goals. Sometimes these attitudes flowed out of resentment, but mostly they emerged from a strong egalitarian instinct that their moral sensibility dictated.

This sensibility led them to turn up their noses at the cultural prizes depicted on television and to scorn the colleges and jobs and lives they saw there. Their young people were discouraged from donning gray flannel suits and climbing corporate career ladders. Knowledge and brains were respected, but most of all in people who had read and educated themselves. Except for a boy or two who went off to learn medicine or law, or a girl to learn some music, they preferred to keep their children home. Their teachers were trained in the local college or other small regional schools.

Old county families not uncommonly raised their boys to think of a job, any job, as a bad thing. Of course, a man was expected to work and support his family, but he should not have a boss if he could help it; he should be his own boss. All authorities—politicians, doctors, lawyers, and especially preachers—were to be mistrusted and should get no more respect or higher status than anyone else did. "That's just a man," my father used to say. He also taught his children that most preachers were crooked, among other reasons because they encouraged people to take stories in the Bible literally. He made a special point of making me understand that the biblical account of the rainbow as a sign of God's promise not to flood us again was just a tale, though with a good moral, and he showed me what happened when light passed through a prism.

In the 1960s, the world that I grew up in succumbed to a variety of blows—mine closings, farm failures, emigration, and the homogenizing power of television—but it had been an anachronism long before then. It had lasted two centuries. At thirteen, I was just old enough to have been thoroughly enculturated before it crumbled. My siblings and I were mystified by the lives of the rich children we saw on television. Our games, houses, school, and play were nothing like theirs. I had gone to a church in whose yard my eighteenth-century ancestors were buried. I recited the same jump-rope rhymes as my great-grandmother, knitted with the same overhand motion, and sewed a gored skirt on her treadle machine. On television, grown men came to blows only in westerns and crime shows, but I knew that my father, with my uncles standing behind him, had punched a man for publicly insulting him—hard enough to knock him off his feet and leave him half-conscious. In my world, my parents, who recited poetry to each other and on winter nights read *Pilgrim's Progress* and *David Copperfield* aloud to their children, were not unusual in having married at seventeen and having had their first four children before they were twenty-five. When we left the county, at thirteen, I, too, expected in four or five years to be married and a mother.

From that world and those expectations, I moved almost overnight to the high-tech suburban world of central and coastal Florida that was later described vividly by Tom Wolfe in *The Right Stuff*. The shock was severe. I was in the same country and spoke the same language, but all the social signposts had been torn down. Florida in the sixties was undergoing a massive influx of newcomers. Cape Canaveral and NASA brought to the region astronauts, scientists, engineers, and air force and army personnel, and they in turn created a boom economy that drew huge numbers of distressed people looking for work, sun, beaches, and better lives. Florida became a society of strangers.

The thrill of the space program and the heated economy created an excitement that was more dark and desperate than hopeful and high-spirited. It was a rootless, lonely time and place. The high school students I was thrown in with were cool in a way that even television had not led me to expect. Misbehavior I had seen plenty of, but open commitment to it was something surprising. The egalitarian, antiauthoritarian attitudes I had absorbed at home were absent; money and status were openly worshipped and the poor viewed as inferior and misbehaving. On average, my classmates seemed to me to be rich; they took it for granted that they would go to college. I, of course, assumed that I would not, even though I did well in school. The outdated, demanding curriculum in our country school back home, it turned out, had given my siblings and me a good preparation. I won a scholarship and went to college after all, over my father's objections.

A chasm began to open between me and my family after I graduated from the University of Florida, and I widened that chasm by going to graduate school at the University of Rochester. There I studied philosophy with an emphasis on ethics. The further down the academic road I went, the more incomprehensible my life seemed to my parents, who began to mourn the loss of their children along with their world. I, on the other hand, found a sort of kindred in the academy, where I met many people whose strong sense of moral vocation was familiar and comfortable. I did not connect my interest in moral philosophy or my attraction to the academy with this personal sense of comfort, but in retrospect I saw that they came from the same source.

Nonetheless, I could not think of the moral life or moral philosophy in the ways my colleagues did. Dissatisfied with the indifference of professional philosophy to the cultural and psychological determinants of moral thinking, in graduate school I began to read history, anthropology, psychology, and psychoanalytic theory. It seemed to me that, on the one hand, philosophers were alone in insisting on taking the moral life on its own terms, but that, on the other, this very respect confused their efforts to understand it. With my professors' encouragement, I ignored these doubts and joined the philosophy department at Purdue University, hoping that independence would end my qualms. In fact, it increased them, and I soon had to admit that I had taken a misstep. Despite my degrees, I thought that I did not know what I needed to know, and I accused myself of doing a disservice to my students by teaching material that I regarded as mostly empty. I left the university, hoping to write and pursue independent study and someday to return.

With the idea in mind that law would supply an empirical approach to the moral life and the moral mind, while also making it possible for me to support myself while continuing my work, I entered Harvard Law School. Once again I found myself in a world that seemed skewed and opaque. I had expected a second dip into the academy, but this was different—and not a little disturbing. While studying law, I continued to write on academic moral philosophy and published in academic journals, but after I graduated, my philosophical writing stopped. I began practicing law, starting out at what was called a "white shoe" firm—that is, one founded and still, in the 1980s, dominated by Ivy League–educated WASP gentlemen, though Jews, Catholics, women, and blacks were beginning to appear among the partners. I chose the firm for its reputation as a generous supporter of pro bono work, for its tolerance for odd career paths, and for attracting lawyers who wrote novels, took sabbaticals to pursue other interests, and were upright and uncompromising.

Until that time, I had encountered only in novels the world of the Harvard and Yale clubs, Park Avenue, and country houses. But the firm's older generation were welcoming and generous, despite the fact that I was in so many ways an unlikely addition to the firm. I was struck by their self-conscious and confident moral approach to their profession. They encouraged candid debates about professional ethics and took seriously their obligation to teach high standards to young lawyers. Even if I sometimes thought their ethical aspirations fell short, I admired their sharp sense of justice and their fluent and courageous response when someone outraged it. I began to think that I shared more common ground with these elders of the firm than with many lawyers my age and younger, whose narrower and at times more cynical ways of thinking about the practice of law I had already encountered in law school.

I now lived in Manhattan's melting pot, and the first of its many subsocieties that I encountered, through my job, was its Upper East Side. These were the years of the hot Reagan economy, and this Manhattan world was increasingly dominated by newly rich people who openly rejoiced in their wealth and status, openly disdained those poorer and less successful than themselves, openly voiced what were to me outrageous claims of entitlement, and openly justified their privileges as simply what their personal superiority merited. These attitudes have frequently been described and skewered—more potently than I ever could. I mention them here merely because it was an extraordinary experience to encounter them in the flesh, and had I not done so, I would probably never have believed in my heart that such people really existed.

But Manhattan had many other worlds, and I eventually found my way to a number of them. Among the musicians, scholars, doctors, psychoanalysts, social workers, writers, teachers, and others I met there, many obviously shared the squarish moral mentality that I had seen in remote Appalachia, in the academy, and in sophisticated white-shoe law firms, even though none of these new friends came from any of those places. Indeed, they came from all over the country and all over the world. This mentality, so immediately recognizable and warmly familiar, transcended the ordinary social divides of class, religion, race, education, and nationality and created unexpected common ground. Individuals sometimes seemed to invent it for themselves, but cultures sometimes seemed to breed people up in it as effectively as it trained them in their native languages. It was cultivated by subgroups in all the world religions, though all those religions also seemed to harbor antimoral contingents.

I did not stick with the practice of law, which never allowed enough time for reading and writing. In the early 1990s, I worked out an accommodation with the academy and professional philosophy and taught occasional courses in philosophy and the philosophy of law at Columbia and Barnard. The rest of the time, I studied and wrote in ways that approached my subject from various tentative and oblique angles. Finally, in this book, for the first time since my law school days, I feel bold enough to address the subject directly—not in a scholarly work, though it will be obvious how deeply I am indebted to many scholarly thinkers. Instead this is something shorter, more polemical, and more direct.

THIS BOOK ENDORSES several views that are often mistakenly regarded as inconsistent. It claims that a system of value that is characteristically and historically Western, one that depends on a specific, typically Western psychology, is in a meaningful way a universal system of values despite its local origins. It also recognizes that these values and this psychology sometimes arise independently outside the West, in individuals, religious groups, and a variety of subsocieties. It defends morality yet deplores the politics and theories of today's rightists, who have claimed the word for themselves, and regards their ideas and the kinds of religion that support those ideas as antimoral. Taken one by one, none of these views is unusual, but their combination has become uncommon. Together, I hope, they express a coherent moral framework, one that is, on the one hand, tolerant, respectful, and embracing and, on the other, free of the double-talk and concealed self-justifications of moral relativism.

The last chapters of this book look at some of the ways the academy has failed in its historic moral mission, but they address in any detail only the kinds of academic moral studies that popular media now disseminate to the general reading public. Today, media attention focuses no longer on the social sciences but on evolutionary science, not only on biology but also on the subdisciplines of neurology, psychology, and philosophy that explore the implications of evolutionary science.

Unfortunately, insofar as the book argues that the moral value system and the moral psychology* are in decline, with ominous consequences, it may seem to dovetail with the many varieties of nostalgia that are today so tempting. Moral nostalgia is a serious error, with serious consequences. For one thing, it is not true that "people" used to be better in the past than now or that "our way of life" was better in some lost world. Such ideas lead to futile, cruel, and destructive forms of conservatism that try to mend the present by constructing a fantasy version of the past—complete with home-abiding women, unregulated corporations, subservient minorities, and closeted gays. What *is* true is that there are

---

* In this book, the phrase "moral psychology" does not have its usual sense, in which it refers to universal human feelings and motives. Here, it refers to a specific set of psychological traits that in the chapters that follow I describe as belonging to the moral mind—traits that are not universal but depend on specific kinds of learning and experience.

reasons to think that earlier social and economic conditions in the United States may have supported a somewhat greater proportion of moral-minded individuals in the population and that these individuals often had far more social and political influence, relative to their numbers, than today.

The moral mind nonetheless continues to evolve and now understands many moral questions in better ways than anyone understood them before. Though today there may be a smaller percentage of people with a moral outlook, wielding ever less power and influence, in many ways they tend to surpass their predecessors—especially in merciful understanding and in the largeness and inclusiveness of their moral perspective. Meanwhile, like their predecessors, they are dogged, patient, kind, and driven by the kind of courage that springs from conviction and refuses to take immoral means toward moral ends. It is a great handicap to them that they so often fail to recognize one another and that, misled by the hostile attitudes toward the moral mentality that today are so common and that feed so much false theory and false moralizing, they often do not understand themselves.

THE MORAL MENTALITY went through a great shift in the twentieth century. In the first half to two thirds of that century, the dominant moral attitudes were those of people who were born before or during the world wars and fought those wars. The 1970s were a crucial period of transition when influence began to flow to their children and grandchildren, opening a deep generational divide, not only in moral thinking but in dress, taste in music and art, political ideas, and social demeanor. That transition is now mostly completed.

In matters of morality, generational division is less pronounced today than it has been in nearly a century. The painful
conflicts in moral, social, and political opinions, and in taste—in
books, music, film—that estranged the postwar children from
their parents are now muted, and the jarring disparities in codes
of conduct have diminished or disappeared entirely. People today divide not along generational lines but along ethnic, cultural, religious, and class lines. Some are so strongly united in
these ways that they function almost as members of tribes, with
quasi-tribal loyalties and suspicion of outsiders and their ideas.
Most important, people today divide along the fault line that
separates what I call premoral and moral mentalities, and that
line cuts across all the others. On the premoral side of this line,
antimoral fervor has developed that now fuels attacks on fundamental moral ideas and presents antimoral values as "true" and
"traditional," or sophisticated and advanced, or even scientifically valid.

The evolving moral outlook in the premillennium decades
came under criticism not only from antimoralists but from the
elders whose moral ideas it challenged. Some of them insisted
that it rationalized passivity, that it selfishly withdrew from social obligations into private life and disregarded others' needs.
These criticisms occasionally hit the mark, but more often they
missed. The new attitudes were not so much indifferent as realistic; the turn inward was a strong moral imperative. Toward
the end of the twentieth century, people were called on to sort
through the debris of the postwar past—to parse a host of dangerous ideologies, a dozen varieties of corrupted moralism and
religion, and ever-increasing hostility to the moral mentality
itself erupting from many different sources. At the same time,

they had to struggle to bring order to the chaos that in those years had often all but overwhelmed intimate and family life. Amid such confusion, old-fashioned calls to "action" were merely absurd. To sort it all out, moral-minded people had to live more inwardly and develop delicate sensitivities, broad knowledge, herculean objectivity, good humor, and tenderheartedness capable of embracing all sorts of unlikely—and, to minds formed in a different mold, distasteful—objects. The moral sensibilities of today reflect what they learned in this decades-long journey through the social wilderness that they inherited and the courage, strength of judgment, and nimble sanity that they developed in the face of a world that often seemed to be not just corrupted but deranged.

In order to change in these ways, the moral mind had to turn a morally critical eye on itself. This focus led it to more tolerant and less tense attitudes toward the desires, ego, and emotions that conscience presides over, and from there to a strong distaste for moral rigidity and punitiveness. A robust capacity for guilt is still the hallmark of the moral conscience, but today conscience is more alert to the irrationalities and malfunctions of guilt than it was six or seven decades ago and devotes more effort to toning down its own excesses. One's own and others' sexual desires, sadistic urges, envies, ego, murderousness, covetousness, and the rest are less hidden from us than they used to be. The reach for increased moral openness, rationality, subtlety, and flexibility sometimes goes wrong; at its margins it is overtolerant and readily distorted into justifications of wrongdoing, indifference, and cruelty. But by and large it results in more mercy and kindness, more steadfastness and fulfillment in love, and a stronger ability to achieve ordinary decency.

This more open acceptance of guilt and greater insight into the dark dimensions of human nature inspire, in turn, the strong emphasis that so many people today place on redemption and atonement—a natural consequence of a heavy sense of sin. Their preoccupation with this theme explains why they have little sympathy for fare that does not acknowledge at least some sympathy for the devil. So we are regaled with many tales of vampires, but the vampires may well fight their bloodlust and struggle to acquire souls and humanity. On television, we see people trapped on a mystical island where they are surrounded by evil and engage in evil but are offered opportunities to redeem their terrible crimes and misdeeds. Or we read about a hard-bitten police detective and his thirteen-year-old daughter who, having caused suffering, together dedicate their lives to atonement. "Everyone lies" becomes a byword, and TV characters engage in misbehavior aimed only secondarily at its ostensible objects and primarily as a statement on what good and bad really are, in a sort of meta-naughtiness. Courage, too, is a major preoccupation, as that virtue is so often a precondition of the others—especially of a capacity for genuine remorse.

Because the new moral mentality has a more rational sense of guilt than it used to, it can more readily acknowledge the sufferings of wrongdoers and wrongs that they suffer, which in turn enlarges the capacity to forgive—something quite opposite to the broader social trends of our time and a source of constant friction with them. The changes in the moral mind also render it resistant to the pull of tribalization and comfortable with cultural differences and with the tolerances that decency requires in a shrinking world. It tends to find party affiliations uncomfortable, even though it does not always abandon them and recognizes that some moral goals can be met only through politics. But, in the end, people who share the moral mentality have ethics, not politics.

People with the postwar moral mentality have given morality a new inner reality but a new public face as well, a social demeanor suitable to their new sensibility and self-understanding. The irony with which they so long greeted a world unfriendly to their ideas and goals gradually gave way to a wry, many-layered openness, the knowing innocence of today's young adults. They are cautious, being anxiously aware that they are surrounded by pitfalls. They do not claim to be more or better than they are and do not burn out striving for the impossible, but they also persevere and keep things that matter in sight. They have keen humor, and they make jokes about things that were once tabooed to joking, in order to render enormities human-sized, so that they do not overwhelm reason and emotion. They demand to be confronted with death, evil, and horror in film, fiction, gaming, music, and sport because they feel compelled to experience darkness before they can believe that they deserve anything else.

Although millions of people whose minds fit the moral mold still exist in the United States, their ability to lead and to influence is waning. Because this book is addressed to them, it puts forward many controversial ideas with little argument. Such readers already understand the arguments and already accept the ideas. What is presented here is a moral geography, a map of those places in the moral realm and the dangerous territories surrounding it where in our time it has become easy to get lost. It is intended to help us orient ourselves in a world increasingly dominated by antimoralism: to understand who we are, where we live on this map, how we got there, how to speak the language, and why moral suasion has never in the United States' history seemed so little capable of reaching people's hearts as now.

Chapter 1

A MORAL GEOGRAPHY

All this vivid sympathetic experience returned to her now as a power: it asserted itself as acquired knowledge asserts itself and will not let us see as we saw in the day of our ignorance. She said to her own irremediable grief, that it should make her more helpful, instead of driving her back from effort.
—GEORGE ELIOT, *MIDDLEMARCH* (1872)

MORALITY IS ABOUT the self and a kind of judgment that implicates the self. In moral judgment, what is always at stake is the sort of person we are. We decide not just what we ought to do but who we will be; and when we decide who we will be, we bring into question our own human worth. When Macbeth decides to commit murder and when Abraham Lincoln resolved to free the slaves, each chose not only to perform a specific action but also to become a certain sort of man, different from what he had been, and in doing so, each roused a self-judging part of his mind and opened himself up to his own condemnation or approval. In each of us, that self-judging part of the mind is who we feel we really are. Thus morality ultimately concerns action, and moral judgments are those judgments about how to act in which our truest selves are both judging and judged. In this judging, they make use of our mind's moral capacities.

These moral capacities depend on other, nonmoral, capacities that all human beings share. All of us are born with native mental equipment that will enable us to learn to feel with and for others, to be fair, and to exercise some sort of restraint over impulses of greed, fear, anger, egoism, and sexual and other appetites; and every civilization shapes these universal nonmoral capacities into its own code of right and wrong. But morality itself is not shared by all human beings. It is best understood as *one* of those shapings, as a historically specific cultural molding of the nonmoral capacities, an artifact of the civilization shared by a group of European countries and their colonies. This moral culture dawned around the time of the Protestant Reformation, furthered by a spirit that influenced not only the Protestant sects but also Roman Catholicism, Judaism, and Islam. It evolved, reached a peak in the eighteenth and nineteenth centuries, and began to decline in the twentieth. Although the characteristic moral psychology frequently arises outside the West, sometimes with independent roots, sometimes under Western influences, it is most common in the West. In the West, far more than anywhere else, it shaped governmental structure, the forms of civil society, and social custom, and it has its fullest elaborations in Western arts and letters. Thus only in the West did an elaborate, all-encompassing moral culture develop.*

---

* Of course, this does not mean that Western peoples and governments have done more good in the world than others or that they have not done horrify-

Naturally enough, the moral mind develops most reliably in places where social habits are designed to promote the moral character, so that moral culture tends to perpetuate itself. But those subgroups and individuals in nonmoral cultures who have a moral mentality—the Essenes, for example, or Mahatma Gandhi—often show unusual moral depth and courage. American frontiersmen frequently reported having met Native Americans whose moral nature was deep and subtle. Wherever and through whatever means the moral mentality comes into existence, it tends to come to favor certain basic values. This is what makes it possible to speak of moral truths—large moral ideas that are eventually accepted by all people with a moral mentality. Tecumseh, a moral man who belonged to a nonmoral society, disapproved of torture and valued freedom—and did so on the same rationale as Quakers and abolitionists and Enlightenment moralists, all distant from him in time, space, and culture.

Although morality is loyal to a characteristic set of values and ideals of conduct, *it is not a code or a set of rules*. Its characteristic values and ideals are generalized, rough-and-ready conclusions reached through exercise of moral psychological capacities. That mercy and equality, say, are moral ideals means that long, shared experience in a broad range of important social situations has

---

ing evil. "Moral" has both a descriptive and an evaluative meaning. It can mean "having to do with, or related to, morality," or it can mean "morally good." When used descriptively, its opposite is "nonmoral" or "outside the moral." When used to judge or evaluate, its opposite is "immoral" or, sometimes, "amoral" (without morals). In the sentence this note refers to, "moral" is used descriptively, not evaluatively. "Antimoral" means "opposed to" or "against" the moral.

proven them desirable. To understand those ideals properly is to understand when and how social realities call on them and to have a firm, reliable sense of how and when to enact them—an ability that may require, besides one's moral capacities, knowledge of history, experience of life, and understanding of human nature. The ideal of equality, for example, works differently in politics, the classroom, and families and requires different kinds of knowledge and understanding in those contexts. When individuals with moral capacity have a strong understanding of moral ideals, they are often able to adapt them to novel and complicated situations and to confirm one another's judgments about what morality requires in those situations.

We often speak of the world's diverse systems of right and wrong as "moralities" and refer to the different *moralities* of the Bedouin or the Hopi or the Aztec. In doing so, we make use of an antiquated sense of the term, in which it refers to social mores and little more. But I prefer to use "morality" to refer only to the psychology and values of an originally Western moral culture, a usage more true to the fact that, within this culture, the term strongly suggests specific inner dispositions as well as specific kinds of outer conduct. This usage helps avoid the confusion and skepticism that come from being forced to say, for example, that evils such as slavery, genital mutilation of young girls, or the sacrificial murders of children are "moral" among some peoples. Besides, to use the term *morality* to refer to a specific local ethic, the psychology and ideas of right that are originally Western, though increasingly met with everywhere in the world, is only to use its own word for itself.

I refer to other codes of right and wrong, with their own histories and psychologies, as "ethics" or as nonmoral codes and cultures. Some human beings—Plato, for example—are admirable and great although they are not, in our sense of the term, *moral*. This is not to say that Plato was immoral or that we cannot measure his merit on a moral yardstick, for we easily can; that is why we can admire him. It is only to say that his admirable qualities reflect a different ethic and organization of mind from the moral. He had a different susceptibility to guilt and shame, and his judgments failed to achieve the universality that is characteristically moral—for example, in his tolerance of slavery.

This is a slightly cranky but, I hope, clarifying use of the term *morality*. It lets us talk about morality in a way that recognizes that it combines culturally and historically unique roots with universalism. For although morality is a cultural product of the West, it does not govern or belong only to Western peoples; it has a kind of universal validity, and it is committed to a universal brotherhood of man, to recognition of all human beings' equality, rights, and autonomy, and to recognition of each person's potential obligations to all others. But the universal nature of morality is a much-debated and misunderstood phenomenon. Most attempts to salvage this aspect of morality from skeptical and relativist attacks do so by abandoning all its local, historical content—a grave and morally destructive error.*

MORALITY IS ONE of many ethics that admonish people to aid the suffering, whoever and wherever they are. On the most obvious level, the universality of morality refers to this sense of

---

* Some of these efforts to defend morality's universality by emptying it of historic content are addressed in chapter 10.

obligation to all people—no matter what tribe, nation, religion, or race they may belong to—simply by virtue of their humanity and their need. In saying so, we do not deny that moral peoples sometimes fail to render aid when it is desperately needed and at times have done evil under the moral pretext of "helping." "Aid" has sometimes served only as a means of buying political advantage; and religious organizations, while ostensibly fulfilling moral duties and "improving" those they help, have too often only sought converts, power, and authority. Despite all this, it remains true that wherever there is moral culture, there also arise civic and religious organizations, governments, and individuals motivated by moral concern, who strive to feed, clothe, cure, and empower strangers, often at the cost of huge personal sacrifice and tireless work.

A second dimension of morality's universalism is far more difficult to understand, and it is unique to morality. Morality claims governance over everyone, not only over particular peoples, tribes, religions, or nations. It not only establishes duties to everyone, but in an important sense it *imposes* duties on everyone and insists that none of us is free to decline them. All people are morally bound, whether or not they choose to be, and the moral point of view is a common, objective, or shared point of view. This claim, paradoxically, rests on the fact that moral values are those that people adopt when they are endowed with distinctive, in many ways culturally dependent capacities for love, reason, and feeling—moral capacities built on, but not identical with, native or noncultural human endowment. These moral capacities make up the moral mentality or psychology. They make possible the whole, rich rationality of the moral, the kind of rationality that calls on the whole person. Because this mentality makes the sanest and happiest life possible, because no one who understood it would choose to be without it, moral values stand as those that well-judging human beings everywhere recognize. Wherever and whenever people exhibit such moral capacity, we feel justified in making moral demands on them just as they do on us. It is by virtue of those capacities that we are members of a moral community that overflows national, tribal, and religious boundaries and unites all of us in something human; they give morality its objectivity. Moral truths are a historical distillation of such people's stable choices and ideals over the centuries. Moral errors are those choices and ideals that time and experience have taught them to abhor.

The moral psychology is complex, and it is different in every person. It may be only partially achieved and may be compromised in subtle ways. Sometimes we decide that people have chosen their own moral limits. Such cases aside, we recognize that the moral demand must alter when culture, natural endowment, or rearing has impeded individuals' development of moral capacity. Moral culture has therefore developed elaborate ideas about how to deal with individuals or groups of different mentalities. While it rejects the idea that it does not apply to those who lack moral capacity, it bows to their incapacity in morally required ways. This bowing can take many forms—from tolerance and inaction to persuasion, teaching, working to help those they may have harmed, and preventing them from causing harm. To claim that others are subject to the moral demand even when they cannot respond to it is to make a moral judgment whose sense is something like this: These individuals' truest selves are the moral selves that life has prevented them from achieving.

★　★　★

MORALITY'S CLAIM TO universal governance is sometimes
scorned as naive and hypocritical, sometimes as a dangerous
parochial delusion. But the claim is valid and, properly understood, not particularly controversial, while to deny it is to mis-
construe the geography of the moral terrain and undermine
moral conviction and motivation.

Those who deny morality's universality in favor of some
version of relativism usually do so because they hope to promote tolerance and understanding. They have in mind familiar
confrontations of Western morality, past and present, with
practices in nonmoral cultures that are licit under those cultures' local codes or rules, especially cases where false moral
values were foisted on subject peoples. Examples of these morally condemned practices have included, in different times and
places, extramarital sex, the genital mutilation of girls, the use
of torture to induce confessions to crime, the ritual murder-
sacrifice of children, the burning of widows on their husbands'
funeral pyres, child marriage, slavery, and polygamy. *We* may
think ill of polygamy, slavery, torture, or genital mutilation—so
goes the familiar argument—but *they* think differently. What
makes our ideas better than theirs? All of us think our own
values best, and ultimately "it's all relative."

This kind of thinking is not only mistaken, but it makes a
poor foundation for tolerance. If one's ideas of right and wrong
reflect no truth, but simply the accident that one was born in
one place rather than another, then just as there is no good
reason to think one's own values superior, there is also no
good reason to think anyone else's merit much tolerance or
forbearance. Their values become simply another set of local
prejudices that reflect no truths. Denying the universality of

moral values, that is, tends to undermine the sense that right and wrong are *compulsory*. If morality is merely local custom, then even tolerance loses its morally compulsory quality and becomes, at best, a piece of cosmopolitan etiquette, easily disregarded in favor of compelling self-interest or even less worthy goals.

If tolerance is one's goal, then true morality with its universalism, not a relativistic skepticism, is the better support. The ineptness of the relativist argument for tolerance is especially obvious when it confronts those many local ethics that preach intolerance and disrespect of alien ways and punish outsiders' violations. Morality does not dictate these things—even though it claims that its values are universal and govern all human beings. It insists on tolerance and forbearance, and these moral ideals are rooted in historical, cultural, and psychological understanding. These kinds of understanding also lead to moral disapproval of claims to racial, tribal, religious, and national superiority and any attempt to shore up one's ego by identification with tribes or nations or religious or charismatic leaders of these. Moral humility dictates that we judge ourselves as individuals, and moral rationality confronts us with the fact that others are as helpless as we are, in the short term, to be or wish to be something other than what our worlds have made us.

Slavery is evil everywhere and always, but we do not expect a tenth-century Viking or even Plato to understand this, and people in the United States do not judge them as they would one another or as they do Thomas Jefferson, Robert E. Lee, and Jefferson Davis. When slavery is practiced today in places where we have no governmental or social control, we feel obliged to oppose it to whatever extent we can, even if those responsible do not understand that it is wrong or if they insist, in all sincerity, that it is not. On the other hand, we also know that we are not morally bound to fling ourselves and our resources at all problems indiscriminately. We have stronger obligations to protect the innocent and helpless in realms where we have better control and resources. (Other things being equal, we have a greater responsibility to protect children in our own city than children in an African war zone, though we have obligations to protect them in both places.) And we recognize that sometimes when others are doing wrong, it is wrong for us to try to stop them. The point is that there is no contradiction between saying that slavery or child prostitution or political oppression is evil always and everywhere and in regarding it as an open and difficult question, in any given case, what anyone should do about someone else's engaging in it. In the same way, we understand that genital mutilation of young girls is an evil and that we are obligated to help those who suffer from it; but we also understand that this does not imply that we must send armies to Sudan or Somalia to prevent it or that we need not attend to or seek understanding of the complex cultural maze in which among some peoples the practice seems indispensable. We are called on to engage in a moral balancing act, poised between respect for others' ways and the need to render aid, and to strive for sensitive and creative ways to meet these obligations.

THESE IDEAS ABOUT the nature of morality and its universality help sidestep many mean-spirited attacks on moral talk and action as well as much befuddled moralizing. For example, they make it clear that nothing in morality requires us to be narrow, stupid, and rigid; we need not reject morality to reject the sins committed in its name. They also make it clear that there is no reason to identify moral judgment with bad moral judgment and thus no reason to regard morality per se as "judgmental"—as do so many people today who have never heard the word *morality* uttered except by the blinkered and blinded.

Efforts by "Christian" groups to prevent the distribution of condoms in AIDS-stricken regions of Africa and their insistence on sexual abstinence as the sole means of protecting health are cruelly mistaken, but regarding those efforts as mistaken requires no rejection of morality but only the adoption of an intelligent moral perspective. More generally, the sad fact that history is full of egregious moral errors made by people who were convinced they were doing good deals no fatal blow to morality. (We do not reject physics because most people can't understand it.)

The presence of the moral mentality and moral ideals in cultures, subcultures, or individuals does not guarantee their wisdom or virtue. They may nonetheless be ignorant, misguided, weak, or perverse, either throughout or in more or less limited realms of conduct—in sexuality, say, or in covetousness or violence. The moral mentality is a set of broad capacities, not a warrant of merit. It docs not necessarily result in more kindness, generosity, or prosocial behavior than other ethics and sometimes has led to less. Conscience once dictated that Hester Prynnes be tormented and shamed, that children be beaten with leather straps, and that the poor be confined to workhouses where they were poorly fed, clothed, and housed and forced to labor beyond their strength. Some Native American tribes, observing these and other customs of the whites, thought them a shockingly cruel people (and, of course, some Native American tribes were themselves far more cruel).

The recognition that morality rests on a complex of rational and emotional capacities precludes another error: that of treating morality as a simple code or set of principles or rules. Certainly, clear and generally accepted moral values crystallize into helpful rules that we can all recite: Assist strangers in need, keep promises, tell the truth, and treat others as we wish to be treated. But these rules are merely shorthand for immensely complicated moral convictions that reflect intricate attitudes and social realities. In real life, violations of the "rules" are rarely as simple as the rules themselves sound, and following rules is no safe route to virtue after the age of five.

Because morality is a set of psychological dispositions that are imbued as a cultural habit and lead to various shorthand rules expressing shared values, those values are what they are only within the context of a moral culture. When moral ideas filter singly or partially into nonmoral frameworks and are taken up by nonmoral minds, their meaning may alter dramatically. Egalitarianism became a force for evil when taken up by Mao Zedong. This was no reason to question our own moral ideal of equality, but it was sometimes treated as though it were—and still is, for example, when civil libertarians are denounced as communists. Within morality itself, there is a parallel to this sort of extramoral abuse of moral value. Sometimes individual moral ideals or values are taken singly and applied mechanically, disregarding how they are embedded in the moral cast of mind or character or in whole moral ways of life, or how they are addressed to specific dimensions of life. The result can be fanaticism, rigidity, or ordinary misjudgment. So, for example, the idea of equality is abused within the moral context when, wedded to a shallow and inadequate concept of "disability," it is made to serve as a weak foundation for whole complexes of obligations owed to people who have nothing in common except an ill-fitting label.★

All such confusions and all the bitter moral debates and errors of the past half century are to a great extent the effect of a decline in moral culture and the rise of a widely shared antipathy for the moral—an antimoralism. But what this book refers to as antimoralism has little overlap with what the "moral majority" of the 1980s and its various angry heirs protested as degeneracy and immorality. On the contrary, right-wing defenders of "morals" are as antimoral as the explicit proponents of antimoralism who have arisen at other points on and off the political spectrum. Their combined influences have caused, overall, a dramatic decrease in the social and political weight of what we might call the moral point of view, the moral type, and, it

---

★ The misfortunes of amputees, paraplegics, dyslexics, the crippled, the blind, the deaf, those with Down syndrome, and many more leave them with strikingly different needs and capacities both from one another and from those who have not suffered their misfortunes. To group them together under the label "disabled" may be legally adequate, but it is morally inadequate. With its reliance on the badly fitting civil rights model and its implicit equation of equal treatment with the same treatment, it reduces sensitivity to vast differences in needs and capacities. It is all but certain to create the very kind of stigma that we want to avoid because it groups people together on the basis of abstract misfortune. This invites other people to feel themselves one of life's superior "fortunates" and tempts them to adopt a global response to "misfortunates" that is superficially positive but on a deeper level perceives them as inferior and is fearful and hostile.

seems, in the number of people who are of that type.★ For decades, people of the moral type have lived with the experience
of repeated moral shock—as over and over they see their neighbors and leaders defend what is all but self-evidently immoral, as
over and over they struggle to explain moral good and evil to
minds ill-equipped to grasp it, as the language of morals is
adopted and used specifically and pointedly to defeat the moral.

Morality has always existed as a difficult human *achievement*, in
some instances individual and in others social, the result of successful patterns of child rearing and social education. The moral
mentality may never have formed a numerical majority of any
nation's population. There are towns in the United States in which
most people seem to have the moral mind, houses of religion in
which most of the congregants do. But it also seems true that those
communities are themselves unusual, and even in communities
dominated by a genuine moral mentality, merely conventional
"morality" is all but sure to arise. There will be some people who
conform to others' moral expectations only because, and so long
as, doing so is a means of protecting their respectability and status,

---

★ This book often speaks of *kinds* and *types* of characters, minds, or people.
Scholars debate whether "types" and "ideal types" of people exist and, if so,
what that means. I use the terms in a commonsense way and trust readers to
understand how they work and to assume that I do, too. Types should play a
minimal role in face-to-face interactions. They are useful only as rough
analytic tools. Stereotyping and reducing people to types are only two of
many possible abuses of reliance on types, and both involve moral as well as
intellectual errors. But talk of types is a necessary shorthand, an efficiency of
speech without which discussion of some subjects is hardly possible. In morals, literature, and psychology, we would be tongue-tied if we could not talk
about types.

and some who are obedient to moral values only because they are obedient to whatever authority commands it. Such people become morally lost when social change results in mixed cues, and then they may begin to approve of bad or questionable behavior or seek some other source of external guidance, for example in strict religions that prescribe clear, rigid rules of conduct. So in the postwar sexual revolution, some people defended adultery or engaged in the fads of "swinging" and wife swapping while others took refuge in religious sects that insisted on sexual abstinence outside marriage, banned contraception, and enforced those prohibitions with threats of biblical punishment and ostracism.

In the past, for a variety of historical reasons, moral thinking repeatedly achieved political dominance in America despite fierce and powerful opposition. A number of American presidents, as well as men and women with lesser political influence, had a moral mentality, and until fairly recently the world of writers and thinkers was dominated by moral minds. It should not surprise us that moral men and women achieved so much influence. Moral people tended to be sober, strong-minded, rational, truth telling, promise keeping, dutiful, compassionate, and self-critical; their value to political life will have been evident even to observers ruled entirely by self-interest. Moral traits are as obviously desirable in those holding political office as in tradesmen, doctors, lawyers, and farmers.

Wherever morality has existed, it has been merely one way of acting and thinking among others and has often inspired hostility. The moral mentality, conceiving of itself as free, equal, and self-governing, sees all people as owning these same rights—even when they do not understand this or deny it. These ideas naturally inspire detestation wherever prevailing attitudes and codes render some people subject to others as a consequence of their sex, class, birth, race, or caste and locate their virtue, as inferiors, in their obedience and submission. But such quarrels often occur within moral cultures as well.

The American Revolution, which in one aspect was a war of moral protest against England, was in another aspect a moral battle among the colonial people themselves. The Civil War was, among other things, a war of the moral against another set of mind. The history of American society in the twentieth century was sometimes that of moral leaders presiding over a people whose morality was increasingly merely conventional and thus vulnerable to suasion by the antimoral. The decline in moral capacity in the American voting public has rendered it more vulnerable to flattery and greed and more easily deceived by a facade of respect for conventions and authorities that make them feel safe. The result is that today the moral type is weaker and more despised than it has ever been in American history.

Public discourse in the United States is now dominated by a four-sided debate: The parties include a profoundly antimoral group tied to a rightist political ideology; an antimoral group with a leftist ideology; a small, motley group that openly disdains the moral; and the genuine moralists who may be found in all political persuasions but now are usually called liberals no matter what they actually believe about government. Some of these groups promote various forms of *pseudomorality*, nonmoral and antimoral doctrines or value systems that claim the moral mantle, insisting that their antimoralism is actually true morality. Given that each of these contingents is itself splintered, it is no surprise that public debate is as confused and shallow as it has ever been, and that politically and economically we have veered dangerously near chaos.

Chapter 2

DEMOCRACY, THE MORAL PSYCHOLOGY, AND THE MORAL INDIVIDUAL

The test of every religious, political, or educational system is the man which it forms. If a system injures the intelligence it is bad. If it injures the character it is vicious. If it injures the conscience it is criminal. . . .

Civilization is first and foremost a moral thing. Without honesty, without respect for law, without the worship of duty, without the love of one's neighbour—in a word, without virtue—the whole is menaced and falls into decay, and neither letters nor art, neither luxury nor industry, nor rhetoric, nor the policeman . . . can maintain erect and whole an edifice of which the foundations are unsound. . . .

The ultimate ground upon which every civilisation rests is the average morality of the masses, and a sufficient amount of practical righteousness.

—HENRI-FRÉDÉRIC AMIEL,

JOURNAL INTIME (1885)

The more democratic republics become, the more the masses grow conscious of their own power, the more

do they need to live, not only by patriotism, but by
reverence and self-control, and the more essential to
their well-being are those sources whence reverence
and self-control flow. . . .

—JAMES BRYCE, *THE AMERICAN*
COMMONWEALTH (1888)

HISTORIANS SOMETIMES TALK of governments' moral failures as though they evidenced whole peoples' shared "weak" or "failed" morality, and occasionally that is fair, but not usually. More often than not, the moral faults of nations are better thought of as the effect of the political dominance of nonmoral people over moral ones. Strictly speaking, morality, a type of mind or mentality, belongs only to individual human beings, and only they can have a strong or weak moral character. We speak of peoples, cultures, and governments as moral when the influence of moral minds within them is strong, but that influence is never absolute. In Western nations, the moral mentality had an unusually powerful influence on the shape of government, but nonetheless it has often failed to guide governmental action.

Those peoples who best cultivated the moral mind and allowed it the greatest political and social influence were also history's most vigorous and successful promoters of democracy and the familiar social habits that support it and flow from it, including those that protect good governance. Within moral cultures, governmental power tends to be reliably subject to law; business and administrative and civil services—postal systems, tax collection, traffic regulation, and so on—are tolerably efficient, fair, and honest; judges are not assassinated; civil order is at a high level; and peace and safety are maintained with maximum freedom and minimum oppression and tyranny. Obedience to law in predominantly moral cultures is furthered by people's expectations that others will be kind, fair, and rational—expectations that breed social trust, loyalty, and reduced motives for misbehavior. Civil servants, police, and legislators are far less likely to take bribes when they know that citizens are willing to be taxed so that they can be paid properly.

Moral cultures invariably promote learning and research in the arts and sciences, and they create excellent schools and colleges to make these things possible. Their educated populations are immune to superstition and magical thinking. Moral cultures enjoy high levels of sexual and racial equality and a broad, egalitarian distribution of wealth. Eventually all of them abolish polygamy, servitudes, and privileges of caste and class. Within a moral community, the insistence on these goals is powerful. Failure in them is felt as an intolerable moral lapse and can inspire revolutions.

Although a strong moral culture guarantees neither the power nor the inclination in government officials to do justice, it creates a continuing pressure toward it that tends to limit the sway of cruelty and evil. The very existence of democracies, their success in establishing the rule of law and its freedoms, and their prohibition of servitudes and caste—all this depends on the continuing struggles of moral citizens to maintain these good things against other forces that constantly strive to destroy them. Moral achievements are not like buildings that, once erected, stand by themselves without buttressing. They need continual reinforcement and renewal. Democracies provide institutional incentives to engage in that work, but these incentives presuppose moral citizens with sufficient integrity, understanding, and strength to carry it out. In the absence of a moral culture that produces such people in adequate numbers, the institutional barriers of democracies against evil and oppression are fragile or nonexistent.

The past influence of the moral type in Western democracies has created a reservoir of potential good that we still draw on, but it will dry up if we do not reproduce the moral culture that shaped and sustains those democracies. This culture is endangered, as most people who belong to it know, but it is also resilient. Moral injunctions are perceived as neutral, disinterested, and compelling, often even by those who despise them. Thus, in their very nature they carry a certain authority. Moral culture, more than any other, has the tools of reason and understanding at its disposal, and this gives it the great advantage of being able to fathom the forces that oppose it. And the moral mind enjoys a heightened capacity for self-understanding, which enables it to nurture itself and strengthens its courage and patience—two of the moral qualities essential to endurance.

MORAL AND PREMORAL PSYCHOLOGIES

Morality arose as a response, first psychological and then social, to feudalism and its hereditary hierarchy of human value and privilege, and to the psychology of dominance and submission which that hierarchy grew out of and depended on. Just as feudalism required that people be psychologically fitted to submit or dominate, according to their place, and to think in patterns consistent with their status, so morality requires people who, internally, resist submission and dominance and are capable of freedom, self-judgment, and self-determination. Morality thus blurred and then gradually undermined feudal statuses; it revealed them as unjust and unnatural.

The English word *morality* first appears in the late Middle Ages and comes into its modern sense in parallel with the development of the moral psychology and moral values in the modern sense. Thus, in the fourteenth century, Chaucer, with all due irony and skepticism, depicts a world in which right and wrong turn on a person's "degree" or place in the social hierarchy, in which specific vices and virtues belong to specific classes, trades, and social positions, and in which inferiors are expected to obey superiors and superiors to take care of inferiors.★ Shame and dishonor attended violation of the duties and virtues that belonged to the various rungs on the feudal ladder.

Morality quarrels with all this. From the moral point of view, a person's value is determined by things within him, not by his place in the world. Birth and life's circumstance do not define

★ The first recorded uses of the word *morality* may be in Chaucer, where it has not yet acquired its modern meaning. "Derived from the Latin mos/moris, 'a custom, usage, or fashion,' *moral* and *moralite* [in Middle English] retain a flavour of public probity, as opposed to private piety, throughout the period" (Richard Firth Green, "Morality and Immorality," in *A Concise Companion to Chaucer*, ed. Corinne Saunders [Malden, Mass.: Blackwell Publishing, 2006], p. 199). See also Chaucer's poem "Gentilesse," in which he distinguishes true nobility from mere rank and points out that only the latter is heritable. But Chaucer still makes an equation between the gracious nobility, the gentilesse, that those of high rank should have, and the true virtue that makes Christ first in gentilesse. Later moral thinking far more carefully distinguishes noble, aristocratic qualities of character and moral merit.

one's quality, one's deserts. From this idea flows the moral sense of universal compassion, or compassion not conditioned on membership in any particular family or group or on fixed social relationships; the sense of injustice that cannot be satisfied by feudal reciprocities; and the elevation of loving kindness—kindly love—to the summit of human virtue. All of this wars against the premoral, feudal sense of right and value; its preoccupation with honor, shame, submission, and role; and its concepts of the sexes and their relations.

By the seventeenth century, and with continuing force thereafter, this new ethic—morality—had achieved great cultural momentum in the British Isles, many European nations, and their colonies. Moral values were practiced as a devotion and taught and disseminated by houses of religion. Of course, precepts of right and wrong had always been taught by religions, but now these teachings were taken up by people with a different mentality and absorbed into culture in new ways. The eighteenth century saw denunciations of cruelty in every form and a growing abhorrence of torture, slavery, beatings, and brutal punishments. Moral subtleties were explored by great minds in works of philosophy and political theory and in works of art—especially in the novel. This meant not that most people became morally good, or even that most people had this moral mentality, but that everyone lived and breathed in an atmosphere in which the moral demand was constant and was articulately voiced. The idea that the serious business of life was to strive for goodness was an ancient one, but it developed a new character as people with a moral psychology developed new ideas of goodness in accordance with the demands of the modern moral conscience.

Their moral earnestness, evident to us in their diaries, their books, and their letters, would have seemed natural to many people even as late as the mid–twentieth century, but it strikes the contemporary reader as quaint and foreign.★ Of course, moral piety was often faked and often served as a front for egoism; moral fanaticism repeatedly veered into pointless asceticism; and sometimes overstrict and intolerant conscience caused enormous, pointless suffering to self and others—flaws of moral character depicted in Charlotte Brontë's St. John Rivers, Dickens's Mrs. Jellyby and Uriah Heep, and Ibsen's Brand.

★ The letters of John and Abigail Adams are typical of their time in their pervasive and humane moralism. Consider, for example, this response by John to the news from Abigail that Samuel Quincy's house in Boston was among those that suffered "abominable Ravages" inflicted by Quincy's "own merciless party." Quincy was solicitor general, an old acquaintance of the Adamses, and a British loyalist whose siblings and father, however, supported the revolutionists:

> What shall I say of the Solicitor General? I pity his pretty Children, I pity his Father, and his sisters. I wish I could be clear that it is no moral Evil to pity him and his Lady. Upon Repentance they will certainly have a large Share in the Compassions of many. But let Us take Warning and give it to our Children. Whenever Vanity, and Gaiety, a Love of Pomp and Dress, Furniture, Equipage, Buildings, great Company, expensive Diversions, and elegant Entertainments get the better of Principles and Judgments of Men or Women there is no knowing where they will stop, nor into what Evils, natural, moral, or political, they will lead us. (Letter from John Adams to Abigail Adams, April 14, 1776, in *The Oxford Book of Letters*, ed. Frank Kermode and Anita Kermode [Oxford: Oxford University Press, 1995], pp. 142–45)

And here is how Louisa May Alcott described one of the wounded men under her care as a volunteer nurse in the Civil War:

Nonetheless, the cultural ideal was moral, and it was universally understood that no one achieved that ideal without strenuous effort. Bringing up a child properly meant not merely teaching it a catechism of "our" rules, but, more important, endowing it with a faculty of self-judgment and critical self-analysis. Those in whom upbringing and education were successful would exercise moral oversight of their own thoughts and actions. They would be morally autonomous, and they would insist on being so as their right and demand the freedom from others' control necessary to exercise that right. Moral autonomy required political and religious freedom and obligated people to seek it.

The adult moral mentality legislated its own moral law. In its later, most mature forms, the moral mind assumed an absolute power of self-determination and, echoing religion's claim that God's laws were superior to those of kings and states, insisted that sometimes the laws of conscience overrode the law of governments. From the beginning, the United States, a nation founded by people in whom the moral mentality was unusu-

---

John Sulie, a Virginia blacksmith, is the prince of patients. . . . Under his plain speech and unpolished manner I seem to see a noble character, a heart as warm and tender as a woman's, a nature fresh and frank as any child's. He is about thirty, I think, tall and handsome, mortally wounded, and dying royally without reproach, repining, or remorse. Mrs Ropes and myself love him, and feel indignant that such a man should be so early lost; for though he might never distinguish himself before the world, his influence and example cannot be without effect, for real goodness is never wasted. (Louisa May Alcott, January 1863, from her Journal, Union Hotel Hospital, Georgetown, D.C., in *Louisa May Alcott: Her Life, Letters, and Journals*, ed. Ednah D. Cheney [Boston: Roberts Brothers, 1890], pp. 116–17) ally strong and widespread, established a still remarkable degree of protection for the autonomy of conscience. The existence of conscience both entitles people to democratic freedoms and equips them to carry out the obligations of democratic citizenship. Democracies are created to serve people of this mentality. When democracies lack a substantial proportion of citizens of this type, they are likely to turn into something else.

THE MORAL PSYCHOLOGY

The Moral Character

Democracies depend upon the presence of the moral psychology in enough of their citizens, just as feudal systems depend on its absence. The moral mind suits people for life in a democracy. They resist tyranny and oppression; they are not inwardly compelled to tyrannize and oppress others.

Moral individualism is something psychologically distinct and opposed to the "individualism" of egoism and unrestrained greed. Those who develop the moral mind enjoy a sense of self that enables them to resist and moderate the temptations of wealth, rank, power, fame, status, and beauty and, in some cases, to enjoy happiness even in their absence. Moral characters seek such goods with less appetite than others, and when they acquire them, especially wealth and fame or rank, they are less likely to be harmed by them and inflated with them. They tend to be modest and to feel uncomfortable trumpeting their success. Their restraint flows not from fear of others' envy but from the reduced value of those nonmoral goods to the moral mind. The victory dances at today's sporting events reflect diminished public morality, which is now so distant from the sensibility of modesty that it no longer objects to the victors' public triumphing in the presence of the defeated; it does not understand why and when winners are obliged to be magnanimous to losers.

Because all societies require some degree of cooperation to survive, most ethics recognize many of the same character traits, in some form, as desirable and praiseworthy. Integrity and truth telling, promise keeping, generosity, and similar traits are recognized as virtues almost everywhere. The prominent moral ideals of forgiveness, egalitarianism, universal obligation, rationality, and autonomy, however, are not. While humility and modesty are accepted as virtuous in some nonmoral codes, they tend to be seen as the virtues of inferiors or of the inferior sex; but in the moral character they extend to everyone and even to its own qualities. It is a paradox of morality, one that moralists constantly warn of, that moral striving leads easily to false pride—to smug moral superiority, self-righteousness. The person who is good and does right, even when he sees correctly that others around him are falling short, must not boast about it, not even to himself. We are morally permitted—in fact encouraged—to enjoy self-respect when we have acted well. But this self-respect is not a sense of *social* superiority; we experience acting well, morally, as being obedient to objective ideals commanded by conscience, and we have a good feeling from doing so even if it results in a loss of social standing. We also recognize our common nature with those who do less well, and we see how our moral achievements always depend on things and people other than ourselves.

Morality also differs from other codes in its heavy reliance on the capacity for self-observation, self-criticism, and self-knowledge—a set of abilities that underlie the equally important moral qualities of mercy and forgiveness. Because the moral mind tries to estimate its own failures with a cold, objective eye, it more readily forgives others their flaws and more readily detects the infiltration of its judgments by its own ego, envy, vengefulness, desire, and anger. Morality calls on the individual to stand up to wrong, condemn it and fight it, but at the same time approves of those who are tolerant and slow to point the finger. Morality demands that we make judgments but condemns being judgmental—a particularly tempting moral error because it offers a combination of covert pleasures, allowing us to feel righteous and superior to those whom we condemn while also enjoying pleasure in the pain our condemnation inflicts. It is why judgmentalism is both widely despised and widely practiced.

We frown on people who enjoy disapproving. No one likes Mrs. Proudie, Anthony Trollope's finger-wagging scold. The highest moral characters are kindly, warm, and forgiving—never what we call, with appropriate distaste, "moralistic." They do not scour every casual remark, every pleasure, and every laugh for signs of moral offense—the great sins of the politically correct. They do not equate pleasure with wrong. Most important, they know when and how to raise the moral issue. For a second paradox of moral striving is that it is often morally best to be morally oblivious. It is wrong to be overly conscious of others' flaws and wrongs, and it is a mistake to intrude the moral into every moment and aspect of life, which is entitled to its light, silly, and pleasure-filled moments. Indeed, these are all the better when experienced with the support of a silent morality.

Most of the moral life is lived unconsciously and automatically, and much of life falls outside moral parameters. This is as it should be. Someone who brings moral consideration to bear on teeth brushing or on choosing a tie or a seat on the bus suffers moral insanity. Someone who brings it to bear on his behavior as, say, CEO of a large corporation may well be seen as mad by his colleagues, but he is not.

The moral mind is inherently, necessarily, egalitarian. This is what Abraham Lincoln meant when he said, "If slavery is not wrong, nothing is wrong." Morality also condemns slavery as an interference with moral autonomy; those who claim the right to control their own acts and thoughts in accordance with conscience cannot help but regard others as having the same right. From the moral point of view, any distribution of social benefits and detriments that is based on nonmoral criteria is to some extent suspect. Morality is suspicious of all claims to superiority, including its own. Other moral values reinforce the moral insistence on equality and autonomy; people disposed to kindness, compassion, and empathy find the cruelty of enslavement intolerable.

Observing the strictures that the moral mind imposed on itself, Friedrich Nietzsche concluded that morality turned natural value on its head. What he regarded as natural value was very much like what Thomas Hobbes or, in today's world, Richard Dawkins would: strength, power, and success in a Darwinian struggle. Dawkins and Hobbes both insist that nature has little use for altruism, compassion, or justice except when they serve oneself or one's own. Nature often favors gross inequalities and rewards the strong. Nietzsche—but certainly not Hobbes or Dawkins—thought morality degenerate, effeminate, and weak, a set of lies promulgated by the weak to protect themselves from the strong by afflicting them with a bad conscience.★

Even today, many people try to defend morality by showing that it is natural, a function of built-in biological capacities. (Chapter 10 explores contemporary attempts to shore up morality this way.) They are right insofar as morality is built on natural dispositions rooted in the very structure of our brains. But morality is also a highly cultivated, culture-dependent phenomenon that is itself non-natural and often counternatural, one of many value systems that such natural abilities may be shaped into. Morality and moral insight rest on a distinctive moral psychology; they feel natural and instinctive to those who have this psychology. But this only goes to show the remarkable plasticity of our minds, that all the quick immediacy and vitality of instinct and intuition may be put at the service of such a thoroughly invented, learned, and history-laden phenomenon as morality. Morality is a second nature, not a biological nature.

Narcissism, Individualism, and Happiness

Psychologically speaking, to have developed a moral character is a piece of good fortune. While from one point of view, morality

---

★ At least Nietzsche seems to think so sometimes, being one of those philosophers who was fond of giving every shard of truth, every partial fact, at least a brief chance to posture as the whole.

restrains narcissism,★ from another it is itself the product of the rising narcissism of individualism.

In the premoral mind (the psychology common among Western peoples before the moral era), narcissistic goals dominate the sense of value—wealth, power, fame, status, pleasures, and beauty, including handsome clothes, jewelry, and the increased attractiveness resulting from practice of the various arts of grooming and manner. In premoral cultures, the pursuit of these goods is governed by ethics based on shame, or codes of honor, that accept them as true goods or values. Such values instinctively and intuitively guide premoral choice, and the worth of the self is defined and experienced in accordance with its possession of them or its rights to them. All human beings, including those with the moral mentality, seek these natural goods, but in moral people such ambitions are reshaped and re-formed and the natural goods' value is diminished or outright denied.

Morality subscribes to the ancient insight that money, power, status, and the other natural goods do not ultimately satisfy—a truth that has only a weak hold on the common sense of our times. Morality teaches that happiness is both possible in the absence of such worldly goods and never present in those whose opinion of themselves rests on their possession. It points out the self-defeating logic in the search for happiness in such things. For if they are what make me worthy, then in myself, apart from

---

★ Freud's "On Narcissism: An Introduction" (1914) is the classic, ground-breaking analysis of this phenomenon, and it still both rewards and frustrates close reading. On the Freudian view, narcissism has natural and normal roles in a well-balanced mind, but there are also specific mental dysfunctions that are best described as disturbances of narcissism.

such goods I am not worthy. A nagging sense of inner worth-lessness might well set people off on a Hobbesian "restless search of power after power" in a vain attempt to overcome it. Their lives are an endless struggle to keep a grip on the things that support their fragile sense of personal value, and they are prone to excruciating envy of those who have more than they and contempt for those who have less.

Wherever a premoral mentality is culturally dominant, right and wrong are determined by social rank and codes of honor that establish conditions for preserving rank, and people's lives are dominated by the need to live so as to avoid losing face and being shamed. This might mean that men must, if insulted, fight duels or launch blood feuds or that women must bear male children. In some such societies, a girl who fails to bear a son may be beaten by her husband's family, and there are cases in which women have been burned alive for bearing only females. Or a girl who has been forcibly raped may be regarded as having dishonored her family and be murdered by her male relatives as a means of restoring the family's honor. Their families' treatment of them will not be faulted by their neighbors. That the young women are not wrongdoers in a moral sense does not matter. The girl who provides no sons has deprived her husband and his family of a good that they bargained for in their marriage. The girl who has been raped has been shamed, and her shame dishonors her family. In ethics of this kind, her life is valued according to nonmoral, external standards of utility and purity, not according to her own intentions and wishes.

Among the powerful, the premoral mentality makes little or no distinction between what is good and what I want. Hence their characteristic sense of entitlement and their tendency to adopt the dangerous view that failure and inferiority deserve deprivation, suffering, or ill-treatment—to find it fitting and natural that the low and powerless should have less and endure more. But it is important to remember that in such premoral cultures, not only the rich and powerful but the low and powerless think this way. The serf has little, but in his own mind he deserves little; he thinks ill of himself and his rights. Only with moral insight do people acquire the self-respect that resists servility and refuses to accept one's station and its deprivations (or its privileges) as fit and natural or as self-defining. Moral self-respect can arouse hostility in those who, lacking it, seek others' envy, obedience, submission, or worship as a means of boosting their sense of worth. It is correctly perceived as a challenge to their superiority.

In the moral mind, the narcissistic need for power and rank is moderated, and all but obliterated in the most admirable characters, because people with the moral psychology enjoy a group of substitute satisfactions that, with caution, might be considered moral forms of self-love or narcissism. The first, and largest, source of this feeling is simply the self-respect of the egalitarian. Those with a strong sense of equality grant respect to themselves just as they do to their neighbors; they do not feel inferior. (In Charlotte Brontë's *Jane Eyre*, Rochester admires Jane when she displays just this kind of moral self-respect and claims equality with him even though she is his penniless dependent and employee.) When people act according to their own moral ideals, satisfying their own consciences, they also experience self-approval, a heightened self-regard, for doing right, and this is a second dimension of moral self-love—a morally licit narcissism.

But beneath these two aspects of moral self-love is a third that is more subtle and even more important. This is the intrinsic positive feeling, the inherent internal reward, in the psychological integration of the moral character that makes us into genuine individuals. Simply in acquiring the structure of mind that confers such moral capacity, the individual gains a pleasurable background awareness of existence, of simply being who one is. It is an easy reliance, taken for granted and never thought of, that one exists and is oneself. Psychologically far distant from worldly pride and a sense of superiority, it is a comfortable feeling that arises in the moral psychology, a sustaining, constant, and continuing form of self-acceptance that goes far to give life a sense of meaning and purpose and to mitigate emptiness and despair.

These kinds of moral self-love are what enable moral characters to minimize the sufferings, the envy and anxiety, of offended narcissism and to find life worthwhile even when the world withholds its goods. Their satisfactions multiply, too, because the moral character has a heightened capacity for pleasure in work, in love, in nature, and in the arts.

The rechanneled narcissism of the moral mentality is nearly the opposite of Buddhist calm, which is psychologically a kind of ego obliteration, and quite different from ordinary pride. It is also nothing like the good feeling of winning an election or race or prize, accomplishments that give a pleasing sense of social value or significance. When moral self-respect is weak or absent, people are likely to seek to comfort themselves with the rewards of pride, shoring up the weak sense of self by trying to be something or someone. In the absence of these rewards, they may experience depersonalization, emptiness, or a hungry feeling of being no one or of being a chameleon, taking their identity from their place or situation. People who suffer such feelings comfort the resulting agony however they can. Premoral and nonmoral cultures provide many well-trod paths of life that enable people to avoid their pain. They can subordinate themselves to superiors and in this way share in their superiority or gain their superiors' approval; they can idealize others from whom they receive identity in reflected glory; they can dominate others in one way or another and find consolation in that form of superiority; or they can identify themselves with, or lose themselves in, professions, religions, political movements, or ideologies. Such psychological maneuvers are, of course, unstable and emotionally costly. Yet in most times and places, most people are forced either to resort to them or to endure misery. Thus moral capacity is a strikingly successful psychological solution to the unhappiness that most people are otherwise doomed to.

Moral Capacity

Moral capacity is not a single thing but a combination of several mutually reinforcing capacities:

Self-government and self-restraint. The capacity for autonomy or self-government is the central moral fact. The moral mind demands the right to govern itself because it is capable of doing so; but its commands to itself take the form of compulsory laws that apply to everyone. The capacity for self-restraint derives from the internal rule of self-imposed values. Moral autonomy is a great part of what underlies the egalitarianism and universalism of morality. If my right to self-government rests on this capacity, then anyone who has a similar capacity also has the right; and if it is what entitles me to moral respect, then others like me are entitled to my moral respect.

Weakness in this respect leads to a familiar form of moral failure, one that everyone sometimes falls prey to: the inability to stand up against peers, authorities, and institutional values. Thus the dean of a major law school may defend one opinion about presidential war powers while he is dean and a very different opinion when he becomes an adviser in the State Department. This weakness is one that tends to be pronounced in politicians and others with a chameleon-like ability to adopt, in all sincerity, whatever beliefs offer them the most politically protective coloration or best conform to those of their bosses.

Social capacities. The capacities for love and empathy, and the ability to feel *ruth (pity)*, *compassion*, and *sympathy*, are all crucial to the moral life. Love and empathy are essential to the existence of pity, compassion, and sympathy.

People who have limited insight into others' feelings must, of course, fail in sympathy and compassion.* Lack of empathy

---

* The terms *sympathy* and *empathy* have begun to be used interchangeably, but they mean different things. "Sympathy" itself has two meanings. The first is a kind of catching of someone else's feelings. This sense of "sympathy" is illustrated by Adam Smith in *The Theory of Moral Sentiments* (1759), where he describes how people react as they watch a man walking a tightrope. They unconsciously twist and bend and sway as though they themselves feel in danger of tumbling. The second sense of "sympathy" is warm concern for another's troubles or pain. In this sense, "sympathy" is synonymous with "compassion." Empathy is yet a third thing. The term was invented by a psychologist to name an intentional act of cognition—a kind of trial identification. Empathy, strictly speaking, is not a feeling or sentiment, but an ability to project oneself into another's mind. In empathy, we place ourselves by imagination (or "projective identification") in other people's shoes so as

also results in an inability to love, which requires, among other things, the ability to see others as persons, independent beings with their own thoughts, wishes, goals, and feelings. Incapacity for love has many causes and forms, but in all of them it cripples the moral life. When other people serve merely as receptacles for projections of one's own thoughts and feelings, or when loving someone is experienced not as delight but as a diminishing of self, or when aggression, envy, or paranoid fears stand in the way of warm feelings—in all these circumstances, morality is undermined. It is nearly impossible to do right by others when that must be done catechistically, by rote, as it must be for those who do not react to others as independent persons and have no idea who they really are. George Eliot depicts precisely this painful combination of rote morality and incapacity to see others for what they are (and thus to love anyone) in *Middlemarch*'s Mr. Casaubon.

The capacity for love plays many roles in the moral life. Early in life, in the intimacy of parental and familial love, we get an indispensable education in how to understand others. Children's eventual success in understanding what they owe, mor-

---

to understand them by feeling what they are feeling. At the same time, we know that the feelings are theirs, not ours. Note that we can be empathetic without being sympathetic. For example, one might register empathetically a would-be killer's murderous rage yet lack warm concern for it or him. It sounds slightly self-congratulatory to claim that one empathizes with someone and implies no kindness; whereas it is almost always kind to express one's sympathy. This analysis of sympathy and empathy is borrowed from David M. Black, "Sympathy Reconfigured: Some Reflections on Sympathy, Empathy, and the Discovery of Values," *International Journal of Psychoanalysis* 85 (June 2004): 579–96.

ally, to strangers begins with their passionate love for a few intimates; love for a few teaches kindness to all. The experience heightens our sympathies, our goodwill toward strangers, and amplifies our moral motivation. People who, because of negligent, cruel, or neurotic parenting, grow up with a limited capacity for empathy are also stunted in their ability to love; they do not understand what others need from them; they can find little reason to help others get what they need; and their moral opinions tend to be either irritable, harsh, skewed, and contrarian or merely conformist.

A strong sense of what is owed to others, altruism, and an emphatic condemnation of cruelty and sadism all derive from the natural, universal capacities for sympathy and empathy combined with the moral belief that everyone is entitled to equal moral respect or consideration. Always egalitarian, the moral mind extends compassion and protection to all other human beings, not only to its own family or group (although in most matters we owe more to our own family, friends, and colleagues, with whom we have more direct and complex relations). To the moral mind, there are no strangers, no outsiders, and human beings are entitled to moral respect just because of their human vulnerabilities and capacities. In this way, the moral mentality creates a community, a warming sense of *us* and comfort in our shared life, our mutual care and respect. But it is having become an autonomous individual that makes it possible to belong to this community. A strong sense of self is the precondition of a strong sense of others' rights, deserts, sufferings, and vulnerabilities as beings like oneself, and of the ability to feel with and for them intensely enough to make heavy sacrifices of personal interest to aid them. Individuality, in other words, is not an obstacle to other-regarding emotions and actions, altruism and compassion; it is the foundation for them. But as a historical and psychological achievement, not a natural or biological endowment, it is dependent on the support of certain kinds of familial and cultural patterns.

Self-criticism, self-observation. A strong ability to observe and criticize oneself, to be objective about oneself, is necessary to ensure conformity to one's own standards. Those who cannot see themselves accurately and critically—who rationalize or blind themselves to their own flaws and errors—cannot recognize when they have defied their own rules of conduct.

Rationality. The moral mind's strong conscience reinforces its grasp of reality and its obedience to reason and logic. Thus a decline in moral culture inevitably leads to widespread irrationality and to a flourishing of extrarational ways of fixing belief. This might mean growth in magical and crackpot thinking or in people's willingness to believe that some dictator can do no wrong or in dismissals of scientific theories about vaccines, global warming, and evolution. Or these forms of irrationality may coincide; a totalitarian government can force minds into scientific molds for economic and military purposes while also training them in grotesque defiance of reason in politics.

Obedience to reason includes the ability to bow to what is true even when we are strongly tempted to disavow it, and in morals to be able to see the implications of one's ideals even when they run counter to one's fervent wishes. In the psychoanalytic framework, the "ego," or the rational self, is responsible for reality testing and logic, and a strong superego, the seat of conscience, helps the ego by controlling emotions and wishes and demanding certain consistencies as a moral imperative. The mind with moral capacity is less prone to a number of psychological mechanisms that undermine rationality and distort thought: projection, "splitting," rationalization, denial, magical thinking, and all invasions of reason and integrity by wish and fantasy.* Rationality, the ability to follow logic and the lessons of experience to reach truth, requires a conscience with strength sufficient to control our temptations to exaggerate, to blind ourselves, to ignore facts, to fall back on superstition, to believe what serves our interests or our anger, and to think as everyone else thinks or some authority dictates.

Guilt. The capacity to experience guilt is needed both to be able to perceive what is right and to be able to bring oneself to do it. Guilt arises from a judgment that one has violated one's own standards or ideals, or that one wishes to do so. In psychoanalytic terms, guilt is the punishment meted out by the super-ego, or conscience, for such violations. Conscience is also the source of the warm sense of having lived up to one's ideals. (See page 63)

The capacity for love is a precondition for the capacity to feel guilt. Remorse and guilt are first experienced when, as small children, we undergo the inevitable, painful experience of having aggressive or angry feelings against someone we love. Our love curdles the aggression and turns it back on us as the powerful and crushing sensation of guilt. We speak so lightly today of feeling guilty, in fact, that it is worth reminding ourselves of the potential force and pain of guilt. Even mild guilt is a hollow,

---

* See footnotes page 79 in chapter 3.

restless feeling, a kind of mental nausea. Someone "struck" with heavy guilt experiences emotional agony that manifests itself in a blood-drained face, sagging features, slumped shoulders, and haunted eyes.

Guilt reflects the conviction that one has done or been what one shouldn't, in one's own opinion, according to abstract, impersonal, internal standards, regardless of what anyone else knows or thinks.* Conscience, in its negative aspect, uses guilt both to signal the danger of a breach of conscience and to prevent an actual breach. In its positive aspect, it rewards us with moral pride and self-respect when we live up to our own values and resist violating our inner standards.†

The capacity for guilt is the capacity to do right simply because it is right, rather than from fear of punishment or hope of admiration. But the feeling of guilt is also an imperfect guide to right and wrong. Irrational and unmerited feelings of guilt are a familiar, painful malfunction of moral capacity and can be extraordinarily hard to cure. If we have been wrongly taught, for example, we may feel guilty about things that are right and approve of ourselves though we have done wrong. We may feel compelled to fulfill unreasonable parental expectations as to our career or marriage when there would be nothing wrong in failing to fulfill them. Or we may find ourselves split between some-

---

* In religion, this aspect of conscience is expressed in the idea that God knows all, that what He knows matters and what people know matters less or not at all.

† See generally David Milrod, "The Superego," *Psychoanalytic Study of the Child* 57 (2002): 131–48. See also the footnote on page 63.

thing we have been taught and ideals that derive from deeper sources. Huck Finn feels guilty when he does not tell Miss Watson that her slave Jim has run off, though, of course, Huck's choice to protect Jim is the expression of a truer kind of conscience. One can feel irrational guilt over violation of some moral value in thought or wish, even though there is no chance we will act out the wish; guilt may also arise as a result of unconscious ideas and or irrational thinking, as when a child feels guilty because it thinks it caused its parents' divorce or because it is a better athlete than some envious friend or sibling. Most of us must, at times, struggle to correct a conscience that errs or is too strict, too rigid, too lenient, too weak, or blind and blunt. Conscience may also display "lacunae," gaps, that are more or less serious, as for example in the otherwise honest, compassionate, and generous person who cheats at cards or displays odd stinginess toward family or lies freely about his war record. In an ominous and destructive kind of misfunction— sometimes produced, paradoxically, as a result of weak or inadequate discipline in childhood, not, as one might expect, excess discipline—the superego becomes tyrannical and cruel; the individual endlessly torments himself for minor or imagined transgressions.

Guilt dominates shame in the moral mind and often wars with it. We sometimes use the terms *guilt* and *shame* interchangeably, but they name different feelings that occur in different circumstances. Most important, we feel guilty if we have done wrong in our own eyes, but shame is consciousness of standing low, or deserving to stand low, in others' eyes—that is, knowledge of one's actual or threatened social

diminishment.* Those to whom the distinction seems unclear might find it clarifying to note that guilt yearns to confess, whereas shame wants to hide. This is because guilt is
self-condemnation; the guilty go to others because they want
punishment or forgiveness—either of which may help to re-
lieve their guilt. But shame is deficiency in the eyes of others.
Thus exposure and confession ordinarily increase the pain of
shame.

Although it is common to feel guilty and ashamed at the
same time and about the same things, morality often overrules
shame. It makes a virtue or moral necessity of enduring shame,
contempt, or dishonor for the sake of a moral good. Sometimes it fails, and guilt yields to shame: For example, a socialite
breaks off her longtime friendship with a loyal friend who has
fallen on hard times. And it sometimes succeeds: A Jewish
lawyer asked to undertake the legal defense of neo-Nazis
comes in for intense disapproval in his home community but
accepts the case anyway because he believes that it is right to

---

* Shame is a secondary moral emotion, but, like guilt, it can be extraordinarily painful. In some societies, agonizing shame is a frequent cause of suicide. In recent decades, some observers have begun to argue that shame's
role in the moral life is not secondary. See, for example, Bernard Williams,
Shame and Necessity (Berkeley: University of California Press, 1993); and Fa-
brice Teroni and Otto Brun, "Shame, Guilt, and Morality," *Journal of Moral
Philosophy* 8 (2011): 223–45. My own view is that while Williams and others
make welcome corrections of misunderstandings about how shame works,
their conclusion about its proper role in the moral life is weak. It is an opinion whose appearance coincides with the increasing prevalence of premoral
concepts of right and wrong.

do so.* It is morality's control of shame, through the higher mechanism of guilt, that enables people to endure poverty, insult, aggression, danger, and humiliation for the sake of what they think is right. Morality makes use of shame as it can to reinforce moral values, but it disdains shame as an ultimate motive for doing right.

Conscience exists in nonmoral character types as well as moral, but in them it works differently, especially in its far greater reliance on directions from external authority and on shame. When nonmoral or premoral individuals obey their societies' rules, they are likely to do so out of either fear of punishment, conformism, or a wish to stand well before their fellows. So, for example, in the *Iliad*, the Greek warrior Phoenix explains that he decided not to murder his father because he did not want the *reputation* of a parricide. In such people, shame, not guilt, is the dominant mechanism of self-control. They are ruled by externals: Laws, police, religious or other authorities, and social opinion govern their behavior; when these are absent or conflict, such people readily go wrong. The noble premoral character who refuses to lie or keeps his promise out of a sense of honor obeys a value that morality, too, enforces, but does so out of nonmoral motives—to maintain pride and to avoid loss of honor or worldly standing and thus to avoid shame. The adult governed by shame may abide strictly by a highly developed and rationalized set of

---

* In novels and movies, a moral hero often endures shame for the sake of right—losing the promotion or getting fired or being thought a coward—only to be publicly vindicated and rewarded in the end. In real life, the reward for such difficult actions is often only internal and private.

social values, but internally they function as a means of being someone, achieving a certain social identity or status that the world will respect.

GROWTH OF CONSCIENCE: THE MORAL INDIVIDUAL

The behavior of very young children is controlled only by external authority—the parent's actual or anticipated voice. A toddler leaves the stove knobs alone in mother's presence but immediately and guiltlessly experiments with them if she leaves the room. At this early stage, what is right is simply what the parents enforce, and true conscience does not exist. In the later preschool years, the child begins to internalize depersonalized, abstract values. Where once it knew simply that the parent prevented hitting the sibling or taking the toy, now it regards causing pain and stealing as wrong, and it feels a moral dislike of them. That is its own opinion, and it feels guilty if it breaches these rules even when the parent is ignorant of the crime. Right and wrong begin to be expressed not in terms of its own or its parents' wishes, feelings, or commands, but in objective and necessary terms. When we say that the very young child's concrete ideas of right in terms of parental commands give way to abstract, general ideas of value that now command it in its own voice, we do not mean that it is *as if* they were its own. They now *are* its own, and it has achieved an important degree of self-governance.* At the same time, the child now understands

---

* The capacity for self-restraint is buttressed by an effective unification of all the parts of the mind into a single, relatively consistent identity. The these commands of its own conscience as being independent of its wishes. Its values, laws, and ideals are experienced as rational requirements, not mere personal inclination. As it reaches primary school age, the child begins to show the primary schooler's strict moralism about those moral values it understands; cheating in games, cutting in line, and taking others' things are prime examples of bad behavior that six- and seven-year-olds strongly condemn.

Because conscience begins as the internalization of parental prohibition and exhortation, conscience not only punishes but also protects and comforts with good feelings that can be traced back to the sense of being approved of and loved by one's parent,* and these good feelings lead to moral aspiration. By our teenage years, we have developed strongly held and deeply personal convictions about abstract, impersonal moral ideals. The term for all those things that we would like to be—the aspirations, values, and ideals we attempt to live up to—is the "ego ideal." When we move closer to fulfilling the ego ideal, we experience our own approval, a moral self-respect.

As the child grows toward adulthood, its moral sense grows flexible and subtle. No longer does it see moral questions in black and white terms (unless they truly are black and white). Most

---

moral self unifies or integrates the personality, so that it can reach as much of itself as possible: Our left hand must know what our right hand is doing. But this integration is never absolute. We are never absolutely one person, never absolutely consistent in our behavior, but only more or less so.

* See Roy Schafer, "The Loving and Beloved Superego in Freud's Structural Theory," *Psychoanalytic Study of the Child* 15 (1960): 163–88, especially the closing summary.

important, moral maturity brings an increasing ability to hold to one's own values and beliefs despite lack of social support and, in the strongest characters, even in the face of powerful opposition.*

The process of forming a conscience is not entirely passive. From the very beginning, the child by no means merely takes parental and cultural imprints. Its own temperament, beliefs, insights, and experience and the exercise of its reason determine which influences it absorbs and in what form. The child seeks out models, too, and accidentally encounters others. Its admiration and idealizing of parents and others may be based on misunderstanding or misperception of the parents' true qualities, yet the child nonetheless models itself on what it thinks it sees. Likewise, children for a variety of reasons often reject or ignore some aspects of their parents' character or values. The moral mind is always at least partly its own creation. These active, self-determining aspects of moral development grow stronger and stronger as the child reaches its teen years and, finally, adulthood.

The development of conscience continues throughout life. The older we get, the more conscience reflects individual temperament and personal experience along with individual capacities for self-observation, self-reflection, and self-criticism. To a great extent, becoming an individual and becoming a moral individual are one and the same thing; individualism and morality are not opposed but mutually reliant.

Each of us grows up with a unique set of moral strengths and weaknesses, insights and blind spots. Having acquired a moral

---

* Supported by ego rather than conscience, strength of mind is no virtue but what we call being pigheaded and, taken to an extreme, as in Anthony Trollope's Louis Trevelyan (*He Knew He Was Right*), becomes a kind of madness.

mentality, by itself, does not make us into guiltless, respectable, or even what we think of as good people. Those with a moral psychology may be odd, deluded, rageful, inconsistent, weak, neurotic, or misguided, or they may reason poorly or be poorly informed or educated or be overthrown by various temptations and inhibitions. Ordinary moral capacity guarantees neither goodness and wisdom nor a life whose moral challenges are proportioned to our individual strengths.

Although moral self-government develops throughout life, perfect moral control and absolute moral certainty do not exist. The moral self is never fully in command, never fully independent of its environment. Few, if any of us, completely outgrow the need for others' support of our moral resolve and understanding. At times, everyone finds it hard to resist wrongdoing, especially when it will go undetected, or to stick with what one knows is right when others disagree—less hard for those whose conscience is strong and harder or impossible for those in whom it is weak.

As a social phenomenon, morality is a repository of knowledge— the gleanings of generations that have been recorded in histories, expressed in religions, stories, novels, paintings, songs, and poems, and analyzed in philosophies. This shared heritage enables us to have common reactions and shared insight when our individual experience would not have put insight within reach. It enables each of us, as individuals, to know more than our own lives could teach us and so to be bigger people than we could otherwise hope to be. Its common ground is what enables us to go beyond frigid tolerance and value our differences in temperament, perception, experience, ability, and desire, as a boon to understanding and as the essential foundation of democracy.

Chapter 3

PREMORAL AND MORAL CULTURE

When ambition has set up ideals of its own, in order to attain its ends, what duties does it not outrage, what feelings of humanity does it not stifle? What laws of honesty, equity, and fidelity does it not subvert? A conscience may remain, but, corrupted as it now is by ambition, what damnable intrigues will it not hatch, what trickery, what treason will it not resort to, to obtain its object?

—LOUIS BOURDALOUE (1632–1704),

SERMONS

[The narcissistic personality's] attitude toward others is either [exploitative and] deprecatory—he has extracted all he needs and tosses them aside—or fearful—others may attack, exploit, and force him to submit to them. At the very bottom of this dichotomy lies a still deeper image of the relationship with [others]. . . . It is the image of a hungry, enraged, empty self, full of impotent anger at being frustrated,

*and fearful of a world which seems as hateful and
revengeful as the patient himself.*

—OTTO F. KERNBERG, "FACTORS IN THE
TREATMENT OF NARCISSISTIC PERSONALITIES"
(1970), IN *ESSENTIAL PAPERS ON NARCISSISM*,
ED. ANDREW P. MORRISON (NEW YORK: NEW
YORK UNIVERSITY PRESS, 1986)

FROM A HISTORICAL point of view, the moral psychology arose in opposition to the social values of feudalism.
The social hierarchy of feudalism, in turn, came about as a
result of some people's successful pursuit of social dominance,
power, wealth, and status, goals that are all, in a straightforward way, narcissistic in that they enhance the kind of self-
love that is felt as superiority, pride, and importance. Thus in
its origins and essence, morality *is* an attempt to transform and
restrain this kind of narcissism. Likewise, from the moral point
of view, narcissism, understood as a spectrum of character
traits in which self-love and self-interest are pronounced, and
in extreme cases disturbed, in specific ways, *is* countermoral
and often antimoral. Naturally, then, in the West, a decline
in the dominance of the moral mind is one and the same
thing as an increase in narcissism, or the rise of a "culture of
narcissism."*

---

* The phrase is, of course, the title of Christopher Lasch's immensely influential book, *The Culture of Narcissism: American Life in an Age of Diminishing
Expectations* (New York: W. W. Norton & Co., 1979).

PREMORAL AND MORAL CULTURE

A premoral culture, or culture of narcissism, reemerges when morality collapses. When premoral thinking becomes culturally dominant, moral values begin to seem unconvincing and uncompelling. People may continue to pay lip service to them, but in their hearts they respect other values far more. Compassion is seen as weakness, mercy as injustice. Eventually the narcissistic goods—wealth, power, success—replace moral ones. Then premoral culture quickly denies equality and reestablishes social hierarchy; it removes moral restraints on the status that is granted to wealth and power or, perhaps, even makes wealth and power the sole criteria for determining rank; and it redefines right and reshapes government in terms that serve the interests of those with status, wealth, and power.

The United States has been in the process of reversion to premoral thinking for more than a century, but the trend accelerated in the mid–twentieth century. Its causes were ill understood, but it was easy to see that its effects were negative. Narcissistic people were themselves unhappy, and they created misery and social damage all around them, in business, politics, sports, marriages and families, and all other aspects of civil society. Because democratic societies lack strong social controls and rely heavily on individuals' self-control, they are far more vulnerable to these kinds of damage than are societies in which individuals are subject to strong external restraints.

The spread of what I call premoral thinking was first described by social critics as a rise in "narcissism" in the 1960s and 1970s, and before long that term was being flung back and forth as a weapon in the culture wars. Today it is a household word, often used to denounce ordinary selfishness, egoism, or self-absorption. But in the sense in which it is meant in this book, the term refers not to these sad but ordinary moral failures, which occur commonly in moral as well as nonmoral characters, but to a specific psychology that promotes a premoral culture when it becomes a socially dominant psychological type. In individuals, that psychology may be more or less pronounced, narrowly or broadly present in personality traits, subordinate to other, moral, dimensions of character or dominant over them, although it will often be convenient to describe it and analyze it in unqualified terms.

The moral call for self-restraint is addressed to individuals' narcissism just as it is to their greed and sexual and aggressive instincts. Morality asks us to evaluate ourselves on a scale of value that is incommensurate with other kinds of social values. If an individual is poor, low-status, and limited in attractiveness or ability, morality offers him a separate source of self-approval, an independent basis for self-evaluation. If he is rich, powerful, beautiful, famous, or talented, morality will save him from the dangers of immoderate self-love. By placing moral qualities above these, by restraining excessive, destructive pride and ego and providing alternative satisfactions, especially those of love, it increases security and diminishes fear of competition, dread of age, the need for conquests and admiration—in general it boosts sanity, contentment, and well-being. In these ways, morality makes equals of those who, according to other measures of value, are superior and inferior and gives everyone reason to accept its measure as the most important. When a person succeeds in conforming to his own moral standards, the satisfaction he experiences is narcissism transformed, redirected and abstracted from its "natural"* sources and made to serve moral goals. Morality does not do away with narcissism but in some respects controls and in others modifies it.

When morality is culturally dominant, some people earnestly strive to conform to its ideals from mostly narcissistic motives. George Washington, for example, seems to have been a highly ambitious, somewhat narcissistic man whose uprightness may have reflected not a moral psychology but his wish to fulfill an ideal of gentlemanliness that in many ways reflected the influence of the dominant moral culture. When the surrounding moral culture fails, narcissism cannot serve itself this way, and it resumes its premoral shape, with a demotion of moral value.

To the degree to which people's personalities are narcissistic, they also tend to have flawed moral perception. They lack what we might call moral common sense, and, in fact, in a moral culture, shared moral perceptions form a large part of what is always called common sense. The loss of this aspect of common sense is a sign of the breaking up of moral culture—for example, when moral language and categories are used in matters that are not moral, as when people make a morality out of prudence, say in adopting healthy habits; or when people insist that we have moral obligations to nature, to the earth, trees, and rivers, whereas in fact our moral obligations to protect and preserve nature and the things that exist in nature are owed to other people (including future generations), not to the things we must preserve and protect for the

---

* Strictly speaking, this underlying narcissism itself has a historical and culture-bound shape, but I often refer to it as natural because, in its acceptance of these "natural" goods as the truest and highest, it is closer to instinct than the moral.

sake of those people. The daily newspaper brings us many examples of this loss of common sense and common ground, presenting us with striking examples of poor moral thinking, often on the part of "experts." So, for instance, a story in the *New York Times*★ describes research into children's moral development with experiments in which psychologists, by means of deceit,† induced guilt in toddlers and then "for 60 seconds . . . recorded every reaction as the toddlers squirmed, avoided the experimenter's gaze, hunched their shoulders, hugged themselves and covered their faces with their hands." The reporter finds nothing to object to in this procedure and points out that when the minute was up, the experimenters "absolved" the children. But if the experimenters would not be permitted to slap toddlers, why may they inflict emotional pain that probably hurts more? And why is it all right to trick small, trusting children into thinking that they have caused harm—especially when the goal is to learn something that could be (and has been) learned in so many innocent ways? The author does not ask, and reports the experiments with lively, approving interest; the scientist gets a moral free pass.

In the premoral mind, in place of moral individualism—the individual's moral autonomy and capacity to think and act according to conscience—there is mere egoism: the demand, or wish, to be allowed to do and have what one wants. The

------

★ John Tierney, "Findings: Guilt and Atonement on the Way to Adult-hood," *New York Times*, August 25, 2009.

† The ethics of using deceit on subjects in psychological experiments has often been questioned. To the extent that research psychologists must do so, they must also be people who can overcome moral inhibitions about deceiving others and, sometimes, making fools of them.

premoral individual who confronts a moral culture, or the remnants of one, must cope with social demands that he experiences as illegitimate. Because his sense of entitlement, his greed, and his demand for superiority feel right to him and are not internally moderated as they are in moral minds, moral restraints may provoke him to outright rage and hatred. Such rage, of course, is especially likely in those who wish desperately for the kinds of superiority that morality devalues or condemns and in those who wish to engage in morally condemned behavior—especially greed, but also sensualism, hedonism, sadism, and domination.

The premoral mind in a democratic, egalitarian society finds no social structure that answers to its needs and demands or that channels them in socially useful or harmless directions. In feudal society, such people would have been forced into a position in the social hierarchy and reared to accept their value as that belonging to this inherited status. If it was low, they would have been accustomed to humility and subservience, under which resentment and hatred might have smoldered, ready to burst out, sometimes opportunistically, sometimes in service to the manipulations of the powerful. If it was high, they would have become accustomed to grandiosity and pride, the attitudes that would have seemed proper to people of exalted status.

This kind of socialization does not exist in egalitarian societies. In such societies, premoral characters feel moral restraints as a yoke imposed by external powers. Morality does not speak in their own voice as their own wish. And because morality restrains narcissism—pride, grandiosity, desires for superiority and domination—they experience moral demands as a rebuke to such feelings and wishes and hence as an offense against pride. Again, the result is humiliation that inspires rage and hatred and rebellion against morality—antimoralism. This is especially true when, as is often the case, the narcissistic mind equates strength and standing with masculinity. Then moral condemnation of power and wealth gained or used unethically is felt as emasculating, and compliance with the moral demand is regarded as effeminate and weak.★

In these respects and others, the premoral mind is primitive and childish. It presents itself as the defender of morality, but it fails to condemn what morality sees as wrong and sees as wrong what is morally innocent. It confuses the disgusting with the wrong. It may retain infantile attitudes toward sex that can lead, for example, to fearful, angry condemnations of homosexuality and abortion.

IRRATIONALITY AS A PREMORAL TRAIT

Irrationality is a prominent characteristic of premoral thinking. As moral thinking declines and premoral thinking spreads, we see more and more people disregard truth and science—in the birther movement, literalist readings of the Bible, attacks on Darwin and the theory of evolution, and the growth of fringe populations attracted to Scientology, UFO theories, astrology, magic, and modern varieties of witchcraft. Irrationality has produced a legislative overthrow of the economic and

---

★ Refusal to retaliate may issue from, and be perceived as, moral strength, not weakness and cowardice. This was once a tired, familiar insight, but the present-day love of vengeance gives it renewed freshness. Of course, moral error in the opposite direction—weakness and cowardice—is also possible.

financial lessons of the Great Depression. On the right, it has led to ideological rejections of the weighty scientific evidence substantiating the reality of global warming. On the left, it has led to ideological attacks on anyone who dares to question aspects of that science; Freeman Dyson, a liberal, rational dissenter who questioned not so much the evidence for global warming as hypotheses about its dangers, inspired hatred and was demeaned as a heretic and a villain.* Irrationalism is also visible in some people's emotional displacement of feelings onto rationally un-

---

* Hitlerian analogies have by now been so abused by ideologues on both the left and right that they seem suspect even when valid, but there is a stark likeness between right-wing antiscientific trends in our own society and the Nazi abuse of science. The madness of Nazi eugenics is the most familiar example of this, but the Third Reich also scorned theoretical physics, which it denounced as "Jewish science," ensuring that the United States, not Germany, first created an atomic bomb. Hitler often became attached to quacks and quackery. He dabbled in occultism and astrology and admired the cosmology of Hanns Hörbiger, who believed that the earth had had a second moon that crashed into the ocean, caused Noah's Flood, and formed Atlantis. This second moon, Hörbiger claimed, also destroyed the dinosaurs, which must therefore have been on earth at the same time as man. Hitler commissioned an architect to design a planetarium and observatory in Linz with a gallery in which Hörbiger's image would be placed alongside those of Copernicus, Galileo, and Kepler. At the same time, the "Einstein Tower" observatory in Potsdam, which was designed to study phenomena relevant to Einstein's theory of relativity, ceased all research on relativity because of Hitler's prejudice against Jewish physics. See John Cornwell, *Hitler's Scientists: Science, War, and the Devil's Pact* (New York: Viking, 2003), especially pp. 33–34, 59, 106, 178–79, 184, and 194). In obvious ways, in the United States religious fundamentalists and others on the right make similar attacks on theories in climatology, biology, and astronomy with pseudoscientific ideas.

connected causes: for example, in those unfortunate people whose rageful feelings of helplessness, unimportance, and mistreatment lead them to identify with embryos or animals and to become fanatic about stem cell research, abortion, and animal rights; in paranoia that takes political forms; and in people whose resentment of authority or sense of inferiority leads them into fascism, anarchism, totalitarian-style communism, or fanatic left-wing politics. These displacements serve such people simultaneously as a means of feeling superior and of protesting the way they are treated by the world. Such perversions of moral judgment are often accompanied by rage against those who oppose their causes and an alarming, murderous willingness to see them harmed. The underlying rage so prominent in personalities with narcissistic tendencies is repeatedly tapped by right-wing demagoguery to fire up opposition against "liberals" and "elites" and others who are seen as claiming superiority over them or challenging their dominance or superiority or restraining them from thinking and doing what they please. They turn painful feelings into pleasure by making these political opponents into objects of outrage and hatred, even though this sometimes leads them to support political goals that undermine their own political interests and to vote for politicians whose main attraction is that they rationalize and provide an outlet for their perpetual feelings of envy, resentment, and rage.

VENGEANCE AS A PREMORAL VALUE

Morality's rejection of the code of vengeance arouses anger in the premoral mind and impels rightist fundamentalists to favor the Old Testament book of Leviticus—"Breach for breach, eye for eye, tooth for tooth" (24:20)—over the New Testament Gospel of Matthew: "Ye have heard that it hath been said, An eye for an eye, and a tooth for a tooth: But I say unto you, That ye resist not evil: but whosoever shall smite thee on thy right cheek, turn to him the other also" (5:38–39). The reasons for their fury go to the heart of the differences between moral and premoral mentalities. Retaliation, return of evil for evil, is the natural, instinctive response to having suffered a wrong—a blow, theft, or insult. Such wrongs inflict suffering that goes beyond pain and loss; they also cause a wound to narcissism. The one who inflicts the evil is felt to have gone "one up" on his victim. Thus the need to return evil for evil, whatever else it is (such as a deterrent to further wrongs), is also the need to erase a narcissistic injury by undermining the other's superiority; revenge is always partly a means of shoring up wounded pride, status, or standing. The prevalence of this premoral psychology of revenge is obvious when we consider how common and how instantly categorizable are the endless incidents of road rage, air rage, horrendous domestic murder-suicides, and shootings in schools, workplaces, and public events. These incidents are so familiar that they are now cultural memes as identifiable in the United States as running amok was in Malaya. Strikingly often, they are cases in which vengeance is sought in response to an intolerable feeling of having been wronged on the part of someone who does not appear to have been wronged at all—a clue that feelings of entitlement or superiority are at work or that pride has been wounded.

But morality devalues wounds to pride; it demotes them and offers moral understanding, moral self-respect, and moral gratifications as alternative means of restoring narcissistic balance. It enables the wronged person to feel that despite suffering a wrong, his value is intact. By making narcissism more vulnerable to conscience—to guilt—than to shame, by offering moral revaluation of the injury to pride, and by providing the balm of narcissistic gratification in the satisfaction of conscience and ideals, it both requires and enables the moral individual to overcome the retaliatory impulse and reduces or obviates the need for the satisfaction of vengeance. Morality does not *take away* the impulse to return evil for evil, which continues to exist as a temptation in the moral mind, as it does in all minds; rather, it reduces the temptation and offers the means of resisting it.

PATHOLOGICAL NARCISSISM

Narcissistic disturbances in self-regard occur on a spectrum that ranges from mild and ordinary to pathological levels of severity, but after the mid–twentieth century they seemed to increase along its entire span. Narcissistic traits became more visible in people free from pathological extremes. Outside the therapist's office, people became increasingly focused on narcissistic rewards (success, status, power, wealth, and the privileges of youth), less able to invest themselves in other people and activities for their own sakes (in the absence of narcissistic rewards), more likely to compromise higher—moral—values. At the same time, narcissistic disorders became more and more common inside the psychotherapist's office, too, and investigation of these shed light on the broader social phenomena.

Psychoanalysts and psychologists confirmed the common lay observation that narcissistic people suffered moral confusion and were sometimes strikingly amoral. Pathological narcissism always involved some degree of compromise of the superego. At the extremes, narcissistic characters were inordinately hungry for admiration, self-seeking, self-absorbed, cold, dishonest, greedy, grandiose, and highly manipulative—traits that sometimes went unnoticed because they were concealed behind talent or a charming, sociable front. Pathological narcissists felt, or wished to be, "special." They used others as means to their ends and dropped them when they were no longer useful. They were often Iagos, ruthless and crooked, willing to lie and betray when it served their ends. They tended to be frustratingly unempathic and to combine poor social judgment with an outrageous sense of entitlement. No matter how badly they behaved, narcissistic personalities experienced little guilt, as though they regarded themselves and their own interests as the measure of right. They reacted with scorn and skepticism to moral criticism, for they tended to believe that others felt and behaved as they themselves did. They interpreted evidence to the contrary as self-righteous posturing: Only a fool really believed in moral ideas.

The most talented among those suffering narcissistic character disorders were sometimes charismatic individuals who achieved positions of power and leadership—televangelists, crooked CEOs, and all the great dictators of the twentieth century. Often they were masters of image making and manipulating appearances or were inordinately concerned with their appearance and image in others' eyes. But no matter how great their success, they remained painfully vulnerable to envy and resentment of good fortune or superiority of any kind in others— in ability, happiness or contentedness, wealth, beauty, talent, luck, status, class, or even goodness. Such feelings are what drive Iago to attempt Cassio's murder: "He hath a daily beauty in his life that makes me ugly." Pathologically narcissistic characters sometimes envied even others' relative freedom from envy. They sought others' envy as a means of boosting their own pride and at times experienced another's lack of envy as a challenge to their self-importance. Because people with moral character are self-respecting and less prone than others to envy, narcissistic characters often react to them with rage, experiencing these qualities as an affront. In some present-day circles, in fact, the mannerly response to news of others' good fortune is to assure them that it makes one very envious.

Alongside these traits, narcissistic characters displayed others, in themselves morally neutral, that strongly affected the moral life. Rationality and a sense of the real are often skewed or compromised in people suffering narcissistic pathologies. They are prone to strong tendencies to project,* splitting,† and magical

---

* To project is to see in another what is actually in oneself; a greedy man, for example, may see his child or his mate, not himself, as greedy, or a woman who is sexually interested in a man may see him as seductive toward her even though in fact he is unaware of her. In these examples, projection serves defensive functions. The projecting persons save themselves from feeling greedy or guilty, but at the cost of believing false things about themselves and others.
† Splitting is the division of the perceptions of one thing into two or more. For example, according to some psychoanalysts, the infant early on splits perceptions of its mother into the good (satisfying) mother and the bad (frustrating) mother. So long as these perceptions of the mother are split—kept apart in the child's mind—the child can hate the one and love the other and need not feel the pains of ambivalence or guilt. The ordinary child's eventual merging of images of the good mother and bad, its recognition that they belong to the same person, is a giant step toward normal development and sanity.

thinking; their fantasies, wishes, and fears overcome their perception of objective realities. They also experience underlying rage, paranoia, a powerful fear of aging and death, and lesser or deficient abilities to sublimate.* They have a tendency to feel empty, lonely, and bored and a related inability to be interested in anyone or anything except as a means to success, admiration, or some other form of "narcissistic supplies." Most devastating, they suffer from an inability to love. Behind these sufferings, psychotherapists repeatedly found not insuperable self-love, but its opposite: a bottomless sense of worthlessness; feelings of being unimportant, dirty, contemptible, humiliated; and a vulnerability to unendurable shame. When people with narcissistic disturbances fail to win success in life, they may overtly display these feelings instead of obviously egoistic ones.

Narcissistic parents tend to raise narcissistic children, and this is one significant means by which premoral thinking achieves cultural dominance. Narcissistic trends have been linked to cold, neglectful, cruel, and unloving parents or to tendencies on the part of parents to treat the child as a means of stoking their own narcissism with the child's achievements, beauty, or popularity. A failure of empathy on the part of narcissistic parents is often remarked on. Such parents may focus intently on

---

* Sublimation is the unconscious diversion or rechanneling of instinctual energy—aggression or sexual passion, for example—into cultural and social activities. Someone might channel aggression into a surgical career or sexual passion into writing poetry or missionary work. Those with less capacity to sublimate are forced to live on a more instinctual level and are less capable of pursuing interests, arts, hobbies, or professions and less able to find satisfactions and pleasures in life. They may be more volatile, more antisocial.

the child but shower it with a kind of cold, mechanical attention that is not geared toward the child's actual needs and feelings. This produces enormous frustration and rage in the very young child and causes, in the language of psychoanalysis, a "merger" of its images of self and ideal self that enables it to escape its painful feelings. Such a child manages to feel better by equating its actual self with the self it wants to be. It becomes, in its own mind, the measure of good and right; hence what it is and wants must be served. This is the source of the characteristic grandiosity of the pathological narcissist and, in less troubled characters, the source of the sense of entitlement and willingness to treat other persons as means to their ends that was all but definitive of people despised as "yuppies."

Narcissism in the parent often combines with authoritarianism to create some specific failures in child rearing. The parent's own narcissism, being bound up in the need for power and superiority, is expressed in harsh or cruel discipline and demands that the child (and employees and others regarded as inferiors) be submissive. This is why child-rearing advisers on the Christian right often teach that the parents' job is to break the child's will.★ Parents whose narcissism is vulnerable in this way will experience the child's disobedience or rebellion as a narcissistic wound and react to it with fury, even murderous

---

★ See, for example, "Bible Study on the Christian Home—Handout 7, Developing a Christian Home Environment," Grace Bible Chapel, March 6, 2011, Pastor/Teacher Jim Bryant, accessed November 16, 2011, http://www .gbcsa.org/Christian%20Home%20Study/ch7handout.pdf; and "A Biblical View on Behavior Management," accessed November 16, 2011, http://www. rsts.net/proactive/behavior.html.

rage. They ignore or misinterpret the child's inner life and enforce its outer conformity by severe discipline that inculcates not a coherent set of values to which the parent also bows, but only the principle that the parent's wish is law. The child is likely to grow into an adult as authoritarian and narcissistic as its parents.

In any fanatical group, charismatic, narcissistic figures easily assume positions of power. They are idealized and worshipped by followers whose narcissistic hungers are satisfied by identification with the idealized leader or the group he leads. Or they may display fanatic identifications with ethnic, religious, or political groups. Secretly or overtly, they regard these tribes as flawless, all-virtuous, worthy, and best, and the individual, by virtue of membership, also claims those excellences. Americans are skilled at detecting when their neighbors are bolstering a sense of personal superiority in this way. But when enough Americans do so in the very name of being American, many of the rest will turn off their critical faculties and join the fun.

People who are rootless, empty, and heavily reliant on mass media and mass entertainments for guidance are readily drawn into irrationalist movements, groups, and cults that offer them identities and ideas, that give them someone to be. This goes far to explain the quality of pretense or playacting, rather like that of children's secret societies and clubs, that such groups so often display—as did the Branch Davidians at Waco, polygamous Mormon-offshoot cults, and some cultish right-wing militia groups. In fact, one reason why it is so impossible to convince members of cults that their beliefs are irrational is that, very often, they do not actually hold any beliefs, but only mouth the ideas and mimic the behaviors required for acceptance into the group.

MORALITY AS A SUPERVENING VALUE SYSTEM

Morality creates a double value system. Moral goods always co-exist with extramoral or premoral goods; and moral values exist to govern the pursuit of extra- and premoral goods. Beauty, strength, courage, honor, status, pleasure of all sorts, and the other "natural" goods continue to be desired and valued even as, in moral cultures, they are made subordinate to a higher set of values that cannot be reduced to these and that judges whether, when, and how we may enjoy them. In other ethics, for example, that of ancient Athenians, goodness could be equated with reason, and the virtuous man with the rational man, because in such ethics, reason's job is to establish, in accordance with natural value, how to pursue natural values; in that world it made sense to say that the truly rational man would always want what is good. Where morality exists, however, it is perfectly possible for rational persons to want natural goods in contravention of morality, and all of us do so fairly regularly.

Morality's attempt to integrate itself with natural goods is always incomplete and often goes wrong. Moral people once condemned sexual pleasure; they were misled and mistaken. Today, sexual attractions are still matters of great moral perplexity. Most of us fall in love with people who have more, not less, beauty, status, fame, and wealth, and, even worse, we are vulnerable to loving people with beauty, status, and wealth in the absence of any moral virtues at all—at least for a while.

Pretty girls have more lovers than plain Jane Eyres. (But Charlotte Brontë, a hard-nosed moralist if ever there was one, has Jane refuse a moral partnership with St. John Rivers in his missionary work and give her love to Mr. Rochester, who is rich, sexy, pleasure loving—and who loves her for her sturdy English moral qualities.)

Failures in this struggle of the moral with the world of natural value are also evident in the undying appeal of the film and fiction fantasy of virtue rewarded with fame and fortune. And, though morality condones pleasure and the gratifications of narcissism when they are consistent with the chief moral goals, it leads some people into a moral anhedonia. They become ultra-abstemious sourpusses. They include fanatics and religious killjoys, people who encourage us to wear plain clothes and no makeup; go vegan; retreat to a monastery; give up dancing, cards, alcohol, and caffeinated beverages—and sometimes to take exaggerated pleasure in condemning those who allow themselves more enjoyments.

But these failures are outshone by the extraordinary successes of the moral culture. Moral culture creates the common ground, neutral as to wealth and rank, that can support democratic forms of government. It strives to create regimes of true law, indifferent to rank, merciful, and administered with high levels of integrity. Moral culture in its few centuries made possible a blossoming of the intellect and all the arts and sciences with a brilliance unsurpassed in human history. It gave reality to the ideas of liberty, equality, and the universal brotherhood of man, compassion for all, and forgiveness and mercy for wrongdoing. In these ways, moral culture benefits all people.

By supporting favorable conditions for moral development, moral culture also confers on individuals whose minds are shaped in its mold a capacity for the kinds of substantial and happy lives whose successes multiply in the lives of those around them.

Chapter 4

TWO FORMS OF ANTIMORALISM

Careful observation of prospective jurors during voir
dire *may provide the defense with signs that indicate
a prospective juror is a narcissistic authoritarian. . . .
He attempts to project the importance and dominance
of the self through carriage and dress.*

*Narcissistic authoritarians have a strong need to
devalue others who threaten their self-esteem. . . . A
disadvantaged person charged with an offense may be
automatically devalued. He is guilty (a "criminal")
because he is the defendant. Such devaluation is one of
the ways in which a narcissistic authoritarian maintains a sense of superiority. . . . The narcissistic authoritarian will not identify with a criminal defendant
unless that defendant is an authority figure or another
narcissistic authoritarian. For example, if the defendant were an Attorney General of the United States
involved in a criminal endeavor to commit and cover up
crimes, such as John Mitchell in the Watergate years, the
narcissistic authoritarian would make an excellent defense juror.*

The narcissistic authoritarian stresses . . . power and wealth values. . . . Narcissistic authoritarians in all probability have a significant interest in combat prowess, physical strength and weapons. . . .

Narcissistic authoritarians are drawn to sexual material. However, they . . . profess to find the material offensive and seek to punish persons who possess sexual material. The generally accepted psychological view is that their guilt about their interest in such materials is displaced outward on to others. . . .

—WALTER F. ABBOTT AND JOHN BATT, EDS.,

A HANDBOOK OF JURY RESEARCH

(PHILADELPHIA: AMERICAN LAW INSTITUTE–

AMERICAN BAR ASSOCIATION, 1999)

Narcissistic patients characteristically adapt themselves to the moral demands of their environment because they are afraid of the attacks to which they would be subjected if they do not conform, and because this submission seems to be the price they have to pay for glory and admiration; however, one frequently finds that patients of this kind, who have never shown evidence of antisocial activity, think of themselves as "crooks" and as capable of antisocial behavior "if they could get away with it." Needless to say, they also experience other people as basically dishonest and unreliable or only reliable because of external pressures.

—OTTO F. KERNBERG, "FACTORS IN THE

TREATMENT OF NARCISSISTIC PERSONALITIES"

(1970), IN *ESSENTIAL PAPERS ON NARCISSISM,*

ED. ANDREW P. MORRISON (NEW YORK:
NEW YORK UNIVERSITY PRESS, 1986)

ALL THROUGH THE moral epoch, there has been significant opposition to morality, and the opposition has always taken two main forms. One we might call "anomic" or norm-less.★ The other has long been described as "authoritarian." The two types express contrary attitudes toward the authority of conscience and toward authorities who represent the rule of conscience.

In both types of antimoralism, a voracious need to be superior dominates the personality. In the anomic type, that need expresses itself most obviously in demands for freedom from restraint, whether by rules or authorities or enemies. In private life, such people behave egoistically and, secretly or openly, greatly covet status and admiration. They lie, cheat, and betray. Politically, they are indiscriminate. They are more likely than not to favor liberalism, anarchism, or liberal-leaning libertarianism, and they approve of bohemianism and are often attracted to revolutionary movements, but their rebelliousness can, and increasingly does, take right-wing forms. When being rightist offers more ego gratification than being leftist, the anomic type readily switches sides—as did, for example, Jerry Rubin, Norman Podhoretz, and David Mamet.

In the authoritarian type, the demand for superiority expresses itself in a quest for dominance, power, and rank, sometimes achieved by violence or threats of violence. Authoritarians

---

★ The Greek *anomos* means "without law."

ally themselves with authority and insist on obedience and re-spect for authority and rules established by authority. They adopt a moral facade that, in the name of decency and purity, defends tradition, rank, and the powerful against degeneracy. Although they dislike genuine moral values, they insist that their opposi-tion to morality is actually a defense of true, "traditional" mo-rality. Politically, with exceptions, they are rightist, conservative, or right-wing libertarian.

These two forms of opposition to moral values are certainly not the only ways in which people have come to reject the moral. They are, however, the most common and the most powerful, now and in the past. As tools of analysis, the concepts of anomic and authoritarian antimoralism must be used with caution, as they are abstract types that never occur in pure form and some-times overlap. Both rest on narcissistic dispositions of personal-ity that are as variable as individual people are. Like any character type, the anomic and authoritarian types are not fixed and rigid but exist on a spectrum, from faint to strong, and are always found in combination with other traits and tendencies of mind that strongly affect how they play out in a person's life.★

The redefinitions of Right and Left in modern America are a consequence of the absorption of older political dispositions into the increasingly premoral culture. This process transforms the conservatism and liberalism that were each, ultimately, de-fined by a set of moral insights, emphases, and commitments.

★ To discuss these phenomena efficiently, we speak of types and focus on clear points on the spectrum. However, it is morally urgent never to forget that there are many other intersecting lines of analysis and that human be-ings exist at unclear points on all of them.

The contemporary right wing displays none of the historical merits of genuine conservatism, which include skepticism about religious and other enthusiasms, political caution, respect for heritage and genuine understanding of it, and an insistence on resistance to rationalization and temptation. The contemporary anomic left wing, likewise, lacks the integrity, foresight, compassion, and egalitarianism of traditional liberalism.

Fed with power or success, the two types always come to seem more and more alike. The authoritarian, in the absence of external control, abandons decency and purity, and lies, betrays, steals, seeks wealth without limit, harms and hurts (increasingly through violence), fornicates, and overindulges in food, drink, and drugs. The anomic's sense of entitlement, fattened on power or wealth, leads him into the same evils and excesses, and a willingness to embrace violence, as he becomes more and more convinced that he is unique and special and that the rules that bind others do not apply to him.

The tendencies of the anomic and authoritarian types to align with the left and right political poles must not be taken to imply that moral values are politically centrist and moderate, or that conservatism or left-liberalism is always authoritarian or anomic. Morality is radical, immoderate, and in many ways eclectic from the point of view of politics. It cannot be located at any point on the political spectrum. Morality is not politics.

ANOMIC ANTIMORALISM

The anomic character has been the subject of myth, poetry, and drama from ancient times. Dante and Shakespeare portray it over and over. Sparkling portraits of this character type appear in the high era of the moral in the eighteenth and nineteenth centuries— Jane Austen's Crawford siblings in *Mansfield Park*, George Eliot's Rosamond in *Middlemarch*, Charles Dickens's Harold Skimpole in *Bleak House*, and William Thackeray's Becky Sharp in *Vanity Fair.**

Anomic characters, secretly or openly, feel entitled to do what they want and cannot understand why they may not. They gravitate toward defending certain classes of wrongdoers, especially those guilty of lapses in integrity and sexual misbehavior, often in highly sentimental terms. "The heart has its reasons," Woody Allen told us, speaking of his own romantic misdeeds. Naturally, Allen rushed to defend Roman Polanski on his arrest thirty years after he fled criminal sentencing by a California court for having had sex with a thirteen-year-old.

Anomic antimoralism often finds a home in the "Living," "Style," and op-ed sections of newspapers and online media, where it addresses private life with a contrarian opposition to

---

* Heathcliff's sniveling, selfish son, Linton, in Emily Brontë's *Wuthering Heights*, is another example. All these authors strove to depict character as a product of youthful experience and education and usually offered insightful accounts of the sorts of family and rearing that produced their characters' flaws. Twentieth-century authors began to present characters who seemed to spring out of nowhere or to avoid peopling their novels with real characters at all. They also began to present as main characters self-involved men who were important and superior in curiously vague ways, who for no discernible reason were the center of everyone else's world, attended to, desired, studied, and admired for their naughtiness as much as anything else. Bellow, Updike, Roth, and any number of lesser lights all produced such main characters and out of authorial narcissism refused to subject these, their ego proxies, to the indignity of having been influenced by their upbringing.

moral values, frequently in a vaguely post-countercultural tone. Those who write these articles follow a standard formula; in one way or another they suggest that the wrong—selfishness, adultery, parental neglect—is actually right, or, at least, that the people who criticize those things, not the people who do them, are hateful. Any idea with a taint of "rightness" about it seems to them an appropriate target because what they oppose is morality. They describe antimoral trends as being the latest and opposition to them as out-of-date. Or they present themselves as people who feel resentful about being "judged" so as to ingratiate themselves with angry readers who feel the same way. So, for example, we find an article entitled "Plagiarism: A Seventeen-Year-Old Novelist Defends Herself . . . Are We Just Too Old to Understand?" or a snarky piece opposing family dinners, full of skepticism about their alleged benefits and animosity toward the self-righteous people who eat them (and who obnoxiously recommend doing so to others). Stanley Fish, a master of contrarian antimoralism, likes to play the skeptical gadfly and has a genius for using familiar facts to create inauthentic philosophical doubts about authentic moral goods. So, Fish titles an essay "There's No Such Thing as Free Speech, and It's a Good Thing, Too," and, in the same vein, announces the death of objectivity and truth, and doubts that plagiarism is "a big moral deal."*

---

* Stanley Fish, "There's No Such Thing as Free Speech, and It's a Good Thing, Too," in *Debating P.C.: The Controversy over Political Correctness on College Campuses*, ed. Paul Berman (New York: Dell, 1992), pp. 231–45. See also Fish's " 'Plagiarism Is Not a Big Moral Deal," Op-Ed, *New York Times*, August 13, 2010, and "Condemnation Without Absolutes," Op-Ed, *New York Times*, October 15, 2001.

The anomic type tends to see morality as contemptible—or perhaps as naive, unsophisticated, unworldly, what used to be called square, or, sometimes, hypocritical, priggish, judgmental, tyrannical, or smug. When they do not openly or consciously reject morality, people of this character tend to believe in their own moral superiority, based on their freedom from prejudices rooted in emotion and tradition, their assumption of superior rationality, and what they regard as their courage. There is no wrong or evil that they are not brave enough to countenance in the right cause. Thus anomic narcissists often favor social-engineering approaches or hard-hearted, cold solutions to moral problems and endorse utilitarian, relativist, or iconoclastic moral views. They are the sort of people who "think the unthinkable" for the Rand Corporation; the most extreme among them become devotees of the kind of amoral reasoning that can justify any atrocity as a means because of the extraordinary importance of the end. They make a show of regret at the evils they are forced into, but in fact they feel no regret. Their "moral courage" and "rationality" are mere absence of conscience. The term *technocrat*, which had gone out of fashion, has recently been drafted back into common use, no doubt because no other word so accurately names this subgroup of anomic people and their style of thinking. Although technocrats like to describe their thinking as being neutral, value-free, and "realistic," in fact it is always saturated with antimoral values—especially those of power, dominance, and wealth; it is free only of moral values.

Many winners in the meritocratic struggle for position, too, tend toward anomic antimorality, and they are preeminent among those powerful people in government and business today who readily find reasons to shrug off moral and legal restrictions. Bill Gates exemplifies the businessman of this type. Personally, during his rise, he was often reported to be insensitive and uncomprehending, and his corporate behavior was notoriously amoral, ruthless, and predatory. Yet now that he has turned to philanthropy in grand style, his judgment and motives are never doubted, and there is no talk of ironies in his doing good with the money he gained by unfair and illegal competition. On the contrary, he has become a cultural hero, idolized by the media, and his advice is sought on improving education, fighting disease, and other matters as to which there seems no reason at all to believe him competent or wise.

The anomic mentality is common in the upper ranks of all branches of government, including the very top. Even Barack Obama has repeatedly given at least all the appearance of a man suffering from its psychological and moral disabilities. For example, in his remarkably ineffectual negotiations with the recalcitrant Right, he seemed to know neither when to hold his ground nor what ground to hold nor how hard to fight for it. He repeatedly abandoned positions that he had publicly espoused, even in the absence of urgent political necessity to do so. To the dismay of many supporters and admirers, Harold Koh, former dean of the Yale Law School and a longtime prominent defender of the view that the president cannot wage war without congressional approval, took the opposite view as an adviser to Obama's State Department. A close friend explained his flip-flop as "a personality attribute Harold has—he's exceptionally loyal to institutions." But someone who substitutes institutional loyalties for the morally right or confuses the morally right with institutional interests, is a person with a limited grasp of moral obligation, and he or she will inevitably be, morally speaking, a chameleon.

In the past few decades, the United States Department of Justice has provided many examples of the same phenomena, as it evolved from an independent agency charged with upholding law into a politically dominated agency that served the White House's political aims and, in both Republican and Democratic administrations, justified abuses of government power on grounds of national security or political expediency. In one of the worst instances of this, during the George W. Bush administration, Department of Justice lawyers bent the law far past its breaking point to provide legal justifications for torturing prisoners of the United States, and the Obama administration worked hard to shield from prosecution those in the Bush administration who ordered and engaged in these violations of law. The Bush administration also engaged in a campaign of illegal warrantless surveillance of United States citizens, to which Barack Obama—in clear violation of his promises to do the opposite—responded with draconian, life-destroying attempts to prosecute whistle-blowers who exposed aspects of Bush's illegal campaign.

Or consider the views of a pair of professors, Cass Sunstein and Adrian Vermeule, both of Harvard Law School. In January 2009, Sunstein was appointed by Obama to serve as the White House "regulatory czar," with the title of Administrator of the Office of Information and Regulatory Affairs. Not long before Sunstein's appointment, he and Vermeule wrote a paper proposing, among other things, that the government send covert agents to engage in "cognitive infiltration of extremist groups"— online groups, Web sites, and real-world activist groups—that advance false conspiracy theories about the government. These agents would "introduce informational diversity" into those groups so as to undermine their "epistemological networks."* This, they suggested, would guard the masses against the infectious spread of false beliefs—and increase citizens' faith in government officials.†

But the anomic type, being rudderless, is likely to adopt any political stance that serves its need for attention. Thus, for at least two decades, it has often migrated to the mad or irrational Right, the Right that despises science, adopts outlandish conspiracy theories, prefers fundamentalist religion, and entertains

---

* Cass R. Sunstein and Adrian Vermeule, "Conspiracy Theories" (Working Paper 08-03, Harvard Law School, Public Law & Legal Theory; Working Paper 199, University of Chicago Public Law & Legal Theory; Working Paper 387, University of Chicago Institute for Law & Economics), January 18, 2008, pp. 4, 24, accessed November 16, 2011, http://ssrn.com/abstract=1084585.

In *Nudge* (New York: Penguin, 2008), Sunstein and his coauthor, Richard H. Thaler, argue for a movement they call "libertarian paternalism." This movement calls on government to "nudge" individuals' choices in directions that are good for them or for society rather than dictate specific courses of action. "Choice architects" would determine what directions those are and how to reach them. The book is subtly condescending to its readers, who are gently and affectionately nudged to give up objections to the authors' proposals, and it adopts the tolerant, generous, and over-familiar tone of people who believe themselves very clever trying to explain things to the not so clever. Sunstein and Thaler's concept is radical, and so are some of their specific proposals for nudging. As regulatory czar, Sunstein may be in a position to put some of these ideas into practice.

† See Glenn Greenwald's discussion of this proposal: "Obama Confidant's Spine-Chilling Proposal," Salon.com, January 15, 2010, http://www.salon.com/2010/01/15/sunstein_2/.

itself with megalomaniac fantasies of remaking the country or even of overturning the government and replacing it with a theocracy or something else more all-American.* To one degree or another, Glenn Beck, Rush Limbaugh, Sarah Palin, and Michele Bachmann seem either to fit or *play* to this profile. Members of the anomic, irrational Right feel inferior in the face of a world that both dominates them and works on the basis of truths, rules, and goodness that speak to nothing inside

---

* Or something much closer to a dictatorship than the Constitution contemplates. A clear example of this—and of how anomic thinking, being so often contrarian, rudderless, and attention seeking, often promotes ideas more traditionally defended by authoritarians—may be found in a book by Adrian Vermeule and Eric A. Posner, a University of Chicago Law School professor, *Terror in the Balance: Security, Liberty, and the Courts* (New York: Oxford University Press, 2007). This book proposes that in times of national emergency, lawyers and courts should be prevented from interfering with executive action and that civil liberties, due process, and other constitutional values should give way to executive wisdom, decisiveness, and knowledge. It objects to the Supreme Court's "lawless" (p. 271) hamstringing of the Bush administration in *Hamdan v. Rumsfeld*, which held that the Geneva Conventions constrained its treatment of Hamdan, Osama bin Laden's driver and bodyguard. And it sees *Hamdan* as evidence of how important it is that in future national emergencies, the courts show far more deference to the executive. More recently, in *The Executive Unbound: After the Madisonian Republic* (New York: Oxford University Press, 2011), Posner and Vermeule argue that the American presidency will and should increase in power and that the Madisonian checks and balances of the Constitution have become dysfunctional and dated. We would be better off, they maintain, to prevent executive excess by relying on such political checks as are provided by the media, competition between political parties, and the strength of public opinion—no doubt because those means have worked so well for us lately.

them. Thus they fume about the liberal "elite," they tout their own homegrown common sense and wisdom, and in a hundred other ways they deny that anyone needs to know or understand what they, and those who listen to them, do not know or understand. They subscribe to pseudomoralities so as to be able to see themselves as the good and the wise people of the world; their aim is to create a world in which they do not feel inferior, incompetent, impotent, and bad—and in which they can do what they like without loss of face, status, or respectability.

When it suits their goals, people of the anomic narcissistic type, despite their apparent differences in style or politics, tend to make moral errors in similar patterns. As a result of deficient empathy, compassion, and social sense, they are prone to superficial and confused perceptions of social realities. This undermines their common sense and can induce them to "go too far." They often display a distinctive combination of lack of common sense, social sense, and moral sense* that is illustrated in the following anecdotes, all drawn from real life:

A woman left her young son of five or six alone to run the neighborhood most of the day without supervision. When her neighbors protested, she responded haughtily, "Timmy has his life, and I have mine."

---

* When I refer to "moral sense," I am using "sense" with the meaning that it has in the phrases *common sense* and *good sense*, that is, as referring to good judgment, especially but not only about everyday matters. Philosophers sometimes use the phrase to name a theory about moral judgment that likens it to sense perception. I do not subscribe to that theory.

In a rainstorm, a woman stood on a deserted corner of Park Avenue trying to hail a cab with no luck. After about ten minutes, a cab pulled up, and at the same time a second woman emerged from a doorway just around the corner. As the first woman was opening the cab door, the second came running up, calling out with a completely convincing air of being wronged and outraged, "*Oh* no, you don't. No, you don't, lady. Don't you *dare*," jumped into the cab, and slammed the door.

A philosophy professor, infamous for his involvement in an adulterous scandal involving the wife of a colleague (which ended with many bitter feelings and a permanent swap of wives), regularly taught an undergraduate ethics course. He always devoted one lecture to the subject of adultery, arguing that an adulterer committed no moral wrong so long as he or she kept the betrayed spouse from finding out. Only hurting others was wrong, and a spouse who didn't know was not hurt.

Most of the cultural changes first deplored as "narcissistic" in the 1970s are expressions of anomic antimoralism. Since then, the real-life worlds of business, government, and big-media journalism have increasingly become home to people in this mold. But after the seventies, the more prominent examples of antimoralism are of the other breed, the authoritarian, and this type, unlike the anomic, is less often seen as what it is.

AUTHORITARIAN ANTIMORALISM

Dickens gave us an immortal portrait of this character type in Mr. Murdstone, David Copperfield's severe, sadistic, and piously hypocritical stepfather. Murdstone believes in being "firm" with children. They must be "subdued," "conquered," their will crushed with floggings, deprivations, and humiliations, all of which Murdstone inflicts on David to enforce his obedience. Egoism is at the core of Murdstone's cruelty; the narcissistic rage that lies behind his pretense of religion is frighteningly easy to arouse. Murdstone's sister illustrates how such people are both submissive and domineering; she is tyrannical to David and his mother and at the same time obedient to her brother, whom she idolizes.

In the real world, Dick Cheney, the polygynous sect leader Warren Jeffs, and Osama bin Laden all appear to belong to this type, along with all the authoritarian dictators of the twentieth century. Back in the seventies, so did the Reverend Jim Jones, whose sadism, cruelty, and tyranny were apparent long before he led hundreds of his followers into mass suicide. Occasionally, authoritarian personalities are attracted to communism and other leftist regimes that stand for order, powerful leadership, and, often, an antihedonic culture. Authoritarian narcissistic parents are well represented in show business by stage mothers and fathers—like the Beach Boys' Wilson brothers' father, Murry Wilson, and the Jackson Five's father—and by the parental behavior of narcissistic actors like Joan Crawford. Christian fundamentalist boot camps and schools for "troubled" children have occasionally been closed down for child abuse. Such places aim to produce, above all, children who are obedient and submissive.

Rules and the laying down of rules are central in the authoritarian mentality, which tends to understand rules, and obedience to rules, in a mechanical, legalistic way, as when young women with considerable sexual experience become born-again virgins or insist that they are virgins because they have had only anal or oral sex, or when businessmen think themselves morally innocent of theft and fraud or tax evasion when they engage in technical, hairsplitting evasions of the laws. Or consider this interchange between a member of a right-wing militia in Texas and a journalist:

> "Jesus said if a man is to strike you on the cheek, turn to him the other cheek. But if he strikes you on the other cheek, God leaves that up to you. You can either turn and walk away or you can fight."
>
> But he didn't say that, [the journalist responded].
>
> "No. But the catch is, after he strikes you on the other cheek, God doesn't tell you what to do. It depends on how you're struck[.]"★

All these are cases of childish, literal interpretations of a rule or command and rejection of its real sense. This is a sign of continuing reliance on external authority and external punishments and the absence of the real self-government and reliance on internal sanctions that is characteristic of true conscience.

Because they have inadequate self-control, many such people seesaw between impulses toward dominance and submissiveness. They are readily inflated by success and power and deflated

---

★ Alex Hannaford, "Armed and Extremely . . . Patriotic," the *Sunday Telegraph*, August 15, 2010, p. 12.

by failure; they alternately swagger and cower, meek and submissive to those who are stronger but domineering and arrogant to those weaker than themselves. Like Uriah Heep, they are humble only until power and success embolden them and convince them of their own superiority. Then they easily become bullies. Their need for dominance often means that they find special pleasure in violent or physical domination—in blows, tortures, restraints, or, at the extremes, murders. They project unconscious feelings of worthlessness, effeminacy, weakness, and dirtiness onto others—homosexuals, liberals, Jews, blacks, effete, weakling intellectuals—who are then seen to merit punishment, humiliation, and mistreatment. Sadism toward such people shores up their sense of strength, superiority, and righteousness. Thus Nazism defended German superiority, entitlement, decency, and purity against those onto whom it projected all its own evil, who were then perceived as degenerate, inferior, subhuman, and worthless beings meriting enslavement and extermination. The restraints of law and morality were despised and cast aside. As many worried observers have pointed out, the same spirit of murderousness is now often on display in United States politics, overtly or covertly, as, for example, when in campaigning prior to the 2012 presidential primaries, Rick Perry boasted that if Federal Reserve chairman Ben Bernanke came to Texas, "we would treat him pretty ugly." After Democratic senator Paul Wellstone died in a plane crash in 2002, right-wing Web sites exploded in witty hilarity. There is similar exultation when doctors who perform abortions are murdered.

Punishment, revenge, and retribution are at the heart of authoritarians' sense of right and are essential to their emotional equilibrium.* They are not likely to feel pity for prisoners, or suspicion of the power of authority, or sympathy for underdogs, the poor, and little people; all such feelings are extinguished in this type of mind. It sees genuine morality as weakness and insists that its own, tough premoral ideas of right and wrong are true, old-fashioned morality. It particularly objects to moral demands for compassion, mercy, pity, forgiveness, and equality, and it scorns the "bleeding hearts" who whine about such things. What it denounces as bleeding heart liberalism, as so many others have pointed out, is often actually old-style conservatism. The cultural dominance of this kind of authoritarian thinking is reflected in popular film and fiction in which the pleasures of triumphant revenge are endlessly repeated as the standard happy ending.

Moral constraints produce narcissistic distress in the authoritarian character because they conflict with its need for revenge and for superiority in power, strength, and rank or status. Though sometimes this type is ascetic, more often it is incontinent—violent, cruel, and greedy for food, sex, and money. The kindness and self-restraint that morality calls for it experiences as emasculating, castrating, or effeminate.† The authoritarian antimoralist has no guilt about injustices that make some rich and others poor and no objection to social hierarchies. He has difficulty in seeing success as other than meritorious and failure as

---

* The authoritarian narcissist needs to punish and wants the punishment to be humiliating or degrading and painful. He wants to break down pride and produce a conviction of worthlessness and inferiority—in children, prisoners, or anyone else subject to punishment.

† This is especially true when morality is identified as female or feminine.

other than deserved and contemptible. Fulminating ego dictates these attitudes: Such a person feels superior, strongly entitled to power and control, and reacts with narcissistic rage if challenged.

Authoritarian antimoralism is a psychologically primitive mentality. It projects its fears and self-hatred onto others, whom it demeans and degrades, sometimes mercilessly and sadistically. It is prone to paranoia (and the projective tendencies of paranoiacs) and a variety of sexual anxieties—in males, especially, homophobia, fears of castration, and fear and disgust toward female genitalia—and these anxieties spill over into their political ideas. Men of this type commonly oppose laws they perceive as emasculating—gun control laws, tax laws, and laws restricting vehicles felt to be masculine, such as outdoor sports vehicles and SUVs.★ But almost any government regulation can tap such feelings in them. Such men often loudly avow "family values" while pursuing affairs and divorces because they experience the restraints of marriage and fidelity, too, as threats to their masculinity. Fear of emasculation and a need to dominate, likewise, make them oppose the "liberation" of blacks and females and incline them toward religious sects that call for wifely submission to husbands. Authoritarian Christians have often

---

★ They invariably support the death penalty. In 2010, Kay Bailey Hutchison was running against Rick Perry in the Texas gubernatorial primary and, as part of her campaign research, had voters in a focus group asked how they felt about candidate Perry's having allowed a man to be executed who was probably innocent. She was surprised to find that the voters did not mind, or even approved. One man's now famous reply: "It takes balls to execute an innocent man."

portrayed Christ as a tough he-man. The group has its female members, bullies like Ann Coulter and Michelle Malkin, who pride themselves on being tough and mean, at least verbally, and a group of madcap, exhibitionist women who carefully package themselves as "traditional" through their dress, style, and born-again Christian ideas while wielding or seeking enormous political power—women like Sarah Palin, Christine O'Donnell, and Michelle Bachmann. But this type of authoritarian is usually a male animated by a primitive ideal of manhood and, quite often, tormented by homosexual wishes that he denies.

Though the authoritarian premoral character, like the anomic, is prominent in contemporary politics, it is no more a modern or recent invention than the anomic. This kind of human being was common in fifteenth-century England and even later among the group of peoples historians have called "borderlanders" (southern Scots and northern English and Irish) of the seventeenth and eighteenth centuries, places that sent huge numbers of immigrants to the American colonies in the eighteenth century. In these times and places, the father held great power over wife and children. Women's low status meant that wealthy husbands strayed or kept concubines or, among the poor, that women bore huge broods of children whose labor, along with that of their mothers, was indispensable to their fathers. The fathers readily exposed their children to danger and hardship and used harsh discipline to make them submissive.

Authoritarian antimoralism often finds that it has little quarrel with polygyny. The powerlessness and low status of women and children are always exaggerated in polygynous cultures and in those that tolerate harems or concubinage. The moral mind does not readily arise where polygyny is practiced because poly-gynous families do not provide children with the type of family structure that favors the development of moral psychology. Where morality already exists, polygyny and concubinage will over time undermine it and set in motion generalized moral collapse—sexual abuse of children, abuses of power, greed, dis-honesty, cruelty, and diminished rationality—a conclusion sup-ported by evidence from polygynous American families. In the United States, polygyny was practiced by Mormon descendants of borderlanders—an authoritarian culture characterized by powerful and power-hungry males, submissive women, and comparatively low levels of concern and affection for children. In fundamentalist offshoots of Mormonism that still practice polygyny (whose members number ten thousand or possibly, according to some observers, many times that figure), social pa-thologies are well in evidence. In the worst cases, these include widespread sexual abuses; increasingly bizarre social relations of all sorts; the marriage of girls at, or even before, puberty, will-ingly or not, to much older men—often to middle-aged or old men; the marrying of ten, twenty, thirty, and more wives on the part of the most powerful men and thus the existence of "fami-lies" with thirty or more children by one father.*

---

* Some scholars have recently offered arguments in favor of legalizing po-lygamy. See, for example, Andrew March, "Is There a Right to Polygamy?: Marriage, Equality and Subsidizing Families in Liberal Public Justification," *Journal of Moral Philosophy* 8, no. 2 (2011): 246–72. See also Martha Nuss-baum, *Liberty of Conscience* (New York: Basic Books, 2008), p. 197. Their ar-guments provide antimoralism, which in both its common forms likes the idea of polygamy, with a philosophical rationale. Anomic antimoralism finds nothing to object to in polygamy because its ethical thinking tends to

Societies in which the authoritarian type dominates are always strongly hierarchical and always keep women in subservient positions. In these societies, worth is a matter of status; virtue consists in submission on the part of subordinates, wives, children, and slaves, and in dominance, courage, strength, and power in their lords. Power, wealth, and status are high values. Honor and pride are paramount, and—clear evidence of the narcissistic nature of the underlying psychology—shame is a matter of life and death. Guilt is comparatively weak as a

---

hover near the limited principle that people should be free to do as they like and because it enjoys being contrarian. Authoritarian antimoralism is highly attracted to the power and status of the polygynous patriarch, and polygamy, in practice, almost always means polygyny.

The polygamy of Mormon offshoots in the United States today succeeds in inducing women to enter plural marriages by teaching them that it is a command of God, that a woman can enter heaven only as the plural wife of a polygamous patriarch to whom she swears obedience, and that she must have as many children as possible and tolerate many co-wives doing likewise because a man's status in the afterlife increases with the numbers of wives and children he has. Where polygyny is widespread, it inevitably results in a large surplus of unwed boys. In the grotesque sect led by Warren Jeffs, now serving a life sentence for, among other crimes, raping a twelve-year-old child "wife," the potential threat that the excess boys posed to their elders' plural marriages was dealt with by routinely forcing them out of the community and permanently denying them any contact with their families or friends; boys as young as twelve were expelled in this fashion. The media reported the story of these "lost boys" with an uncommon degree of shock. Journalists, well-educated members of the mainstream, child-centered society, seem never to have suspected that marital and family arrangements quite unlike those of that mainstream might entail attitudes toward children and mates unlike those of the mainstream. (*footnote continues*) mechanism of self-control. Among males, submission is shameful, revenge is essential to honor, and dominance is based on power and cruelly enforced. Such societies typically either practice slavery or rely on other forms of coerced or debased labor.

The authoritarian displays the usual irrationality of the premoral mind. He ignores contradictions in his thinking and does so all the more easily when some authority directs him to.* In present-day America, millions take the word of the

---

In the nineteenth century, aboriginal polygyny in Australia sometimes coped with the problem of wifeless youths by giving them a male child to serve as a "boy-wife." Other polygynous cultures resort to polyandry; in those places, however, the shared "wife" is unlikely to hold an enviable or desirable status comparable to that of the male with many wives. While there are sometimes apparently rational and merciful reasons for polygamy—for example, in simple societies where women would otherwise be in danger of attack or starvation or devastating social displacement—this is by no means necessarily or even usually the case. In any event, these recent arguments for polygamy are not based on claims that any dire necessities require overturning the fundamental social institution of monogamy, or on any research showing that this would turn out well. Scholars' shallow and gratuitous arguments about polygamy provide one more example of the decline of moral common sense.

* Authoritarian narcissism is readily confused with *authoritarian morality*, an early form of genuinely moral mentality that resembles modern authoritarian narcissism only in superficials. Authoritarian morality is identical with the moral mentality per se as it existed in much of its early history. A key moral distinction between an authoritarian moral mind and a narcissistic one lies in the fact that in the former, guilt strongly predominates over shame as a mechanism of self-judgment and control. Equally important, in an authoritarian morality the role of compassion is strong and there is revulsion against

Bible literally and reject not only scientific theories of evolution, but the entire Western system of knowledge and belief insofar as it conflicts with biblical literalism. They create alternative "universities," sciences, histories, and schools and schooling systems, which indulge their needs by certifying a substitute set of authorities that mimic real science and the genuine pursuit of knowledge. In this way, a belief system that is primitive and irrational acquires a facade of reliability, rationality, authority, and legitimacy. At the same time, these social forms enable their ideas to spread and transmit themselves to future generations, and they create an authoritarian culture whose members feel that they belong to a separate society dedicated to an antimoral war.

---

sadism; sadism is rerouted into the superego and cruelly punishes the self rather than the other. In authoritarian morality, love is a deeply held value—between parents and children, husband and wife, and friends and neighbors. In both authoritarian narcissism and authoritarian morality, obedience and respect for authority and tradition are high values and the father holds power over women and children, but in authoritarian morality he does so only *under moral constraint* and only insofar as he himself is obedient to the moral. Authoritarian morality naturally evolves into a broader egalitarianism as its own premises are consistently applied and overcome premoral cultural habits.

Chapter 5

LOVE AND MONEY: THE CONTRACTING ROLE OF THE FAMILY

*The psychological patterns associated with pathologi-
cal narcissism, which in less exaggerated form manifest
themselves in so many patterns of American culture—
in the fascination with fame and celebrity, the fear of
competition, the inability to suspend disbelief, the
shallowness and transitory quality of personal relations, the horror of death—originate in the peculiar
structure of the American family, which in turn origi-
nates in changing modes of production. Industrial
production takes the father out of the home and diminishes the role he plays in the conscious life of the
child.*

—CHRISTOPHER LASCH, *THE CULTURE OF
NARCISSISM* (1979)

TO ACCOUNT FOR the rise of the moral mentality, scholars point to sources in religion, economics, and politics.
These explanations are valid but incomplete. For such causes to
produce this effect, they had to have acted on or through the

chief mechanism by which character is shaped: the family, the social group that bears the first and heaviest burdens of rearing children. The single greatest influence on the malleable portions of character, those not biologically or otherwise fixed, is early experience in the family, and especially a child's early experience with its parents and siblings.

The moral capacity develops most readily in people fortunate enough to have had an adequate experience of a certain kind of intense love, usually from parents who loved them for their own sake and perceived them as separate individuals, with their own fates, rights, and lives, not as the parents' extensions, labor sources, or possessions, or as props for their parents' power or egoism. This affection enables the child to control and redirect aggression, narcissism, and desire and to achieve the sturdy individuality of the moral mind. The moral individual has—and must have—a strong sense of self.

Moral individuals' rationality and objectivity, their moral strength—their ability to guide their conduct according to a sense of right and wrong rather than what others may think or do, the dominance of guilt over shame as the primary inner mechanism of self-control, and the capacity for love, empathy, and compassion for others—all these blossom in children who experience them as part of parental love. Moral characters are able to love their children in the way that matters, and being loved in that way reproduces these capacities, and the ability to love, in their children. Thus the psychology of the moral individual is passed from generation to generation, but the transmission is known to be endangered by accidents of life that deprive the child of one or both parents, their affection, or their influence—or those of an adequate substitute— and by distortions in parental love and aggression.

The village does indeed play an essential role in forming the child's moral character. The older the child grows, the more important outside influences become. Ties with other relatives, religion, formal education, friends, and a wide variety of social and life experiences profoundly affect moral development. But unless the core of the moral psychology is laid down early in life, in the family or in an adequate substitute for the family, it arises only haphazardly. The village builds on the psychological foundation laid in the family, and it cannot readily supply that foundation when it is lacking.

Nor does the family ever cease to play a necessary role in supporting its children's moral growth. The development of moral maturity and strength requires intense, continuing fostering from many sources into adulthood. Still, the moral qualities develop reliably in ordinary, imperfect human children with ordinary, imperfect parents and villages, only assuming that these imperfections do not prevent them from achieving psychological adulthood and a capacity for love.

These straightforward facts about the mutually supportive roles of family and society in bringing up children were hopelessly obscured when the family became a battlefield in the culture wars. Culture warriors on the right defended the "traditional" family, disdained women's rights, and ignored the damage its own favored policies inflicted on families, while some feminists and others on the cultural left maintained that the family was little more than a machine for generating misery, oppression, and injustice. These left-wing critics of the family, many of whom were exemplars of what in an earlier chapter I called "anomic antimoralism," argued for abolishing marriage and denied that single-parent homes added even the slightest risk to children's welfare. Many of their opponents were authoritarian antimoralists who wanted women to resume roles subservient and obedient to men. The loudness of this debate made it hard for more rational defenses and criticisms of the institution to be heard.

THE FAMILY AND THE MORAL PSYCHOLOGY

The Roots of Conscience

The foundations of the moral psychology are laid down in early experience in the family. All schools of thought on child development now recognize that very young children who are deprived of a strong, loving connection with parental figures suffer emotional catastrophe. Current debates concern only the effects of different degrees and kinds of deprivation, especially those that may result from loss of one or both parents or from different kinds of substitute care for children.* What early experiences so overstrain the very young child's need for parental care and love that the child's good development is threatened?

---

* There are also developmental difficulties that stem from insufficient distance and independence from parents; the helicopter parenting of relatively privileged people is justly criticized. The social pressures that are most potent in the lives of most contemporary American children, however, tend to deprive children, especially poor children, of sufficient involvement with parents. But it must be understood that *psychological* distance and physical and social distance are different things. A child may be psychologically merged with or overdependent on a working parent whom it does not see much of during the work week, while a child of stay-at-home parents may be highly independent.

In psychoanalytic terms, conscience is, for the most part, a dimension of the "superego," the self-judging and self-controlling part of the mind.* To explain when and how it develops, Freud famously declared that it arises as "heir" to the Oedipus complex, a stage in child development that occurs in the preschool to early school years. Conscience resulted from resolution of a family love triangle consisting of mother, father, and child, in which the child's love for its mother results in a jealous rivalry with the father; when all goes well in the child's development, love for father and fear of his anger finally neutralize or contain the child's aggression[†] and jealousy and result in a new capacity for internalized self-control.[‡]

---

* For the purposes of this book, conscience and superego may be taken as roughly identical. In fact, the superego issues nonmoral prohibitions and ideals as well as moral ones, and some parts of conscience may lie outside the superego.

[†] Morality neither requires nor approves of the complete overthrow of aggression. A degree of aggression is an essential element of good character and the good life. Masochistic, spiritless, or cowardly characters are no more morally admirable than sadistic and violent ones. Though this is obvious, it must be said because in certain quarters today the restraint of aggression for moral reasons is equated with cowardice and weakness.

[‡] Oedipal theory says roughly this: The small child falls in love with mother and wants her for itself alone; it is possessive. It wants to be loved first and best, which leads it not only to rivalries with siblings for mother's love but to a wish to replace the father in her affections. The wish to push aside the father, however, arouses painful feelings, because the child also loves its father. It fears the father's anger and imagines that he will retaliate or punish the child for its jealous wishes. The child's feelings eventually reach a crisis stage and must be resolved. (Or, at least, the child is likely to arrive at this point of crisis if it has successfully mastered earlier challenges of development, failure in any of which might undermine its efforts to deal with this one.) Out of this

This theory was much criticized, refined, and elaborated in the century after Freud offered it, with the result that it became the subject of a vast, subtle, and contentious world literature. Psychoanalytic thought itself splintered into many schools that took different positions on the theory, and historians and social scientists subjected it to empirical tests that it passed only in part. While they tended to confirm the existence of an Oedipal stage in child development, they also concluded that it is not universal in biology or culture. Rather, it is the product of specific family forms, and it alters or disappears as those family forms alter and disappear within and across cultures. Child development experts and clinicians weighed in, too, with more and better observations of children. They pointed out that the Oedipal plot plays out with far more variety and emotional complexity than Freud saw and that it depends heavily on even earlier events in a child's life.

In light of these many corrections, refinements, and disagreements, it says something about the power of the original insight that its outlines are still respected by many theorists and clinicians,

---

combination of fear, anxiety, and love for the father, or whoever is in the role of father, the child restrains its jealousy and anger and its love for mother. The child bows to reality: Mother and father belong to each other in a way that excludes the child, and it must accept this. The child's comfort in this disappointment is its father's love; this love enables it to identify more strongly with him and internalize his demands, becoming the father's proxy in controlling its own conduct. The process just described happens in gender-reverse, too: The child loves its father possessively and jealously would like to replace its mother in his affections, and so forth. The Oedipal stage is just this time early in life when children find themselves grappling with conflicting and powerful feelings of love, possessiveness, jealousy, and anger directed at their parents. Girls and boys probably face different Oedipal challenges.

who continue to perceive special significance for the moral life in the emotions, jealous conflicts, and realities that the Oedipal triangle forces the child to confront early in life. In the process of sorting out these feelings and conflicts, they believe, a child takes a major step in a long moral journey and in doing so sets in motion a cascade of further good consequences in its development. The new inner restraint that begins to rule over the child's wishes serves as the nucleus around which other internalizations gather.*
Eventually the child internalizes demands, ideals, and values of both parents, as well as those of siblings, other relatives, nannies, and friends whom it loves or admires and authorities outside the home—teachers, coaches, religious leaders, and others. In school, in religious practice, in sport and games, in exposure to literature, film, music, and other arts, the child constantly encounters and absorbs (or rejects) moral teachings, which further shape its character. These all become part of conscience.

This ordinary process can misfire in a multitude of ways,

---

* In the premoral mind (and in the premoral dimensions of mind that persist even into moral adulthood), internalization of the parents means identification; literally, the child "struggle[s] and yearn[s] to attain identity or 'oneness' with the qualities that originally came from idols" (David Milrod, "The Superego," *Psychoanalytic Study of the Child* 57 [2002]: 131–48). The child who sees his parents as skilled and powerful strives to imitate them— literally to become them by becoming like them. The little child totters about in mother's shoes or pretends to drive father's car. At a slightly later age, the child works hard to acquire in reality the abilities of the parent. It learns to throw a ball, to read, or to carry out tasks on a computer. When the child acquires the adult skill, it experiences a rise in self-esteem. When it fails, it feels small, weak, or incompetent. Its self-esteem is diminished; it is humiliated.

and there are multitudes of books and journals devoted to describing them.★ Its success, moreover, is at most necessary and not sufficient to ensure that someday the small child will have a robust adult moral conscience; and "necessary" here does not mean much more than that this is the only way we know how to bring this development about with any regularity. Even this last generalization must be hedged with a dozen qualifications. Accidents of life, birth order, parental temperament and character, children's temperamental differences, their biological endowments, the unique quirks of each child's thinking, and especially their social and political environments—all these and many more factors feed in to the developmental process that shapes adult conscience.

THE MODERN WESTERN FAMILY AND MORAL CULTURE

Family Type

The cultural dominance of morality begins around the time of the Protestant Reformation with the rise of the modern Western family,† the family type most favorable to the development of the moral psychology and the moral individual. The style of

---

★ One important form of failure that it takes is not weak or absent conscience, but a ferocious, cruel, and irrational one.

† Historians of the family have engaged in a decades-long debate about whether the modern Western family is really so different from its medieval predecessors—a debate too complicated and cantankerous to summarize here. It seems clear to me that for purposes of understanding the moral life, the changes matter far more than whatever continuities exist.

family life that then began to emerge was characterized by more intimate relations between the sexes and between parents and children, higher status for women and children, and a greater role for men in domestic life and child rearing. These changes eventually resulted in the intimate, affectionate, informal, individualistic, emotionally intense modern family—a family style now common all over the world. We no longer kneel to our parents, kiss their hands, or address them as sir or madam, and we do not stand or respectfully restrain our speech and emotions in their presence—as in earlier times people did even into adulthood. Neither do we address our husbands and wives as Mr. or Mrs.; we are amused when Jane Austen's Emma forswears modern attitudes and vows that in marriage she will never call her husband anything but "Mr. Knightley."

There are many social and historical preconditions for the rise of the modern family type. It cannot arise, for example, in places where women do not enjoy some minimal level of freedom and status. In social systems with extensive polygyny or concubinage and those in which women are segregated, subjugated, or devalued, children often live with the women in separate women's houses or quarters and males have nothing to do with rearing them until the boys are ejected from the women's quarters and sent to the men's—usually well past the age at which conscience takes shape—and in some places, the boy's maternal uncle will then assume the authoritative role in his life that we allot to biological fathers. It is obvious that in these circumstances the family triangle—mother, father, and child—will fail to exert the same kinds of formative influence that it does in modern Western-style families. These different family patterns naturally produce people whose psychology is unlike those of people raised in Western-style families, and around the world and throughout history, including Western history, such differences are the rule, not the exception.

Although the modern Western family type may not be the only one that can give rise to the Western moral psychology described in this and earlier chapters, it seems to be the type in which this happens most regularly and reliably. The moral mind is thus a cultural product, the result of a specific type of psychology dependent upon specific styles of family life that are in turn dependent on specific forms of cultural support. It can and does arise anywhere, but it becomes an average, expectable development only in those historically uncommon times and places where the modern family style, in one of its many variants, exists. Those kinds of families did not exist in ancient Sparta or Athens or in medieval Florence or London and are infrequently met with today in Somalia or certain wealthy neighborhoods of Manhattan. But families of this kind are now multiplying all over the globe, as women's and children's status and freedom rise everywhere, as Western cultural influences spread, and as other cultures independently undergo experience that leads them down similar paths to those that Western peoples have followed.

To give life to the assertion that family life in feudal Europe was unfavorable to the development of the moral mind, consider one specific way in which this was true: In many medieval Western cities, families with the means to do so, including many of fairly modest means, commonly sent infants out of the home shortly after birth to be raised by wet-nurses for one to two or more years, when they were returned to their homes as small, traumatized, perfect strangers. During this period, they saw their parents infrequently or not at all.★ The system resulted in an appalling death rate among infants and frequent abuse of the tiny, helpless children. In many places, children as young as seven or eight were again sent out of their parents' home into service in others' homes. These practices were consistent with more formal, less intimate bonds between parents and children,† and they were less favorable to moral development and more favorable to that era's premoral, feudal mentality, one that, as we have seen, had pronounced narcissistic traits. The gradual rise of the moral mentality coincided with the gradual decline of feudalism, the transformation of parent-child relations, an increase in love marriages, an increase in participation of males in domestic life, and the growth of the modern kind of family.

The kinds of experiences that would impede moral development and promote other kinds of development are predomi-

---

★ See James Bruce Ross, "The Middle-Class Child in Urban Italy, Fourteenth to Early Sixteenth Century," in *The History of Childhood*, ed. Lloyd deMause (New York: Jason Aronson, 1974), pp. 183–228. Claire Tomalin's *Jane Austen: A Life* (New York: Alfred A. Knopf, 1997), pp. 7–8, makes us aware that the practice persisted in some places even as late as 1775, when Jane was born. All the Austen children, including Jane, were sent out to a nurse for nearly two years. The Austens, however, were said to visit their infants nearly daily.

† This claim falls into a territory hotly debated by historians of the family, one group of which insists strenuously that medieval parents loved their children as much as we do. I am more convinced by their opponents in this debate. The question is not whether our medieval ancestors loved their children—they surely did—but what love was for people like them, whose experiences, early and late, were so different from ours.

nant throughout history. We would not go far wrong if we called them normal, or at least usual, for most of Western history. The evolution of family life and relations between the sexes in directions that favored moral development is what is abnormal and unusual. But because the development of the moral mind did in fact track this evolution, it seems likely that its reversal would have a negative effect on moral development, and, naturally, economic and social forces that harm or destroy this model of family life can be expected to contribute to a reversion to premoral thinking and a decline in the institutions that depend on a minimum social level of moral thinking.

Thus, observers seeking causes of the transformation in moral character rightly focus on changes in the structure, economy, and behavior of the family over the past century and a half, and they point out two arenas of such change that should concern us: first, the gradual separation of males from their families and the rise of the mother-dominated family; second, the gradual decline in family rearing and the steady increase in the institutionalization of child rearing. Both sets of changes tracked the process of industrialization.

ABSENT FATHERS, SINGLE MOTHERS

Fathers Leave Home

Economic factors affect the family roles of fathers and mothers, and historians have studied them with urgent attention. One of the most obvious, a result of the process of industrialization, is the separation of males from their families. Today, artisans, craftsmen, small-business owners, doctors, lawyers, clerks and other white-collar workers, and laborers of all sorts rarely work out of their homes or on their own or nearby property as they once did; instead they spend long hours in factories, offices, and institutions. As changing forms of work required fathers to spend less and less time employed in or near the home, fathers' parental roles contracted and mothers' parental roles widened. Fathers left in the morning and returned late, often long after the children were asleep, and if the children were awake, they might have been ordered not to bother their tired fathers. Women increasingly became de facto single parents. Today, a middle-class man who comes from several generations of a middle-class family is likely to see less of his children than his grandparents and great-grandparents did—even if he sees more of them than factory workers did in 1900.

Today, fathers' separation from home also, more and more frequently, takes the dramatic and tragic form of total abandonment of their children and their children's mother, a phenomenon only partly attributable to economic causes. Women's entry into the workforce is clearly part of the explanation; women who can support their children without a mate are more likely to take on single parenthood than those who depend upon male support. Frequent divorce is another substantial cause; fathers' contact with their children and their commitment to them often diminish radically once they move out of the family home: After two to three years, 20 percent of the children of divorce have no contact with their fathers and many more have minimal contact, a situation that grows only worse with time;* and children whose par-

---

* J. B. Kelly and R. E. Emery, "Children's Adjustment Following Divorce: Risk and Resiliency Perspectives," *Family Relations* 52, no. 4 (2003): 352–62.

ents were never married or never cohabited—an increasingly large percentage of all children—have significantly less contact with nonresident fathers than the children of marriages.

Whatever the causes, the effects are beyond doubt: Far fewer children live in intact families.* Far more children today are raised by single parents.† Between 1900 and 1960, the number of children living with a single parent—who was almost always, as now, their mother—was relatively stable at about 10 percent, and only about half of those were children of unwed mothers or divorce.‡ As of 2008, according to the U.S. Census Bureau, 29.5 percent of all children in the United States lived in single-parent homes, almost always with their mothers, and in 2009 the percentage of black children living with their mothers alone was 50 percent. Although upper-middle-class single mothers by choice get a lion's share of negative attention, in fact the phenomenon is heavily concentrated in lower socioeconomic

---

* All explanations of the historical evolution of the family point to subtle and complex influences and to causal circles and loops. In these processes, frequent divorce and the increase in single parenthood are causes as well as effects, and they are not independent of economic factors.

† In the nineteenth century, children were much more likely to lose one or both parents to death. But far fewer were abandoned by their fathers, and far fewer grew up never having had or known a father. A child's experience of a parent's death is likely to be quite different from the experience of a parent's abandonment, and the psychological effects of death on a child's development are likely to be different from the effects of abandonment.

‡ Margaret L. Udansky, "A Weak Embrace: Popular and Scholarly Depictions of Single-Parent Families 1900–1998," *Journal of Marriage and Family* 71, no. 2 (2009): 209–25.

groups.* Many children of single mothers have at least some contact with a father, but a disturbing number have little or no contact or have never had contact with their fathers. If it is true that the family triangle is uniquely valuable in moral development, then when large numbers of children grow up without fathers (or adequate substitutes for fathers), we have reason to worry that moral culture is threatened.†

If a beloved, reliable father, one with whom the child has an intense engagement, is mostly or entirely absent in its daily life, this means for the child less love and less discipline than children receive when they have two parents and less opportunity to study and internalize the father, to learn from him and take in his values, less opportunity to know him as a real person and thus to reap the greatest harvest from their mutual affection— and a poignant sense of loss and sadness. In cases of divorce and

---

* In 2006–2008, only 6 percent of births among highly educated women were to never married women, but 44 percent of births among moderately educated women and 54 percent of births among the least educated women were to never married women. (National Surveys of Family Growth, 2006–2008, cited in "When Marriage Disappears," *The State of Our Unions: Marriage in America 2010,* the National Marriage Project, University of Virginia, 2010) Births to unmarried women in 2007 totaled 39.7 percent of all U.S. births (*National Vital Statistics Reports* 58, no. 24 [August 2010]).

† See Judith Wallerstein and Julia M. Lewis, "Sibling Outcomes and Disparate Parenting and Stepparenting After Divorce: Report from a 10-Year Longitudinal Study," *Psychoanalytic Psychology* 24, no. 3 (2007): 445–58; Wallerstein and Sandra Blakeslee, *Second Chances: Men, Women, and Children a Decade After Divorce* (Boston: Ticknor & Fields, 1989); and Wallerstein, Lewis, and Blakeslee, *The Unexpected Legacy of Divorce: A 25-Year Landmark Study* (New York: Hyperion Books, 2000).

abandonment, all this often comes on top of these children's loss of their fathers' protection and economic support and on top of the likely negative effects of their mothers' increased stress, insecurity, unhappiness, and, very often, diminished time to spend with her children.

These effects can pose challenges to moral development in many ways, some subtle and some blatant.‡ Children partly or wholly abandoned by their fathers, depending on their circumstances, may have weaker impulse control, weaker judgment, less resistance to rationalization, a tendency to feel inferior, stronger orientation toward peer group approval, less integrity, more encounters with the law, and more rage, especially in boys.§ Such

---

‡ Of course children may also experience negative effects on *nonmoral* dimensions of their development.

† The effects vary widely. Sometimes a fatherless child may feel grandiose and princely or triumphant, as though it has vanquished the missing father. In Jean-Paul Sartre's *Les Mots*, trans. Bernard Frechtman (New York: Vintage, 1981), an account of his early years, Sartre describes his reaction to his father's death when he was about fifteen months old. He did not regret his loss: "There is no good father, that's the rule. Don't lay the blame on men but on the bond of the paternity, which is rotten. . . . Had my father lived, he would have lain on me at full length and crushed me. As luck had it, he died young. . . . Was it a good or a bad thing? I do not know; but I am happy to subscribe to the verdict of an eminent psychoanalyst: I have no Superego" (p. 19).

Or a single mother may respond to the father's absence by becoming overinvested in the child and using it to satisfy inappropriate emotional needs. The child gives her an identity; its achievements make her proud. She may convince it that it is special or superior, and the sense of being special may also be reinforced by the very fact that the father is absent. The child feels abandoned and, as a result of its pain in this loss, develops a sense of bitter children are less likely than others to grow up to form stable families. To make matters worse, there is good reason to fear that even when stepparents earnestly and lovingly attempt to stand in for missing biological parents, they are not as successful in providing the necessary support as those biological parents are. The developmental process relies on kinds of love and identification that are simply much harder to set up outside the circle of the child's immediate family.

None of this implies that single mothers are not usually good mothers, that the children of single mothers do not usually turn out well, and that steps cannot or should not be taken to mitigate the disadvantages that fatherless children suffer. Nor does it justify imposing a stigma on single mothers or their children—a cruel and ignorant response that can only injure and harm. It is only to insist that to regard fatherlessness as unproblematic is to

---

entitlement: "I have suffered unjustly, so I deserve special treatment and exemption from the normal rules."

Children without fathers may also flounder when they strive to separate their lives from their mothers', as every child must do. In early life, the presence of the father or father figure helps the very young child arrive at a sense of identity independent from the mother. He gives the child a second figure to go to and identify with, so that increasing independence from mother is more attractive, less scary, and easier for the child to understand. In later life, the father (or his substitute) helps the child negotiate social and economic independence. Without this third side of a family triangle, the child must leap directly from mother's arms into independence; it may lack the courage to do so, or the lonely mother may resist the child's efforts to grow away from her, or the child may injure itself in landing. When the family triangle is complete, the father mediates the journey to independence, providing a protected stop halfway along, increasing the child's courage and competence, and making it more likely that it will arrive safely at journey's end.

accept greater levels of risk and unhappiness for children and to create potential moral hazards for them and their society.

Fatherlessness makes it harder for boys to learn to be men. If the father is largely or wholly absent, the mother must become the sole disciplinarian. And when millions of single mothers struggle to raise children who have been abandoned by their fathers and the culture as a whole begins to make women into the sole child rearers, it perforce also makes them the voice of the moral. Then children may come to identify the moral with the feminine, and boys struggling for masculine identity may feel that being "good" is being girlish or emasculated. They may feel a need to engage in wrongdoing as a matter of emotional survival. This phenomenon is so widespread that it has led to literature, film, and street culture in which masculinity is identified with criminality and women who want high-status men must choose ill-behaved ones. The mentality in which morality is identified with female authority, and therefore resented, is readily transmitted from parent to child and thus readily becomes a cultural constant.

It is ironic that the mother-dominated home of the 1950s is so often imagined to be the solution to these problems, given the obvious ways in which that familial style strained the mother and left the children hungry for their fathers and deprived of much of what fathers do for children. If the withdrawal of fathers, along with economic function, from the home is one cause of our problems, then to offer as a solution the 1950s model of the home-keeping, child-rearing mother and the commuting, absent father is futile and delusory, though, admittedly, the working father and husband who is little seen is a great deal better than the abandoning one who is never seen.

Jobs and Joblessness

Unemployment and parents' long working hours and decreasing incomes have powerful, negative effects on family life and thus on children's development. The long-standing American habit of frequent family moves for the sake of a new job also puts families under great stress. Repeated moves lead to repeatedly broken connections with relations, friends, neighbors, and local institutions.* Frequently uprooted families enjoy less aid, less social and emotional support, and less education from relatives, friends, and elders than more rooted families enjoy; they are strangers to the professionals and institutions in their new communities that traditionally support families—doctors, schools and teachers, houses of religion; and they experience more divorces. But the causal relation also works in reverse so that these trends, once begun, are self-perpetuating; individuals raised in weak, disconnected families are more likely to form weak families of their own, with loose ties to friends, family, and community, and more easily break them to seek greener pastures elsewhere—in the form of jobs, houses, marital partners, friends, and lovers. All these pressures weaken families' ability to protect their children just as they weaken the ability of a moral culture to help the family maintain itself.

In an economy without adequate safety nets, in which individuals must compete against one another for employment,

---

* Family mobility is much greater in the United States than in European countries and has long been so, although it has decreased since the nineteenth century. The bursting of the U.S. housing bubble in 2007 reduced mobility because many people were unable to sell their houses and could not afford to move.

nonmoral or even immoral character traits—aggressiveness, competitiveness, detachment, disloyalty, egoism—can become highly functional and moral ones a handicap. Another vicious circle results: Moral restraints diminish, and the economic system becomes increasingly immoral and antimoral. It casts out and deprives of power and influence people who might restrain it, and it creates a growing pool of people whose character is well suited to that system's needs and less well suited to the moral life.

INSTITUTIONALIZATION OF CHILD REARING

In recent years, popular culture and fathers themselves have begun to recognize the crucial contribution fathers make in child rearing. This is a hopeful development, but, as it is paralleled by high levels of mothers' employment, it does not change one crucial overall trend: Child rearing takes place less and less within the family, at home, and more and more in institutions, including day care centers and nurseries, schools, and after-school programs. Because the current American economy requires both parents to work long hours outside the home, more and more children spend more time away from their families, especially in institutional settings, at younger and younger ages, and the poorer the children, the less they have of their parents. If family rearing is more favorable to moral development, then we need to ask whether the long-term trend toward extrafamilial care is among the factors that subtly weaken moral culture and its influence in politics, business, schools, and social relations of all sorts.

In the eighteenth and nineteenth centuries, from an early

age children were put to work. If their parents were farmers or farm laborers, they would work at their parents' sides. As the Industrial Revolution took hold, they were often sent to work in factories, mills, and mines; these industrial employments usually, though not always, separated children from their parents. Later in the nineteenth century, compulsory schooling began. The days and hours of schooling increased gradually until all children now attend full-day, full-week school, with summers off, from age five or six to between sixteen and eighteen. Thus the nineteenth and twentieth centuries, sometimes for better and sometimes for worse, saw a trend toward children's spending increasing time away from their families. That process is ongoing in the twenty-first century.

Powerful movements to extend compulsory schooling have paralleled mothers' movement into the workforce. Kindergarten is not yet compulsory in the majority of states, but there are strong movements to make it compulsory everywhere. There is also great pressure to shorten American children's long summer vacations. Compulsory preschool attendance exists nowhere in the United States, but it, too, has vigorous advocates. In many urban areas, a majority of three- and four-year-olds now attend private preschools (or, rarely, noncompulsory government preschools), which often sets up a call for equivalent benefits for poorer children, who, it is justly feared, will show up at kindergarten or first grade even further behind their wealthier agemates than they would otherwise have been. After-school programs for both school days and school holidays are in high demand. ("Latchkey" children are known to be significantly more prone than others to get into trouble.) To these increased hours of institutional life, recent decades have added large rises in the number of babies, toddlers, and two-year-olds placed in full-time day care or other forms of substitute care. In 1999, 48 percent of children under five with mothers who work full-time spent at least thirty-five hours in care per week, and another 18 percent were in care for fifteen to thirty-four hours per week.* Disadvantaged children given access to high-quality programs may derive significant educational benefits from some of these trends. Overall, however, few of these proposed extensions of a child's days and hours in institutions and away from their homes and families have any justification in educational terms.† The real and powerful motive behind them is, of course, working parents' desperate need for child care.

A century ago, when farmers, doctors, lawyers, blacksmiths, and many more middle-class men worked at or near home, as did most women (mostly in unpaid employments), parents and

---

* Jeffrey Capizzano and Gina Adams, "The Hours That Children Under Five Spend in Child Care: Variation Across States," Table 1, the Urban Institute, No. B-8, in *New Federalism: National Survey of America's Families*, March 2000, accessed December 8, 2011, http://www.urban.org/url.cfm?ID=309439& renderforprint=1&CFID=115796631&CFTOKEN=17005871&jsessionid =b230305f49ec19587d31.

† All children can learn some social skills, physical skills, and pre-reading and pre-math skills in preschool. Although these cognitive effects do not seem to result in much ultimate benefit, the children may have fun and learn good attitudes toward school. But preschools offer diminishing returns with decreasing quality of the program. This matters greatly, because high-quality programs are costly. They require a very high teacher/student ratio, exceedingly well-trained teachers, many expensive materials, and carefully constructed classrooms. Most local governments will find it difficult or impossible to finance high-quality preschools.

other mature relatives were able to supervise children while they worked, between patients or chores, and as they planted, repaired, milked, sewed, cooked, and so forth. When their children were not in school, they were likely to be near their fathers and mothers or other adults with whom they shared intense, long-term mutual attachments—relatives, live-in help or other employees, and neighbors—a fact that greatly favored moral development.* These adults were occupied with serious work but were still present to settle quarrels, scold, talk, teach, joke, reminisce, and provide models of behavior and a sustaining sense of emotional security and belonging. Children's experiences with their parents and others employed at home are unlikely to be equaled in relations with low-paid day care workers or spent teachers struggling to cope with twenty or thirty or more tired youngsters in after-school programs. This comparison should not be dismissed as a fantasy about the joys of the good old days (especially of farm life, of which I have had ample unpleasant experience). The point is only to remind ourselves that children raised under the eyes of good-enough parents are likely to have a moral advantage over those who are not, that a lower percentage of middle-class children today enjoy that advantage, and that there is intense pressure on families to reduce, not increase, their contributions to their children's rearing.

Substitute Child Care for Children Under Three

The quality of a child's rearing is not solely a function of the number of hours it spends with its parents. Poor parent-child re-

---

* Of course, long hours spent in the company of criminal, crazy, drugged, indifferent, cruel, or alcoholic parents are not likely to help any child.

lations may occur despite plenty of time together, and excellent relations are often built on little time. Nonetheless, on average, especially with infants and children under three, more time in parental care in a good-enough home means a better outcome for the child, and it certainly means a happier child. There is a consensus that at age three and older, most children are ready for nursery school or preschool, but questions continue on how much time they should spend there, how much benefit they derive, and the negative consequences of placing them in poor-quality programs.

In 1999, 70 percent of three-year-olds, 57 percent of two-year-olds, 53 percent of one-year-olds, and 44 percent of infants under one year were in some type of regularly scheduled substitute care.* In 2010, about 56.5 percent of women with children under one year old worked, 71 percent of them full-time, and the majority returned to work before their infants were six months old.† In 2010, 23.7 percent of children four and under with employed mothers were in center-based care, 40 percent were in a relative's care, and 13.5 percent were in other kinds of

---

* Jack P. Shonkoff and Deborah A. Phillips, eds., *From Neurons to Neighborhoods: The Science of Early Childhood Development* (Washington, D.C.: National Academy Press and Institute of Medicine, 2000), p. 298.

† But see Jeanne Brooks-Gunn, Wen-Jui Han, and Jane Waldfogel, "First-Year Maternal Employment and Child Development in the First 7 Years," *Monographs of the Society for Research in Child Development* 75, no. 2 (2010): vii–ix, 1–147. This study, on page 96, puts the number much higher, finding that 78 percent of white mothers work in the first year of their child's life and that almost all are back at work full time by the time their child is six months old.

care.* Children in full-time substitute care in day care centers and nurseries receive, at best, kindly, decent, but distant and relatively uninvolved care, compared with parental care at home, for most of their waking hours. They experience this kind of care at an age when they desperately want and need to be near familiar and passionately loved people to whom they know they belong, in relation to whom they find their own identity. By comparison with family life, their experience with caretakers and teachers is emotionally tepid, lacking the underlying intensity of even casual, calm parent–child interaction.† Teachers and day care

---

* "America's Children, Key National Indicators of Well-Being, 2011: Childcare," ChildStats.gov, accessed November 16, 2011, http://www.childstats .gov/americaschildren/familysoc.3asp.

† Professionals who study day care are often so wedded to one side of that debate or the other for ideological reasons that they ignore the obvious, and one telling fact is that most American families that can afford to hire a nanny and avoid day care in fact do so. They are probably right to think that this is better for their children and usually kinder, too. When the nanny is intelligent and warm with a reliably stable role in the child's life, we can expect the child to do well and have a good experience. Unfortunately, far too few of today's American nannies meet these criteria. English nannies of a century ago provide a useful comparison. These were mostly middle-class women, part of an established, elaborate social system that was highly dependent on a dearth of other employment opportunities for middle-class women, a system that does not and cannot exist in the United States. Even that system, moreover, imposed a sad degree of cruelty, suffering, and unhappiness on the children reared in it. For a fascinating examination of this subject that includes vignettes of the childhood of such historic figures as Winston Churchill, see Jonathan Gathorne-Hardy, *The Rise and Fall of the British Nanny* (London: Hodder & Stoughton, 1972).

workers who are in charge of many youngsters do not, cannot, know and respond to individual children the way their parents do. Even if they had the time and inclination to do so, they lack the built-in resource that every parent relies on: the great passion children direct toward their parents and every child's conviction that what it is and should be is bound up with those parents.* In fact, one main social function of schools and teachers is to teach children to accept roles in which love, identification, and intimate mutual knowledge are absent—a form of socialization indispensable in any advanced economy.

Child rearing with heavy reliance on institutional care may well be adequate to support what psychologists, looking at the surface of children's lives, would consider normal socialization, especially conformity, but inadequate to fuel the kinds of

---

In any case, few American families can afford to hire nannies, and as so many observers have pointed out, those that can must often hire poor and ill-educated women who are forced to leave their own children behind in order to care for those of their wealthy employers.

It is important to point out, as well, that some experts say that very young children who are cared for by affectionate, competent nannies while separated from their parents for long shifts may spend their days in a low-key mood, winding down their feelings and holding them for the parents' return. Even children in superior one-on-one substitute care, that is, seem to experience painful loneliness. See Patricia A. Nachman, "The Maternal Representation: A Comparison of Caregiver- and Mother-Reared Toddlers," *Psychoanalytical Study of the Child* 46 (1991): 69–89, a sensitive attempt to understand the experience of children in high-quality individual substitute care.

* These comments ignore many standard, valid critiques of typical problems in day care, for example, that staff turnover means that children do not have a consistent caretaker, that staff are ill trained, and more.

independence, courage, and strength needed for higher moral capacity. Children whose rearing relies heavily on group care may become more intensely dependent on their peers, more likely to see right and wrong in terms of what the group says, and more easily led.★

Studies show that while most children in substitute care are well socialized, a small percentage who spend too much time in day care (usually more than twenty hours per week, depending on the child's age) may be more aggressive and uncooperative.† There are no studies, however, that attempt to gauge just how much additional aggression and uncooperativeness

---

★ The Israeli kibbutz experimented with much-analyzed alternatives to the family model for rearing children with moral capacity—with uncertain results. The kibbutz used a communal child-rearing system (a practice now uncommon). In some places, the child's whole life, including its sleeping hours, was spent in the communal center; in others, parents collected the child in the evening and kept it until morning. One result of kibbutz rearing was that the children grew up highly attuned and loyal to the state and to their peers, with ready conformity to social rules and high courage in military operations. But some observers, like Bruno Bettelheim, in *The Children of the Dream* (New York: Macmillan 1969), claimed that they also showed conformism, reduced empathy, relatively shallow emotions and attachments, reduced capacity for intimacy, constricted imaginations and drive, and a lack of social independence. Such claims were much disputed. In evaluating these or any other child-rearing practices, we must not forget that moral strength readily leads to social nonconformity and troublesome independence, and that social conformity is not morality.

† The factors that such studies have isolated include the age of the child in care, the amount of time spent in care, the quality of the care, the quality of its care at home, and, most important, the sensitivity of its mother.

can be tolerated by society and none that focus on whether the children in substitute care are unhappy or suffering. Older teachers today complain bitterly of changes they have seen over the years in their classrooms, even in the early grades, as a result of aggressive, uncooperative students.★ One aggressive child in a first-grade class of twenty, they point out, can wreck the learning experience of the other nineteen. A half-dozen aggressive children on the playground create chaos and intolerable bullying. One new sociopath per thousand or even per ten thousand citizens might produce dangerous social instability.

★ In the past few years, some researchers have voiced concern at what seem to be increasing levels of misbehavior by preschoolers, including tantrums, fighting, and refusing to cooperate. Some blame the trend toward pushing the children toward academic achievements, in pre-reading and pre-math skills; some worry that they have spent too much time in day care before arriving at preschool. See Walter S. Gilliam, "Prekindergarteners Left Behind: Expulsion Rates in State Prekindergarten Systems" (2004), FCD Policy Brief 3, Foundation for Child Development, May 2005. Accessed November 1, 2011, www .fcd-us.org/sites/default/files/ExpulsionCompleteReport.pdf. See also National Institute of Child Health and Human Development Early Child Care Research Network, "Does Amount of Time Spent in Child Care Predict Socioemotional Adjustment During the Transition to Kindergarten?" *Child Development* 74, no. 4 (2003): 976–1005. This report concludes (p. 976): "The more time children spent in any of a variety of nonmaternal care arrangements across the first 4.5 years of life, the more externalizing problems and conflict with adults they manifested at 54 months of age and in kindergarten, as reported by mothers, caregivers, and teachers. These effects remained, for the most part, even when quality, type, and instability of child care were controlled, and when maternal sensitivity and other family background factors were taken into account."

No large study looks at individual children closely enough to let us know them intimately enough to understand what their aggression really means and why it happens. The researchers know little or nothing of the private life histories, the individual psychologies, and the underlying motives and emotions of the children they describe. The children remain strangers to the investigators and to those of us who read the studies. Moreover, adequate studies will never be done, as they would require in-depth, intimate knowledge of the life stories of thousands of individual children—an economic and practical impossibility.

The sorts of studies that are actually carried out make only the grossest measures of the grossest qualities. It is unlikely that they would identify Bernie Madoff or any of the Enron gang as problem children.* The qualities they do measure are ambiguous. If day care children show more independence and less shyness at age two, is that good or bad? Is their behavior assertive or aggressive? Without knowing a child intimately, how can an observer know whether problematic behavior flows from anger, fear, anxiety, or chronic tiredness? Moreover, the

---

* This is not to suggest that these men's moral defects were a result of a lack of family care, but that moral defects like theirs, whatever their cause, could not be detected by the kinds of studies that have been done on the effects of substitute care. For an interesting attempt to link the moral collapse at Enron with the personal histories of some of its executives, see Mark Stein, "Oedipus Rex at Enron: Leadership, Oedipal Struggles, and Organizational Collapse," *Human Relations* 60, no. 9 (2007): 1387–1410 [published by Sage Publications on behalf of the Tavistock Institute, http://hum.sagepub .com/content/60/9/1387]. Stein is a professor in business management and economics who is also trained in psychoanalytic concepts and methods.

standards of "normality" by which today's children are judged have already evolved to reflect the overall cultural changes of which changes in moral thinking are a major part. The behavior that is at present regarded as appropriate to the age of the child is not what was believed appropriate fifty or a hundred years ago. Only subtle and sensitive historical studies could provide a helpful picture of this moral evolution, but these, too, are lacking.

In fact, the relevant effects of substitute care are in crucial respects still not known because the kinds of studies that are done could not determine those effects, and too often those that are done aim less at learning what is best for children than at ideological goals. Either they seek to justify extended substitute care so as to liberate mothers from child care, or they seek to criticize it so as to do the opposite. Critics of day care cite harm to children, while supporters of day care accuse its critics of romantic idealization of oppressive family forms, prejudice against women who work, and adherence to archaic ideals of motherhood.

Media reporting leans toward support of day care, and it tends to be overly sanguine. It typically fails to distinguish among different types of care or to point out that the studies often examine the effects of high-quality care—often in a university setting—for limited numbers of hours. It does not adequately address the low average quality of day care in the United States, the effects of care beyond the maximum recommended hours, or the unhappiness of the many children subjected to it. Nor does it explain that as things stand now, a large proportion of those very young children who are in care are left there for far more hours than is wise or kind or that the average quality of day care is unlikely to improve significantly, given the outlook for the American economy.*

The difficulty of ensuring that institutional care in the United States will be even minimally kind and intelligent is vastly underestimated by those who have argued passionately for mass day care. While we may admire European systems that rely on extensive paid maternal and paternal leave, flexible work hours, shorter work weeks for both parents, superior methods of child care, and—most important of all—superior and well-paid child care workers, in the United States we have moved children into

---

* While the dominant view today is that research has established the safety, and in some ways the positive benefits, of day care, many child development experts (among them Benjamin Spock, T. Berry Brazelton, and Penelope Leach) gave or continue to give ambivalent or grudging approval to day care for infants and toddlers. Jay Belsky continues to raise critical questions despite the furious antagonism he aroused in the past; he cannot easily be counted as either a supporter or a full-voiced critic of day care. But it would probably be fair to describe all of these experts as convinced that the luckiest infants and toddlers are those cared for at home by good-enough mothers and fathers. Burton L. White has consistently advised against the turn to day care for the very young. Selma Fraiberg, a brilliant researcher and writer on child development, always passionately opposed the move away from family rearing of the very young, as did many others whose training was in psychoanalysis. Some reliably neutral studies have been carried out by attachment theorists. They have supported the general proposition that, within specified limits, the mother-child bond is enormously strong and resilient and not readily broken by daily separations—again, a reassuring conclusion, but one that is not adequate to answer the questions raised here, and, overall, attachment studies cannot be read as exonerating substitute care. See also Steven A. Frankel, "The Exclusivity of the Mother-Child Bond," *Psychoanalytic Study of the Child* 49 (1994): 86–106.

care on a mass basis despite an almost complete absence of all these protections given to Norwegian and Finnish children.★ Furthermore, day care, especially full-day care, even at its best, is likely to be an unhappy experience for babies and toddlers, who suffer if they are not in close, intimate contact for most of their waking hours with the people whom they passionately love and identify as their parent figures. Recognition of that suffering is painful indeed for many sensitive parents who have no choice but to put their very young children in care. But painful recognition is preferable to the normalization of this unhappy necessity and the denial of the effects of poor-quality, full-day substitute care for the very young.

Qualms about substitute care must be evaluated in light of the important facts that many families that place their children in extended care produce outstanding children, that many children reared attentively by their own parents turn out ill, and that the most successful moral development may always have been more the cultural exception than the rule. Long hours of poor or lackluster substitute or institutional care do not spell doom for any particular child, especially when its home ties are strong and satisfactory; and satisfactory later experiences—or the inherent resilience of children—often overcome the deficiencies of earlier ones. It is also important to remember that

---

★ Finland's child care system is in many respects the ideal model. Since 1984, it has given a child care allowance to mothers who choose to stay home with children and continues the allowance until their youngest child turns three. This option is very popular among Finnish mothers. Finland also gives every family the right to a place in public day care for each child and has established high standards of staff education and high ratios of staff to children.

warmhearted, humane, and intelligent substitute care is salvation for children whose home life is deficient or pathological and, for almost all children, when offered in the appropriate doses and forms and at the right ages, a beneficial, enjoyable, and often educative experience.

Nonetheless, as part of a great wave of change in child-rearing custom, the declining influence of family rearing seems likely to be a genuine and significant threat to society's ability to transmit the moral mind from generation to generation. Indeed, it is hard to see how it could be otherwise. Yet this conclusion has been tenaciously resisted by those who are invested in defending women's freedom to work—something whose desirability and necessity speaks so strongly for itself that it can only be demeaned by this denial of the obvious in its defense.

The increasing institutionalization of child rearing is not the cause of the moral changes that this book describes; it is an effect of a complex of economic and social causes. Long hours of substitute care are necessary to maintain an economy that extracts eighty hours of labor from each household each week in exchange for a diminishing standard of living, material and otherwise. But it is an effect that becomes a cause, one likely to produce widespread, subtle cultural change that, in turn, diminishes insight into this change and lessens resistance to it. Today, the contracting role of families in child rearing coincides with a more general disregard of children's interests. Voters refuse to support adequate health care, food, housing, and education for children and favor unwinding the protections children used to enjoy in the juvenile justice system. The destruction of "welfare" programs, conceived a century and more ago and painstakingly implemented through tireless efforts by thousands of anonymous moral heroes, is often justified on the grounds that the responsibility for such things rests on the children's families. But voters also refuse to support policies that would enable families to fulfill those responsibilities, especially jobs programs, adequate wages, family-friendly hours, protection of the right to organize unions, and other policies that, directly or indirectly, would allow fathers and mothers to spend adequate amounts of time at home with their young children.

It has always been true that children with inadequate moral development face pitfalls when they grow up and are forced to cope with the society beyond their families. In the contemporary world, these dangers are amplified by television and film, corporatized religion, mass advertising, and the balkanizing influence of the Internet. None of these venues present any dangers for strong, sane, rational people. But in all of them, weak psyches are likely to be invited to identify with a group mind—one that is presented to them by corporate, political, and religious authorities—and to permit themselves moral and rational regression. Personalities with a great need for identifications and idealizations that boost their egos may be readily seduced into the service of any of these. This danger exists for everyone and in some ways always has; it is only exaggerated in our own times. Now, as always, people with strong moral character are best able to resist the danger, best able to become part of a crowd to enjoy the pleasure of sports and other spectacles but return quickly to an independent sense of self when the pleasure is over or when morally necessary. But there are many people who have little independent sense of self to return to, and many others, whose early deprivations have left them emotionally depleted, with ego needs too voracious to resist any source that offers to feed them. These tendencies diminish their ability to meet the obligations of citizenship in a complex democracy, and they are likely to become stronger if child rearing grows ever more institutionalized. There is reason to fear that as family rearing diminishes, more children will grow up better suited to life in mass culture, with its reduced autonomy and rationality, than to the strenuous life of citizens working to maintain the moral culture and everything that depends on it.

Chapter 6

MORAL REFORM AND PSEUDOMORALISM

Wisdom and goodness to the vile seem vile.
—SHAKESPEARE, *KING LEAR*, ACT 4, SCENE 2

The good displeases us when we are not up to it.
—FRIEDRICH NIETZSCHE,
HUMAN, ALL TOO HUMAN

THOSE WHO DEFEND some substantial right to abortion, favor gay rights and stem cell research, and oppose the death penalty are now inaptly called "liberals," even when they hold conservative ideas about government, because vehement opposition to the moral consensus on these subjects arose on the far Right. The far Right, wherever it exists, is dominated by premoral thinking about right and wrong. Until the 1970s, people who called themselves conservative often questioned the death penalty. Barry Goldwater supported abortion rights. Dwight Eisenhower, Senator Prescott Bush, father of George H. W. and grandfather of George W., and Goldwater were all officers

of planned parenthood.* Many liberals were personally less tolerant of gays than conservatives were; hippies and other counter-
culturalists of the 1960s often sneered openly at fags and queers.

Morality has no natural alliance with either the right or left
of recent politics, though it certainly has an affinity with the
sort of liberalism that embraces both Edmund Burke and
Thomas Paine. The Right's opposition to what it calls liberalism is not moral, though right-wingers think it is; it does not
arise out of moral conscience, and its goals defy the dictates of
conscience. If "moral" refers to the mentality described in
previous chapters, together with the historical values that people
of that mentality espoused, those on the far Right are not moral
but antimoral. Likewise, whether or not anomic characters are
politically attracted to libertarianism or the Democratic Party,
and no matter that they often support gay rights and abortion
rights, they are antimoral. They despise moral values that restrain them in their ambition and in the fulfillment of their
wishes. Confucius, the Aztecs, Idi Amin, and Shakespeare's Iago
did not have different moralities from us; rather, they had
something other than morality, and the same is true of Enron's
Jeffrey Skilling, Dick Cheney, and Alberto Gonzales.

The increasing social influence of these types of premoral
mentality implies not only an increase in characteristically *immoral* behaviors, like dishonesty, tyranny, faithlessness, greed,
and cruelty, but also *antimoralism*, antipathy for the moral mentality per se that leads to efforts to undermine it. Antimoralists
rebel against morality and attack it. Some of their attacks are

_____

* In the 1950s, Planned Parenthood had not yet come out in favor of abortion rights.

philosophical (a Mandevillean argues that human selfishness and vice are good things) or scientific (an evolutionary biologist, shedding crocodile tears and insisting that nature makes altruism rare and weak, urges us to tough-mindedness in the face of that sad truth). Some are angry, explicit, and triumphant, without a political front, as with Charles Manson, or with one, as with fascism. Antimoralism often wears a nostalgic disguise and insists that it is a return to some true good of the past. Or it may claim that it is overthrowing wrongs with its superior new grasp of the good. The cult of "cool" that began in the mid–twentieth century, which expressed itself primarily in social and artistic arenas rather than in politics, was highly antimoral, though it sometimes thought of itself as a truer and higher set of values out to expose the shallow hypocrisy of the respectable and square. The dominance of cool, a narcissistic mentality that often seeks superiority through aesthetic and intellectual qualifications, spread through music, film, fiction, and the visual arts and probably made the single most successful attack on the moral in history, and one whose effects are rarely traced to their source.

MORAL REFORM AND ANTIMORAL REBELLION

In the United States, antimoralism was personified in the 1920s by Leopold and Loeb, two young would-be Nietzscheans whose "perfect crime," the murder of a fourteen-year-old boy, was intended to express their superiority to the moral. The Great Depression, followed by World War II, temporarily snuffed out the twenties' spark of antimoralism, but it flared up again in the

1950s and 1960s, when the United States also experienced one
of its several periods of moral awakening.

The surge of moral sentiment in the first postwar decades
favored civil rights, racial equality, women's rights, workers'
rights, sexual freedom, antimilitarism, and restraints on corporations' power, and it frowned at what it saw as the buttoned-
up, smug moralism and conformism of the fifties—ideas that set
off a virulent antimoral backlash. The antimoral reaction to the
moral fervor of the period had both anomic and authoritarian
forms. The former, with its sexual adventurism and open contempt for middle-class virtues, was obviously antimoral and
was widely seen to be, although it rationalized its misbehavior
by appeal to higher values—often, consciously or not, with arguments modeled on the arguments for genuine moral reform.
By the early 1980s, authoritarian, rightist antimoralism had adopted the same tactics. It held protests and formed groups devoted
to its causes. It opposed affirmative action and laws that promoted sexual freedom for women and homosexuals; it insisted
on punitive abortion laws and defended the right of states to
forbid the sale of contraceptives. It demanded a harsher, more
vengeful system of criminal justice; and it was irate about restraints of any sort on the accumulation of wealth and about the
taxes that went to welfare, which it denounced as forced charity to unworthy recipients. These goals and tactics were motivated by fierce antimoral sentiment.

One effect of the combined antimoral force of the anomic
and authoritarian types was stigmatization of "do-gooders,"
especially those dedicated to serving charity or human rights.
Their explicitly moral goals were treated as suspicious and
denigrated. The anomic Left accused international aid organi-

zations of undermining local movements, drawing off energies that should be spent politically, and favoring private rather than state remedies, while the nonpolitical cool saw them as hypocritical, ascetic, or filled with "crunchy granola" types. The authoritarian Right accused them of forwarding "liberal" and "socialist" political agendas. The International Committee of the Red Cross came under right-wing attack for its neutrality in rendering humanitarian aid to members of the Taliban and other enemy groups. It was also accused of engaging in ideological attacks on the United States when its reports of torture and mistreatment of prisoners by the United States were leaked (even though it was apparently someone in the U.S. government, not the ICRC, that leaked the material). Organizations like the ACLU and Amnesty International were seen as evil and dangerous—no matter how carefully they sought neutrality or how reliable their statements and reports—because of their humanitarianism, their opposition to the death penalty, and their devotion to free speech, civil rights, and other "left-liberal" causes. The ACLU earns no credibility among right-wing antimoralists for defending Rush Limbaugh's rights as readily as those of accused terrorists.

Anomic antimoralism characterized many different kinds of people, reflecting the many different psychological routes by which this end point can be reached. Some, the "yuppies," were conformist and conventional, though they prided themselves on being different and contrarian. They recoiled angrily from the portions of the reformers' critiques that questioned their ambition, materialism, and egoism. Otherwise, they were indifferent to moral goals, or mouthed whatever opinions best served their status aspirations. Others were genuinely unconventional; they disdained the ordinary forms of middle-class life and the moral values that sustained them. They included hippies, swingers, proponents of open marriage, left-wing extremists and anarchists, and people with certain kinds of criminal tendencies—drug dealers, thieves, crooked businessmen, fraudsters and scam artists, and others. Because those who defied convention looked favorably on any lifting of restrictions on behavior, they readily supported some of the moral reformers' ideas, especially rebelliousness against war and the draft, civil rights, gay rights, student rights, and sexual liberalism.

The terms *conventional* and *unconventional* in this context are morally neutral. To the extent that moral reformers call for change, they are unconventional, but so are people who want to dismantle *good* institutions and practices. Conventions, or habitual social practices and customs, can coincide with what morality approves or can fail to, and likewise unconventional habits, beliefs, and actions are sometimes good, sometimes not, and sometimes indifferent. The result is that in periods of moral reform, antimoral aims can be disguised as moral reform, which readily confuses the young and naive—and the less young, too, when their morality is merely conventional. In the 1960s and 1970s, many people could not distinguish reformers from their amoral imitators and despised them all indiscriminately and identified all reform with immorality. There were, to be sure, many people with the moral mentality who were skeptical of the genuine programs of moral reform. Eventually, these people were likely to be conservative supporters of Republican presidents like Ronald Reagan and George H. W. Bush.

Self-identified members of the "moral majority" of the 1980s, however, were largely authoritarian and right-wing.

They correctly perceived both the contempt in which they were held by the counterculture and the antimoral Left and the threat that true moral reforms posed to their already parlous status and privileges, and to the sense of superiority and virtue that was grounded in their middle-class respectability. Men in this group, especially, reacted angrily to racial integration, the expansion of women's rights (including the legalization of abortion), and the criminal justice system. Their anger was turned against what offended their claims to superiority, their power, or their status. Because they felt entitled to that power and status, they experienced their own anger as deeply righteous.

They called their attitudes "moral," but on the far Right this was an aping of genuine moral concern, with no real basis in guilt, compassion, or a sense of obligation. This mimicking of moral concern in the absence of genuine moral motives gave rise to something akin to moral playacting, a pseudomoralism or imitation of morality that lacked the underlying emotional content that gives real moral thought and action its characteristic dignity and common sense and its ability to persuade. A pseudomorality restored a sense of superiority and neutralized and replaced legitimate demands for justice. In this pseudomoralism, only the fury was authentic, and it was in large part the fury of offended narcissism.

During the George W. Bush administration, such people exulted in governmental disregard of legal and moral restraints on the conduct of the War on Terror. Cruelty and obedience to principles supposedly higher than those of morals and law were the means by which authoritarians tried to erase their own sense of humiliation and inferiority and to reinforce their sense of masculine power. The adoption of immoral means was rendered palatable by depicting the opposition as so utterly monstrous and dangerous that well-established moral and legal tenets had to be suspended—as though those restrictions were not addressed to just such circumstances. The same disregard was practiced in pursuit of political advantage, and here too lies and political knavery were seen as justified to prevent a delegitimized, demeaned opposition from endangering the country through degeneracy, cowardice, and unmanliness.

REBELLION AGAINST MORALITY: TORTURE

The Bush administration's decision to use torture on prisoners accused of terrorism is a disturbing example of the triumph of authoritarian anti- and pseudomoralism over morality. When President Bush opted to use torture to force prisoners to disclose information, we faced no threat to national survival. No nuclear warhead was rocketing toward us, threatening millions with death. Although terrorists might again manage to cause us terrible loss of life and property, we knew that as a people and a nation, we would survive those losses. We even had good reason to believe that torture would be counterproductive or at least greatly inferior to other means of preventing them. In the past, we had faced vastly greater dangers without resorting to torture.

The Bush government justified torture on the grounds that it would save lives, but the moral prohibition against torture does not permit it even to save large numbers of lives under circumstances in which a specific danger is known and when specific persons are known to be in possession of specific information about the danger. Much less, then, is torture justified to save limited numbers when no specific danger is known and no specific person is known to have information that could prevent the danger. Yet a majority of Americans had no objection to Bush's use of torture and continue to approve of it as a means of combating the indefinite evil of terrorism—this despite long-standing laws, treaties, and universally acknowledged moral principles that forbade it.

The Bush administration also denied—most unrealistically—that the suffering inflicted by its agents amounted to torture, and members of the administration, including Dick Cheney, repeatedly described objections to torture as ridiculous. Even Supreme Court justice Antonin Scalia spoke aggressively in favor of torture, in public and on the record. "It would be absurd to say you couldn't do that," he maintained, speaking of torture in ticking bomb scenarios.* In this and other ways, the Bush administration engaged in antimoral education and weakened the ability of American citizens to understand why our laws and customs have so long and so adamantly condemned torture. This, together with the constant favorable messages about bowing to the necessity of dirtying one's hands, conveyed by popular fiction and film aimed at premoral and antimoral taste, as well as by journalism and some scholarly literature, may well explain why Americans have become more approving of torture than citizens of almost any other nation.

A 2005 AP-IPSOS poll found that 61 percent of Americans

---

* Antonin Scalia, on *Law in Action,* BBC Radio interview, February 12, 2008.

thought torture justified at least on rare occasions. A Pew poll conducted April 14–21, 2009, found that 71 percent said that torture was justified on at least rare occasions. In that poll, 15 percent thought torture often justified, 34 percent thought it sometimes justified, 22 percent thought it rarely justified, and 25 percent thought it never justified. White evangelical Protestants approved of torture more than other religious groups; 62 percent of white evangelicals believed torture justified often or sometimes; 33 percent believed it is rarely or never justified. In the Pew poll, the more often a person attended religious services, the more likely that person was to approve of torture. But members of mainline churches and the unaffiliated disapproved of torture most strongly. When the National Association of Evangelicals (in 2007) and the head of the Ethics and Religious Liberty Commission of the Southern Baptist Convention (2009) belatedly condemned torture, they drew criticism from their members and from the Right generally—in part for appearing critical of the government.

In fact, the Bush administration authorized torture not for any practical reason, but on principle. *It was insisting on its right to ignore moral and legal restraint*, which it experienced as emasculating, and to free its sadism, which it experienced as strong and manly. Torture was not a means to an end. It *was* an end. Torture satisfied sadistic urges and enabled its proponents to overcome a sense of humiliation—in this case on account of the attacks on 9/11 as well as a barrage of cultural assaults on their narcissism. Torture reinforces a sense of superiority to its victim, and those who torture overcome what is in their minds a feminine command to be kind or a feminine squeamishness about being unkind. Interestingly, given their great concern with manliness, those who have condoned torture easily abandon the old-fashioned code of manly honor and see no shameful un-manliness in inflicting agonies on those who cannot fight back.

If those who instituted torture as American policy had genuinely believed that it was the lesser of two terrible evils, only a necessary means, one would expect to find that they had ordered it reluctantly, on the most certain facts, for the most urgent and specific goals, with no alternative, and only when they had every reason to believe it might actually work. But none of this was the case. They did so eagerly, on shaky grounds, for increasingly questionable goals, when alternatives were available, and with highly unreliable results, and in many instances over the objections and qualms of experienced FBI and military personnel. They did so because the torture itself, as much as or more than its results, was their object.

During the Bush administration, arguments by various academics who favored torture in "ticking bomb" and "end of the world" scenarios dominated the moral debate. Among the academic proponents of torture in specific circumstances are Michael Levin (City University of New York), Alan Dershowitz (Harvard Law School), Eric A. Posner (University of Chicago Law School), Adrian Vermeule (Harvard Law School), and Mirko Bagaric and Julie Clarke (Deakin Law School, Australia). John Yoo and Jay Bybee, who, as lawyers in the George W. Bush administration's Department of Justice wrote the infamous "torture memos" that, by breathtakingly crooked reasoning, found no legal obstacle to torture by the U.S. government agents, are now, respectively, a law professor at Boalt Hall, the University of California at Berkeley, and a judge on the United States Court of Appeals for the Ninth Circuit.

Predictably, ticking bomb arguments were used to rationalize the real-world resort to torture in dramatically less dire situations than the armchair scenarios that abstractly justified them. In general, we should be skeptical of arguments that justify evil in the here and now by pointing to armageddons. Similar arguments were commonly appealed to during the Cold War with the explicit purpose of undermining moral qualms in foreign policy. Henry Kissinger and other political "realists" insisted, with disingenuous regret, that national policy should be dictated by national self-interest, not by "ideals" and morals. The only way that those ideals could survive in a hostile world was if our nation survived; and if our nation behaved morally, Kissinger argued, it would not survive. This sort of argument, offered as a tough-minded, higher, and more manly morality, is always rejected by the moral mind, which registers the ideals to be sacrificed as the very characteristics of the nation that make its survival worth fighting and dying for.

Those who defend torture and cruelty to enemies and criminals may have been taught that such things are morally wrong, but real moral knowledge is possible only for certain kinds of people. It cannot be passed from one person to another solely through words and symbols in the way that knowledge about algebra or biology can be. Catechisms of right and wrong give people with moral capacity a certain amount of guidance, a set of sound, if always vague, ideas of some use in testing and shaping their judgment. But people who are not moral cannot make use of such teaching, though they may be able to repeat what good people tell them is good. Osama bin Laden could not have been convinced that he did evil on 9/11 without having changed profoundly from what he was on that day. Nor is a

John Yoo ever likely to understand why we may not resort to torture to counter bin Laden. Neither man approached these questions with a moral mind. Neither, that is, had the mental equipment necessary for such understanding, and neither understood himself well enough to wish to be different.

Rebellion Against the Moral: Abortion

The premoral mind confuses the disgusting with the wrong and retains an infantile fear of things sexual. Its rationality is overcome by emotion, fantasy, wish, and projection. The belief that extracting a ten-week fetus from a woman's womb is murder rests to a large extent on the sense of disgust aroused by the thought of the destruction of living tissue. When fundamentalists insist on risking the life of the mother to deliver an anencephalic fetus, they take this tendency to its extreme. People who think this way are unable to override disgust with rational appreciation of the objective characteristics of the fetus; the ability to do so is an indispensable trait of the moral mind.

Some people condemn abortion because, consciously or not, they view unwanted pregnancy as an appropriate punishment for extramarital or even marital sexual pleasure. They may experience anxiety at the idea of unpunished sexual pleasure, for they regard sex as sinful and cannot feel safe in a world in which sins go unpunished. Their attitude, again, reflects a premoral mentality. Except under the influence of certain religious premises, morality regards the sex act as innocent, though it judges sexual infidelity and careless procreation as highly culpable. An adult who finds sex inherently sinful is usually one whose thinking about sex and whose conscience overall is still childish. His sense of right and wrong is governed by ideas of retaliation and disgust; it is also rigidly black and white. It lacks the supple, shaded, humane qualities of moral reasoning.

Some abortion opponents are adopted or grew up feeling unwanted. Sadly, but clearly, they feel that legal at-will abortion threatens their own right to exist. If their mothers had had a right not to bear them, they seem to think, then perhaps they would never have been born and perhaps now have no right to live. Or they equate their own present right to live with a right to have been born. There are also parents who cannot bring themselves to acknowledge that abortion is not murder because they fear facing their wish that their children had never been born, and in some cases, the fervor of their conviction that abortion is murder rests on disavowed death wishes toward living children. This illogic is a ready trap for those with the right motives and a mind suitably immune to reason.

Morality vehemently condemns murder because the will to live and horror of death are among the strongest forces in our nature. There is a powerful obligation to respect everyone's urgent desire to live and everyone's wish for the survival of those they love. The destruction of the conceptus, embryo, or early-stage fetus is not, morally speaking, murder because the fetus not only lacks a desire to live but lacks physical characteristics that would enable it to experience emotion, thought, sensation, and desire. Moreover, it has never had such characteristics. It has never felt pain, fear, loneliness, or pleasure and is incapable of love, of suffering, and of fearing death and longing for life. For all these same reasons, no one can love a fetus at this point in its development. Expectant parents usually experience a flood of feeling for their unborn children, a sweet and desirable phenomenon that is important in preparing them to love the real infant when it arrives. But until then it is directed at a fantasy of their own parenthood and of the infant and child they imagine the fetus will grow into, not at a baby.

These facts are reflected in sound and sane customs. Nature sloughs off early pregnancies at a high rate, and we do not name or hold funerals for embryos and early fetuses. As many as 60 to 70 percent of fertilized eggs are lost overall, usually silently, without anyone ever knowing that fertilization took place. Up to 15 percent of known pregnancies miscarry in the first trimester. Were we to take seriously the morbid pseudo-moralism of the fundamentalist Right, we would recognize these countless millions of miscarried embryos and fetuses as lost lives and be sunk in a vast and permanent sea of endless mourning for the unending deaths of innocents. In fact, when we wish to become parents—one of the strongest urges in our nature—we may bitterly grieve early miscarriages and failures to become pregnant. But in these cases we mourn not someone's death, not the passing of a child, but the poignant lost possibility of a child and parenthood and the cutting off of happy plans for new life.

When moral attitudes toward abortion rest on factual premises about the human capacities of the fetus, they converge on a rough consensus that termination of a normal pregnancy becomes wrong when the fetus comes *near* the age at which it would acquire a capacity for fear, contentment, pain, and the rest. That consensus tends to put this point (according to my own unscientific and informal surveys), in theory, somewhere before the midpoint of the pregnancy and, in practice, before the end of the first trimester and in any event as soon as possible.* Although neurological science suggests that the fetus does not achieve consciousness or feeling until around six months or a little later, in such matters morality draws the line conservatively. Again, custom reflects this dovetailing of moral sense and what used to be common sense. At about five months, most states require registration of fetal deaths, and many people hold a funeral or naming ceremony; few do so for earlier mis-carriages, no matter how deeply they grieve them or how ear-nestly they had hoped for a child.

To equate the termination of an early pregnancy with the death, indeed the murder, of an infant or child is not merely morally uncalled for but also dangerous. It implicitly demeans the value of real people's lives, both adults' and children's, and confuses the reasons why we protect them so vigilantly. If our moral obligations to one another are abstracted from our ca-pacities for feeling, thinking, intending, and wanting—from everything that makes us human and forms the ground for our care and protection of one another—we are thrown back into a primitive premoral kind of thinking. To regard the destruction of insensate agglomerations of cells that contain human DNA as the destruction of a person's life is to step outside the moral into a brutal and dangerously irrational kind of thought, to substitute taboo for reason. It is a regression to quasi-magical thinking.

Although some people object to abortion on nonreligious grounds, the bulk of the political opposition is religious. Most

---

* This is the *moral* point. At what point law should proscribe abortion is a different question. The overwhelming majority of abortions occur in the first trimester.

right-to-life arguments appeal to religious premises, and the right-to-life movement would be insignificant if the portion of it dependent on religious opinion did not exist. Not all of this opposition is genuine and sincere moral objection, but to the extent that real *moral* objection exists, sincere religious conviction is usually its source. Most often, religious opponents of legal abortion rely on the idea that the soul enters the body at the moment of conception or implantation or on the vaguer idea that human life is sacred. These ideas lead them to maintain that destruction of the fertilized egg, embryo, or fetus at any stage is murder—no matter if it cannot think, feel, fear, love, learn, and so forth. If one accepts the premises, the conclusions follow.

But what if one doesn't? The premises—that the fertilized egg, embryo, and fetus are ensouled or sacred—are ideas that cannot be proved factually and that many people and many religions vehemently reject. Can they be forced to abide by laws based on others' religious beliefs—even if those beliefs are primitive, irrational, and immoral? Do those who oppose abortion on the basis of those religious tenets have the right to impose their religious views on people who reject them?

The moral answer, emphatically enshrined as law in the United States' Constitution, is no. People are within their rights to attempt to *persuade* others to adopt and live by their religious ideas, but not to force them to do so with laws and the power of government. The antiabortion movement is a religious movement that seeks to use political power to force obedience to its own specific, and to many people appalling, religious ideas. Religious right-to-life advocates, who fail to distinguish among the moral, religious, and legal questions, vote to enforce criminal penalties for abortion against women and their doctors. Some supporters of such laws appear not to understand that this is what they are doing. They appear to believe they are merely voting that "abortion is murder" and sometimes are shocked to learn that antiabortion laws impose prison sentences and other severe penalties.

Like the torture proponents, the abortion opponents have succeeded in a mission of moral miseducation, with the result that a significant segment of the public that used to support abortion rights has come to feel qualms about it. Many of those persuaded to change their views still reject the religious and political views that are the core of antiabortionism and are responding only to the new stigma attaching to the pro-abortion position. Asked to explain their view, they usually will reply simply that all human life is sacred. As an argument, such a statement begs the question as to whether a fetus is a "human life" in the morally relevant sense, though it may be living, with human DNA. Those who rely on it are no longer up to a simple moral distinction between live human tissue and real human lives; nor do they have strength of conscience adequate to remain confident of their beliefs and to resist shaming for the sake of what they know is right.

In view of the growing loss of respectability of pro-abortion sentiment and the continuing rage against the Supreme Court that decided *Roe v. Wade*, we should remind ourselves of a few facts about that decision, which was neither close nor "liberal." It had only two dissents, by Byron White and William Rehnquist; and their dissents had nothing to do with a fetus's alleged right to life. They were based, among other things, on legal ideas about states' legislative prerogatives. One of Byron White's clerks reports that White said he would have voted in favor of abortion rights had he been a legislator. Nor can the two dissents easily be read as expressions of politics or ideology. White was a Kennedy appointee; Rehnquist was a Nixon appointee. The same is true of the majority opinion. Justices William Brennan and Potter Stewart were Eisenhower appointees; Richard Nixon appointed Chief Justice Warren Burger, Justice Harry Blackmun, who wrote the majority opinion, and Justice Lewis Powell. Only two who voted with the seven-man majority were appointees of Democratic presidents: William Douglas (Franklin Roosevelt) and Thurgood Marshall (Lyndon Johnson). Polls taken at the time of the decision show a clear majority of citizens approved of it. Pro-abortion sentiment then was a position of moral reform supported across political lines. The Supreme Court justices who decided *Roe* had moral capacities that enabled them to be dispassionate judges and, though they were mostly stuffy, staid, conservative old men, fair-minded defenders of women's rights. There is no reason to feel ashamed to think as they did on this question.

Abortion opponents will no longer say so publicly, as they once did, but many of them begin from a desire to make pregnancy inviolable and reason backward from this to the right to life of the embryo or fetus. Behind this false rationale and its religious rationalizations lie a dislike and fear of the transformation of women's roles in the years after *Roe v. Wade*, transformations to which voluntary pregnancy was so utterly essential. This group hopes to help arrest and reverse the changes by making pregnancy and motherhood involuntary and handicapping, as they used to be. Their antiabortion position is part of a broad, now familiar program of antimodernism that includes male authority and dominance over women and the dominance of religious fundamentalism over science. Their rage, powerful enough to result in cruel harassment, threats, and murders of abortion providers, does not arise out of moral concern. It is pseudomoral, and their often striking air of bad faith and play-acting is evidence of this. Their angry denunciations of baby murder are one more example of the way in which contemporary antimoralism attempts to use the power of moral condemnation to undermine morality itself.

Chapter 7

COOL

Cool. The notion of cool has been destroying the heart for years. I remember when I came to New York for the first time in the early '50s, when cool was starting to be developed as an important position. I remember sitting in a coffee shop in the Village, . . . and taking my paper placemat and writing in big letters "KILL COOL!" Something has crossed the threshold that we never thought would. It's inside, in us. The wind isn't howling out there anymore, it's howling within us, and everyone understands the beast has been unleashed. Extreme caution is advised.

—LEONARD COHEN, QUOTED IN DAVID
SPRAGUE, "LEONARD COHEN AND THE DEATH
OF COOL," *YOUR FLESH* MAGAZINE (1992)

[The great modernists] were also lucky in their first audiences who were honest enough to be shocked. Those, for instance, who were scandalized by Le Sacre du Printemps *may seem to us now to have been old fogies, but their reaction was genuine. They*

did not say to themselves: "Times have changed so
we must change in order to be 'with it.'"
                    —W. H. AUDEN, *FOREWORDS AND*
                              AFTERWORDS (1973)

Clever men will recognize and tolerate nothing but
cleverness; every authority rouses their ridicule, every
superstition amuses them, every convention moves
them to contradiction. . . . And yet . . . in the indi-
vidual, feeling is more than cleverness, reason is
worth as much as feeling, and conscience has it over
reason. If, then, the clever man is not mockable, *he*
may at least be neither loved, nor considered, nor es-
teemed. He may make himself feared, it is true, and
force others to respect his independence; but this nega-
tive advantage, which is the result of a negative supe-
riority, brings no happiness with it. Cleverness is
serviceable for everything, sufficient for nothing.
                    —HENRI-FRÉDÉRIC AMIEL,
                         JOURNAL INTIME (1888)

"COOL" HAS BECOME a nearly meaningless term of general approval, used in place of "good" by everyone under
the age of sixty-five. The attitude that is the source of this usage is a combination of emotional restraint, concealed defiance
or aggression, ironic detachment, skepticism, and alienation
that was exhibited first among jazz musicians and beats, then
hippies, punks, and rappers, and that spread to writers, journalists, reviewers and critics, moviemakers, high schoolers, prepu-

bescent children, foodies, criminals, and television advertisers.★
It has become the dominant style of public discourse. It is how
most of us speak to teachers, salesclerks, and friends. It is the
voice of television and the common denominator in most of what
remains of shared national tastes in music, art, fiction, film, and
architecture. This is unfortunate, for cool is stifling and destructive and very hard to kill.

Cool is a near psychological cousin of the defeated or punished
child's defiant "I don't care" and of reversal fantasies that say, "I'm
really a swan, not an ugly duckling." In all of its many variations,
it is a way of turning bad into good, failure into success, by rede-
fining a disadvantage as a kind of superiority. To accomplish this,
it preserves a safe distance from others and censors sentiment,
warmth, empathy, and love, along with everything that depends
on them, and substitutes feelings that are proof to narcissistic

---

★ Books and articles about, for, and against cool began to proliferate in the
1990s. See Peter N. Stearns, *American Cool: Constructing a Twentieth-Century
Emotional Style* (New York: New York University Press, 1994); Marcel
Danesi, *Cool: The Signs and Meanings of Adolescence* (Toronto: University of
Toronto Press, 1994); Thomas Frank, *The Conquest of Cool: Business Culture,
Counterculture, and the Rise of Hip Consumerism* (Chicago: University of Chi-
cago Press, 1997); Rick Moody, "Against Cool" (1999), in *The Best American
Essays 2004*, ed. Robert Atwan and Louis Menand (New York: Houghton
Mifflin Harcourt, 2004); Dick Pountain and David Robins, *Cool Rules:
Anatomy of an Attitude* (London: Reaktion Books, 2000); Lewis MacAdams,
The Birth of Cool: Beat, Bebop, and the American Avant-Garde (New York: Free
Press, 2001). See also Norman Mailer, "The White Negro," in *Advertisements
for Myself* (New York: G. P. Putnam's Sons, 1959); and Susan Sontag, "Notes
on Camp" (1964), in *Against Interpretation* (New York: Farrar, Straus and Gi-
roux, 1966).

injury. A reliable sign of subterranean rage, cool is often traced to attitudes adopted by blacks to help them survive slavery and racism, and some historians say that the beats learned it from black jazz musicians. Cool is the demeanor of gangs, at least partly an inheritance from earlier styles of criminality and partly borrowed from black street culture.

Whatever its genealogy, cool's cultural spread was greatly promoted by the beats, who sought the public eye in order to spit in it. Among the beats, cool dictated bohemianism* (joblessness, artistic aspirations, sexual adventurism, unconventional family life, drug use); rigorously enforced musical and literary tastes; and a special jargon and style of dress. These were all means of announcing membership in an exclusive club.

Every cool group that succeeded the beats followed its pattern closely. The beret, shades, bongos, and heroin of the beats gave way to the beads, fringe, guitars, beards, and marijuana of the hippies, down through purple-haired punk and do-rags, baggy jeans, crack, and rap. Every reinvention of cool targeted "ordinary" people, whom it represented as straitlaced, stupid, disapproving, timid, conventional, and hypocritical, the same Middle America that had earned the scorn of the beats back in the fifties. As against such people, the cool were special, superior, knowing, nonconformist. They had a chilly honesty about the dark parts of life and their own darkness and a willingness to flout the moral rules that other people, in their cowardice

---

* Not all bohemianism is cool. In romantic and neoromantic periods it was not; its defiance of social rules was accompanied by conscious devotion to feeling, passion, warmth, sometimes to the point of sentimentalism. In our own time, bohemianism usually is cool.

and hypocrisy, insisted they believed in. Cool was the perfect social demeanor for narcissism.

In the eighties, cool's image of Middle America was represented in MTV videos by besuited, nerdy, middle-aged men with jowls and paunches who lusted futilely after teasing young women who looked like Madonna—a satisfying and reassuring fantasy for the young women, though unrealistic, as by the 1980s square men in fedoras were long gone, as were the dour, dim, self-righteous, respectable biddies mocked in falsetto on *Monty Python* in the late sixties.★ Everyone had become cool.

The cool style was often adopted less from private need than from fear of being its target, especially among young people, and the emotional needs that it answered varied from person to person. From the sixties on, some people began to cling to this style as they aged. For them, it was a kind of tonic against the death-in-life that adulthood in postwar America seemed to them, while to others it was a way to maintain the sense of uniqueness and superiority as the narcissistic rewards of youth faded.

THE COOL MENTALITY is likely to forgive and justify what ordinary morality condemns: cruelty, oppression, self-seeking,

---

★ But because cool values are always changing, the cool especially delight in exposing yesterday's cool as today's uncool. When men's fedoras were so long gone that it was no longer cool to make fun of them, it began to be cool to wear them. But there are also nostalgic devotees of cool like Rick Moody, who object to the way cool has degenerated and yearn for the truly cool arts and people of yore. See Moody's essay, "Against Cool," cited in the footnote on page 167.

greed, duplicity, cowardice, hypocrisy, and betrayal. It often does
so through comedy. Comedy always builds humor on human
flaws; Dickens (with Pickwick, Micawber, and many more),
Charlie Chaplin, Harpo Marx, and Steve Martin all do so in
their own ways. Cool comedy, however, covertly or overtly
builds on the implicit release in denying that wrongs and flaws
are wrongs and flaws. *Seinfeld* is cool comedy, with the twist
that it both seduces the audience into affectionate admiration
for wrong and wrongdoers and in a variety of ways assures
them that it is not doing so. It accomplishes this by adherence
to familiar, traditional comedic forms and by means of the
clothes, jobs, tastes, and habits of its characters, which ascribe
ordinary good-guy status to those characters and coax the audience into accepting that status and identifying with them.
This kind of humor is less funny to those who resist the seduc-
tion and the double-think it invites and more funny to those
who do not.

But cool is no more loyal to wrong than to right. It is fickle
and likely to change its tune for the sake of novelty or, when its
standards become too successful, as a tactic to reestablish a division between insiders and outsiders. Ideas about what is cool
become deeply uncool as soon as they become too familiar or
spread too broadly. The cool attitude is experienced inwardly—
and outwardly, by others—as a kind of higher insight. Thus it
dovetails with the increasingly premoral and narcissistic orientation of American culture, in which individuals strive not for
moral good but for superiority and invulnerability. It offers a
way to achieve these things by means of internal mechanisms
that are readily available to anyone not disqualified by moral
qualms. No special power, wealth, intelligence, wit, beauty,

courage, or virtue is required to be cool—a fact the beats discovered and never tired of analyzing. Anyone, it turns out, can be better than other people.

The attitude of cool is always antimoral, and it tends to find moral character traits distasteful. The attitudes of morality and cool are necessarily at odds: Morality is inherently inclusive, respectful, egalitarian, passionate, and committed. Cool is inherently exclusive, sneering, detached, and tilted toward nihilism. Of course, cool is often adopted innocently and lightly by people who are in no way tempted to slip down into cool amorality and who are simply, civilly, adopting the style and tone of the age, the one that most people find comfortable. But there are many others who seek something more potent in being cool, who find in it the psychological means of throwing off moral restraints. The rise of cool as the language of the public square, which drowns out and discredits moral discourse, offers such people a far larger social arena than would otherwise be theirs, and allows their antimoralism to spread and persuade without arousing resistance or shock or recognition.

COOL POLITICS: GEEKS, SQUARES, DORKS, AND NERDS

Cool aestheticizes all evaluation, and its aesthetic is confining. Not only the arts but human beings, politics, religion, and right and wrong—all are measured by the yardstick of cool. It judges everything with an illusory knowingness, and its judgments oppose morality, religions that incorporate morality, and, indeed, any institutions or practices that fail to be cool. Because what seems cool to cool people varies with whatever relieves feelings of inferiority and humiliation, cool moves from the political left to center right with ease.

The world first saw cool united with politics among left-leaning people. Every member of the Weather Underground, the Black Panthers, and similar extreme, protoviolent and violent groups strove to be cool. Today there are many conservative, right-wing, and libertarian cool people. When John Colapinto wrote an essay in the *New York Times Magazine**[*] pointing out, with some condescension, that campus conservatives—hipublicans, he called them—were abandoning the bow ties and pin-striped suits that had produced so much liberal snickering and were adopting a more cool look, conservative columnist Jonah Goldberg retorted that cool was neither liberal nor conservative.[†] Conservative kids, he said, are just normal kids. This was a defense against liberal descriptions of Young Republicans as not only sartorially challenged, but also sexually closeted or repressed or confused, overobedient, power- and status-hungry, sycophantic weaklings—in other words, as geeks. He was right, of course, that cool had become normal in all political circles.

Cool conservatives, dubbed "South Park Republicans" by Andrew Sullivan, lean center-right and libertarian and favor small government and low taxes. They abhor equally the Peace Corps, welfare, and the thought of compulsory military service. Some of them protest having to pay taxes so that

---

[*] John Colapinto, "The Young Hipublicans," *New York Times Magazine*, May 25, 2003.
[†] Jonah Goldberg, "Conservatives in the Mist," *National Review Online*, May 28, 2003.

other people's children can attend school, and many dislike being forced to pay for medical care for anyone, the elderly, children, or the poor. Their view of politics is amoral and self-interested, and they will argue vigorously that this is as it should be. More than other groups, they dwell on the aesthetic offenses of their political opponents: Left-wing rhetoric has the taint of peace signs, beads, graying ponytails, and political correctness; liberals have a nauseating combination of slickness and earnestness; right-wing creationists are tacky and stupid. But cool conservatives are smart and both moderately pro-environmental and socially liberal; they oppose racism, bigotry, and homophobia.

Cool conservatives also have a laughing affection for certain kinds of geekiness, an affection that warms their self-approval and does not threaten their superiority. Unlike others, their inner script says, *I* am capable of feeling genuinely fond of this repugnant, strange, or otherwise inferior human being. This affection masks their contempt but does not replace it; in fact, the secret conviction that the geek is contemptible is what makes possible their self-admiration in these cases. The affection for geekiness often takes the form of fascination with people who are obsessively invested in silly or unimportant things: trainspotters; doormat collectors; fanatic devotées of minor musical genres or groups; socially inept or indifferent masters of chess or Scott Joplin rags; and, in short, all who are passionate and unembarrassed about meaningless goals. In their admiration and affection for these people, the cool at once achieve a sense of superiority (for not being so silly), a surge of fellow feeling, and, their chief object, a backdoor denigration of the very ideas of passion and devotion, as they take satisfaction in geeks' inadvertent satire of meaningful commitment. For similar reasons, cool is fascinated with autism and has fueled an outpouring of books and films about it (*Rain Man*, *Forrest Gump*, *Adam*, and many more). A number of these convey, or invite, the same combination of overt generous affection and concealed contempt. But cool also has a genuine admiration for autism. It sees the autistic as invulnerable to social disapproval, proof against *all* feeling except with respect to their bizarre obsessions and fears to which it reacts with sentimental compassion; and it thinks of them as possessing strange, misunderstood brilliance and insight, as it would like to believe of itself. The autistic are the ultimate cool characters, the cultural heroes of our day.

Political cool provides a poor defense for rights. In today's world, cool conservatives, unlike authoritarian rightists, find no reason to object to any sort of sexual behavior, and in this they appear to adopt moral attitudes. They joke about homophobes and get dewy-eyed about their own goodness in supporting gay marriage, but because their attitudes are not truly moral, they are likely to give them up when they become socially costly. Now that pro-abortion views begin to be stigmatized, they begin to express moral doubts about abortion. Such doubts gain them many advantages, among them the appearance of moral seriousness while giving rein to antimoral feelings and hostility against liberalism. They will have abortions when necessary, but they are perfectly willing to support a political party that attempts to criminalize them. If abortions are not locally available, they have the money to fly to some place where they are legal.

EXTREMISM AND COOL

In the past few decades, cool has repeatedly devolved into madness and murder, and extremists and fanatics have adopted the veneer of cool. Cool has a natural symbiosis with fanaticism. That fanaticism and cool go together seems counterintuitive only until one recalls that cool is *essentially* a veneer, a pose or front, and that it reflects no underlying psychology apart from narcissistic vulnerability. It can be learned and put on by anyone with a grudge. Those with the most intense grudges often gain the most from cool. Because cool neutralizes conflicting values, the more cool the fanatic, the less able he is to restrain himself in accordance with moral inhibitions on sadism or aggression.

Cool may seem the psychological antipode of political and religious extremes, but in fact they are psychological twins. Like political and religious extremism, cool creates an *us* and a *them*, an in-crowd and a set of despised outs: squares, nerds, dorks, and geeks. (These categories are correlates of cool; they could not exist without it.) Cool people, like cultists, fanatics, and extremists, rely on contempt, disrespect, and name-calling. Cool also plays something of the role of religion in the psyche by providing a template for all life's choices and attitudes, a touchstone by which one assures one's own self-approval, demeans others unlike oneself, and immunizes oneself from their disapproval. Fundamentalist religions and extremist politics share with the cool mentality the tendency to project a sense of unworthiness and degradation onto some despised other and thus to see all opposition as contemptible and degraded. Just as many adherents to right-wing varieties of religion are not satisfied to be saved but must be assured that others aren't, and just as the

mad belief systems of cultists, political and religious, aim at providing a sense of secure belonging in some superior group, so the
essence of cool is to establish the existence of an inferior other
(the geek, square, dork, or nerd) and ensure a sense of belonging
to a superior caste. The cool gambit is always aimed at warding
off a painful sensation of inferiority.

These similarities between cool and fanaticism make possible
their mutual borrowings. Cool performs psychological services
that the fanatic needs. It disarms external criticism, in part by providing what is by now a legitimating social pose, an attitude that
everyone understands, and in part by punishing disagreeable
others, for it is in the very nature of cool to punish and control. The
antisocial, the misfit, and even the plain old selfish quickly discover
that cool, the demeanor of choice for the rebel, is the most plau-
sible way of explaining themselves to themselves as well as to others. Cool provides reassurance, helps the fanatic to feel less defeated,
silly, and alone, more sure of himself: The whole world may be
against me, but I'm not wrong, much less a lunatic. I'm cool.

Cool serves as a psychological disinhibitor, neutralizing internal dissent and conscientious doubts.* The very same disen-

---

* For this reason, the cult of cool plays a complicated role in school shootings.
Not only do the shooters usually strive for extreme cool, but they are often
motivated by rage at the school's popular cool crowd. The cool crowd always
includes those who are too attractive, too cruel, too rich, or too athletic to
serve as others' targets and who have both the need and the will to make the
vulnerable into their own targets, excluding them and bullying them. As
moral culture becomes less and less a part of adolescent experience, these
phenomena grow more common and more vicious, and attempts to rein
them in through increased policing and punishments only serve to restrain
the least skillful practioners of these dark adolescent arts.

gagement, skepticism, and scorn it uses against others by its nature undermines its own inner controls and restraints. Cool can set in motion a free fall into extremism and fanaticism by belittling the tug of conscience, the impulse to wonder if the despised other has rights or feelings or ideas as important as one's own. The moral recommendation to walk in other people's shoes before judging, to see how they feel or why they think what they do, tends to come across to the cool as sentimental, sanctimonious, and phony. Thus cool people grow dangerously unafraid of causing hurt. They become invulnerable to mercy or pity or even just a few reservations. In youth and in age, they are prone to become bullies.

Both fanaticism and cool aim to emasculate or annihilate the despised outsider psychologically. Both fanaticism and cool, therefore, lead logically to murderousness, always in spirit but sometimes in fact as well. Cool's tendency to dehumanize is released and magnified by its amorality. The contemptible other is undeserving of fair play or respect or kindness; no humiliation or punishment inflicted on him is going too far because cool undercuts the sense of values that sets inner limits. Cool tends to allow a slide from hip scorn of false values (self-approving, fat, smug, greedy, hypocritical middle-class morality) to scorn for all ideas of good, along with self-certainty and pleasure in superiority; from the comfort of belonging to a gang or group to bullying and cruelty and even violence against those who don't. There is an eerie nexus between cool culture and the cults led by Charles Manson and David Koresh, both of whom yearned to be rock musicians—to a certain kind of mind, the coolest, most impregnable of all roles.

The cool facade is adopted by both the Right and the Left.

Far rightists and right-wing libertarians veer into actual murderousness at their extremes. Their image of the cool man is visible in film heroes such as Dirty Harry, the Terminator, and many subsequent characters who are, above all, cool—utterly impervious, superior, tough, merciless, detached, unemotional, silent—and who have always been terribly wronged. This version of cool is favored by right-wing militiamen of the kind who would bomb the federal building in Oklahoma, or admire those who did, but also by militant antiabortion groups who publish hit lists of abortion doctors on the Internet. These two groups, in fact, overlap to some extent in membership and certainly in their fantasy of the cool hero who fearlessly and mercilessly carries out executions of the evil ones. Similarly, in the sixties, ultracool members of SDS, taking up the weapons of psychological destruction, called cops and senators "pigs" and consciously aimed to humiliate them. A few advanced to real bombs and guns and killed people with the approval of more than a few sympathizers. All such killers, right and left, displayed a chilling incomprehension that someone for whom they had contempt might nevertheless have a right to live and a stupefying failure to grasp the grief and rage of their victims' friends and families. Kathy Boudin, Timothy McVeigh, and James Kopp were in this way all alike. Tolerance toward the opposition, for them, was weakness or even betrayal; they disapproved of compassion or sympathy for the enemy and indulged in none. Few go far enough down the path of unfeeling to be able to plant bombs and pull triggers, as these three did, but many more can applaud and support those who do, just as al-Qaeda and right-wing militants murder hundreds or thousands of innocents with the gloating approval of supporters who find in such acts a means of reversing their own chronic feelings of humiliation and emasculation.

COOL TASTE

The cool style narrows sensibility. It disapproves of the passions and emotions of the moral life and finds its judgments distasteful. Moral qualities—mercy, trust, warmth, egalitarianism, compassion—are incompatible with cool; they war with its need for invulnerability and superiority. Cool cannot accept the tender, the stalwart, the passionate, the engaged, the upright, and the sublime and makes fun of them. It demands that one be uncommitted, skeptical, disengaged, and superior. It both shrivels warm feelings and increases tolerance of cruelty, sadism, and wrongdoing and the ability to take pleasure in these. As it restricts the emotional range, it undermines empathy, self-examination, and other moral capacities; people grow less able to be outraged, more indifferent, less caring.

The constricted sensibility of cool led to a broad change in taste. Cool people tend to find unpalatable the music, art, literature, and moral and political works from historical periods when the moral mentality was ascendant—to the point that 7-Eleven stores famously succeed in driving undesirable teenagers off their premises by playing Mozart on their sound systems. Cool has encouraged composers to produce the unlistenable new music that has done so much to damage the classical tradition and helped to render the plastic and visual arts docile, silly, and absurdly susceptible to the logic of the market. In the pop fiction of today, the moral sensibility has often gone missing.

The popular subgenres of science fiction, fantasy, young adult literature, and romance increasingly express predominantly pre-moral tastes and concerns.

Because it limits emotional range, cool also cuts us off from traditions of literature, music, and art that speak to emotional life beyond that range.* This is dangerous. The books, music, and art of past centuries of moral sensibility do more than entertain. They also fine-tune and develop the moral capacities, remind us of our moral premises and how they interlink and play out in life. New generations cut off from the stories, jokes, music, philosophy, and other cultural products of our past are more easily weaned away from the moral and more readily fall into moral confusion. They become increasingly less able to understand the structure of our political institutions, the motives that guided their creation, and less able to perpetuate the conditions of democracy, just as they become increasingly unable to experience the pleasures and meet the obligations of family and friendship. The rule of law, the restraints on government, the independence of the press—cornerstones of democracy's dispersal of power—are poorly understood and protected by the culture of cool.

---

* Classical musicians, watching their art die, periodically attempt to fight the cultural currents that are killing it by joining the enemy. "Classical music is cool," twenty-something conductor Gustavo Dudamel told reporters at a press conference, and an Associated Press wire (October 1, 2009) noted that he wore "trendy black sneakers and a persistent smile that showed the sheer fun he's having" at his first rehearsal with the Los Angeles Philharmonic. This now familiar tactic, first attempted half a century ago by Leonard Bernstein, has never been particularly successful. Though young musicians may well be cool, premodern classical music is not; and people who like it are unlikely to care for most cool modern and postmodern compositions.

With its rejection of morally grounded taste, cool creates a divide between us and the moral traditions that enable us to maintain and advance our institutions and even to understand why they are desirable. It is not possible to sustain, let alone increase, the fruits of our past—science, humane democratic forms of government, personal freedoms, wealth justly shared among us—when ties to their sources have been cut, when the works of art and thought that elaborate and instruct in their meanings and workings are dead to us.

MORAL SHOCK: TRANSVALUATION

Cool engages in what Nietzsche called "transvaluation," a revaluing of values in which something that is supposed to be good is said to be, in fact, bad and in which something that is thought to be bad is said to be, really, good. In this it parodies morality itself, which also presses for change and transvalues "natural" values. This is why cool inherently tends toward idol smashing. Alone, however, it cannot distinguish between good and evil. So when it fails to borrow these ideas from elsewhere, it has a natural tendency to descend into dark, mad places.

Cool reverses values so as to give cool people, who suffer from suppressed rageful humiliation, a renewed sense of superiority. It always embraces something naughty, always discovers that something you thought was bad is—surprise—at least all right and probably downright good: adultery, drugs, murder, or, occasionally, mass murder. This tendency provides the standard formula for opinion pieces in most magazines and newspapers, no matter how tired and old this values-reversal gambit gets. "Is Adultery Really Wrong?" (You thought so, but aren't there times . . .) Or, "Are Fathers Necessary? A Paternal Contribution May Not Be as Necessary as We Think." One television director/producer praised his new sitcom by pointing out that its characters "work to puncture the myth of the functional family." The idea that a well-functioning family is a myth was used to give the production a claim to be new and cutting-edge and to exploit the envious disgruntlement of the multitudes of potential viewers whose family situations are painful.

Cool thus brings in its wake constant pointless social churning and poses a formidable obstacle both to rational, beneficial change and to preservation of valuable aspects of any status quo. Because cool exists only oppositionally, it favors change for its own sake and attacks the socially good as readily as the bad. Its narcissism, reacting angrily to social restraint and criticism, readily concludes in cases of conflict that it is the rules that are bad, not me. Add to this self-serving tendency the commercial value that novelty and shock so frequently confer, and the setup exists for endless, destructive social change without progress and a status quo of empty gesturing.

Moral barriers, especially sexual mores, are a favorite target of cool. The cool mentality enables people to separate sex from love, tenderness, and all that they make possible: fidelity, care, intimacy, privacy, and mutual respect. This nihilism in cool attitudes toward sex is echoed in every other part of life. Cool slides into nihilism as readily as into fanaticism. Cool nihilism is a further spur toward—in a favorite cool phrase—pushing the envelope. To cause shock is to advance truth, for shock is a sure sign that some lingering false value has been overturned. Among a large number of today's students, it is cool to down-

load movies in violation of copyright, cheat on exams, and buy
term papers online. Cool neutralizes objections to games, music, films, and fiction that permit the viewer to indulge vicari-
ously in sadism and victorious wrongdoing. It does so, in part,
by so successfully ridiculing feelings of moral horror and guilt
that many people become ashamed of having them.★

Cool promotes the amoral and immoral in part because it
anesthetizes. It distances people from their feelings, so that they
become insensitive and numb. But their numbness then makes
them long for intense sensation so that they can feel alive. Cool
numbness enables people to tolerate or even enjoy the depiction
of torture and psychotic violence. In film and fiction, the cool
seek a sense of extreme danger and tension, along with vivid displays of blood, cruelty, sadism, and mayhem to which they have,
compared with others, muted reactions.

Their numbness also gives the cool an odd appetite for observing others undergo intense fear and pain or moral shock.
The depiction of moral shock being inflicted on the uncool,
indeed, is a cliché now. It remains a favorite device in film and
fiction because it is a means of feeling something rather than
not feeling at all. The sight of others' shock gives the cool an
intense vicarious and sadistically pleasurable experience. It sat-
isfies the longing for feeling on the part of people who are
afraid of feeling, and it uses others' shock to reinforce the sense
of being superior, stronger than the vulnerable and shockable.

★ This trend in popular entertainments tends to drive away people with the
vulnerability of the moral mentality and creates audiences dominated by a
distinctly premoral or amoral sensibility in which shame trumps guilt, rather
than the contrary—the reverse of the moral psychology.

Cool tends to limit the imagination, both because it reduces sensation and because it vigorously resists standing in anyone else's shoes—one of the chief uses of the moral imagination. If cool people do succeed in imagining the sensations implied by the suffering depicted in some contemporary fare, they tend to imagine inflicting them on someone else, not experiencing such things themselves. No one would argue that it might be a good thing for an individual or for society that great numbers of people be oblivious, numb, and morally unimaginative. Indeed, it is questionable whether such people could perform the duties of parents, neighbors, friends, lovers, and citizens of a complex democracy, or whether an intelligentsia that is numb and limited in these ways could serve, or even understand, the goals of a liberal, tolerant, and humane society.

Chapter 8

VENGEANCE AND THE EROSION OF LAW

Revenge is a kind of wild justice, which the more man's nature runs to, the more ought law to weed it out.

——FRANCIS BACON, *THE ESSAYS, CIVIL AND MORAL* (1625)

The narcissistic authoritarian as juror is not going to be truly interested in the law. For him the law on burden of proof, presumption of innocence, the elements of the offense, the admissibility of evidence, and so forth, will be largely irrelevant. . . . He comes to the case with a mental set that introduces distortion into the process of decision making. His personality traits . . . determine how he votes on guilt or innocence. . . .

Contemporary international law and American constitutional and statutory law provide wide-ranging rights for all persons. . . . The narcissistic authoritarian rejects most or all of these rights and the overarching Western principle of the rule of law.

——WALTER F. ABBOTT AND JOHN BATT, EDS., *A HANDBOOK OF JURY RESEARCH*

(PHILADELPHIA: AMERICAN LAW INSTITUTE–
AMERICAN BAR ASSOCIATION, 1999)

LAWS WRITTEN ON paper are impotent or dead unless they are applied by people who have specific moral capacities. They must be able to weigh subtle degrees of wrong, to be outraged by what is really outrageous, to see what facts are relevant in light of the moral presuppositions of legislation, to disregard offense not relevant to the legal determination, and to see and apply the law as it is, not as they wish it were. They must grasp how law embraces facts and when its spirit is more important than its letter. They must be able to respect precedents and their spirit in a highly intuitive way. Of course, they must also protect the inviolacy and dignity of the law; they must not take bribes or make decisions on political grounds. Indeed, whole books could (and should) be written about the moral character that the legal system presupposes in judges and lawyers. But law also requires strong moral capacities in the citizens it governs. They must be disposed to obey the law, they must be so immersed in moral culture that they intuitively understand how laws and legal rights function and what are legitimate and illegitimate goals for law, and when laws and judges are what they should be. And they must vote and otherwise behave as citizens in a way that protects the rule of law.

Law, morality, and democracy comfortably coexist and support one another. When the moral mentality is culturally weak, and when self-governing, rationally judging citizens are either few or lack influence, the rule of law and democratic institutions begin to crumble—a matter easily observed everywhere in the world. In the United States today, law is being eroded by several forces, but most powerfully by the fierce and wide-spread commitment to revenge that has arisen as a result of the weakening of moral influences and the strengthening of a pre-moral sense of values.

For nearly forty years, a relentless and now much-debated trend has moved American law toward harsher, longer punish-ments, limits on judges' ability to exercise discretion, an expan-sion of criminal liability, and increasing insistence on citizens' rights to call on law as an aid to vengeance. Only very recently have these changes aroused much public concern, and then mostly because economic recession rendered local governments unable to meet the enormous costs of their extraordinarily high rates of incarceration. This growth of cruelty and harshness in the law originated as part of the backlash against the postwar moral awakening.*

In the 1950s and 1960s, that moral awakening inspired both legislation and two decades of landmark Supreme Court deci-sions that began with *Brown v. Board of Education* (1954) and came more or less to a close with *Roe v. Wade* (1973).† The dominance of right-wing politics has meant that today all these decisions are dubbed "liberal," but in fact they reflect a variety of political

---

* Altered moral consciousness affects the law in other ways and legal arenas than those taken up in this chapter, among them politicization of courts' decisions, federal policies relating to terrorists and detainees, campaign fi-nance, abortion, the separation of church and state, and many more.

† The consensus usually visible in these earlier cases disappeared in *Furman v. Georgia* (1972), which effectively halted executions in the United States for five years. *Furman* was decided 5–4, on several distinct rationales.

values and complex realities. Among the many true things worth noticing about them that are no longer said, and that are not obvious to those who grew up after the era in which such court decisions were possible, is that they reflected the heightened sense in the postwar years that personal freedom, privacy, equality, dignity, and the rule of law that protected these rights were what Allied victory in World War II stood for. The passion that lay behind the war effort transferred itself to the need to shore up these rights and to ensure that they were guaranteed to all—to women, the poor, and blacks and other minorities. If they were not, then we were no better than the nations we had defeated in what was universally and correctly understood as a monumental moral battle, one in which the very survival of morality and law was at stake.

Many courts of the postwar era set about ensuring that the law protected these rights, which, in their opinion, were both natural and legal; that is, they were laid down both morally and in written law. They regarded it as legal error to construe large, open-textured concepts of the Constitution in a manner detrimental or indifferent to those rights. Given that morality is at once the condition, the goal, and the justification for the imposition of legal restraints in the first place, it is always dangerous to tolerate wide gaps between natural or moral and legal justice. For when the law is put to wrongful purpose, sooner or later it is corrupted; it becomes a means for some people to control, impoverish, or abuse others. It loses the dignity and impartiality of true law and fails to inspire loyalty and respect. The rule of law eventually collapses.

Consciously or not, judges of the 1950s and 1960s had in mind as a negative model the totalitarian regimes of the twentieth century and their destruction of privacy, equality, due process, and all other real values incorporated in law. It was no accident that these regimes both broke the law and enacted appalling "laws" that defied the very idea of law. If we were to be safe from the distortions of law that permitted the horrors of fascist and communist dictatorships, our own legal system had to be placed on a firmer moral footing, and our Constitution enacted broad principles that gave courts the means to carry out the needed reforms.

The burgeoning radical right wing of American politics, however, opposed the reforms and launched a decades-long effort to reverse them and their aid to racial and sexual equality and their protection of the poor and ignorant against governmental power. This authoritarian premoralism preferred, as it does wherever and whenever it occurs, a harsh social hierarchy of superiors and inferiors, status for wealth and power, the subordination of women and those whom they perceived as other, alien races and peoples, and cruelty in punishment.

In obvious and familiar ways, subsequent trends in law reflect the successful deformation of law by premoral ideas. The United States now has the highest rate of imprisonment in the entire world, both in absolute terms (2.3 million people incarcerated in 2008) and as a percentage (about 1 percent of all adults).* In many states, there has been a near cessation of pardons, and pardons are drastically reduced almost everywhere—a development that all prior generations of Americans would have found incomprehensible. Prisons are brutal, harsh, and merciless, relying heavily on humiliation and sadistic treatment

---

* Russia has the second highest rate of imprisonment.

of prisoners to create deterrence to crime. Prison rape, which is horrifyingly common, is the subject of constant joking, and in film and fiction it is repeatedly presented as a satisfying means of punishing and humbling villains. Other problems within prisons include crowding;* grossly inadequate medical care; the use of solitary confinement for years, even decades, torturing and driving inmates into insanity; the dismantling of rehabilitation and education programs; the imprisonment of inmates in privatized jails, often in other states and locales far from their homes, families, and lawyers; the quasi enslavement of inmates hired out to private industry to work for paltry wages; and the imposition on inmates of endless fees that trap them in debt.

There is little public outcry against the barbarous and exploitative treatment of prisoners. A large segment of the public *wants* rape, beatings, and other atrocities to characterize the prison experience and complains that humane prisons are country clubs. Politicians are terrified of being labeled "soft on crime"— with good reason. In a presidential campaign debate in 2011, the audience cheered mention of Texas's execution of 234 death row inmates during Rick Perry's term as governor, more than in any other state, and Governor Perry affirmed calmly that this

---

* In *Brown v. Plata*, on May 23, 2011, the Supreme Court affirmed by a 5–4 vote a lower court decision that called on the State of California to release more than thirty thousand prisoners. The majority concluded that appalling conditions due to overcrowding had caused loss of life and suffering that violated the Eighth Amendment's prohibition of cruel and unusual punishment. Justice Antonin Scalia's dissent denounced the decision as "absurd" and "perhaps the most radical injunction issued by a court in our nation's history."

record gave him no qualms of conscience and that he did not worry whether some of the executed might have been innocent.

The society-wide belief in the propriety of cruelty against prisoners has produced well-known and well-documented unhappy results. Our current prison system incapacitates prisoners for readjustment to outside life; it is a major cause of the spread of gangs; and it establishes a particularly brutal criminal culture in impoverished neighborhoods where rates of imprisonment are staggeringly high. But other dangerous effects have gone unnoticed.

One particularly insidious consequence of the United States having become the prison capital of the world is that in the United States the prison model has come to be widely imitated outside the criminal justice system. Techniques for handling prisoners and prisons are more and more often applied to law-abiding citizens, with consequent abridgments of freedom and dignity that should be protested but rarely are. Schools and colleges, for example, are repeatedly put on "lockdown" when violence is feared; armed security guards prowl hallways and campuses. More and more commonly, primary and secondary schools call in the police to handle garden-variety disciplinary matters with handcuffs and arrests and even Tasers in situations that principals, teachers, and parents used to handle themselves. In ordinary encounters with ordinary citizens, police have begun to exercise the same brutal authority that they are taught to use with criminals. They react violently to back talk. A police officer no longer instructs citizens to "come along" in an arrest but shouts for them to get "down on the ground," kneeling or prostrate, and cuffs their hands behind their back—no matter how unlikely it is that the arrestee will resist or be violent.

Ordinary Americans, having lost the ordinary self-respect and dignity of the moral mentality, submit without protest.

An avalanche of punitive legislation—a favorite way for politicians to curry favor with thoughtless voters nursing inchoate grudges—has caused grave damage to the legal system. Three-strikes laws and mandatory minimum-sentencing schemes result in bizarrely long sentences that are grossly disproportionate to the offenses. The death penalty, after years of disuse, is applied almost exclusively to the poor, the stupid, the mad, and the broken and disproportionately to blacks. Sexual offender laws that are scarcely lawlike exist in most states, ruining the postrelease lives not only of dangerous sexual criminals but also of people who were never particularly dangerous or who no longer are. A motley set of laws criminalizes whatever makes us most angry most recently. All are examples of law succumbing directly or indirectly to the demand for revenge. Their effects are aggravated by drastic cuts in funding for legal representation for the poor and by a loss of moral compass in too many prosecutors, who have come to see not justice but conviction as their goal.

The dignity of law and confidence in the criminal justice system is now undermined by media revelations of hundreds of false convictions that these factors have led to, proven conclusively by indisputable DNA evidence. The parade across the television screen of innocent men who have been locked up for ten, twenty, or more years on disgracefully inadequate evidence seems unending. Most are cleared of rapes and murder convictions, cases in which DNA evidence is often available. Such serious cases are also among the most carefully tried, however, which suggests that the rate of false convictions in other kinds of cases, especially drug cases, where perjury by both police and other witnesses is common, is likely to be shockingly high.

The system of plea bargaining also provides an easy means for prosecutors to abuse people who have been charged with a crime. People who are wrongly accused or face exaggerated charges enter plea bargains rather than face the interminable sentences that they might receive if they should exercise their right to trial and be convicted. Even innocent and wrongly accused defendants often enter false guilty pleas in exchange for moderate penalties rather than go to trial in light of the substantial risk of false conviction and harsh sentences that trial entails. Jury trials, in myth the crown jewel of the legal system, in which defendants have a chance to plead their case to citizens like themselves, now occur in only about 5 percent of felony cases. A system built on the principle that protection and exoneration of the innocent always take precedence over conviction of the guilty has been turned on its head. Conviction is now so important that prosecutors, reversing this fundamental principle, give the public wrongful convictions rather than let a crime go unpunished when we are in reasonable doubt about who did it.*

The premoral mentality insists on having revenge to reestablish narcissistic equilibrium after an injury. It believes that criminals merit inhumane treatment and permits itself pleasure

---

* There are still many prosecutors, judges, and police who are guilty of none of these things and who strive courageously to make the system work the way it should. Some judges have even refused to try cases under laws that would have required them to pass unconscionably severe sentences.

in cruelty. So deeply entrenched in law have premoral attitudes become that many people now react with outrage to the truth: that the law insists on the humanity even of criminals and guarantees equal respect and humane treatment even to those who have committed terrible wrongs. If it did not, law would be merely one more tool the strong may use to whip whoever offends and challenges them. Of course, to those who so abuse the law, their own behavior seems right and good, even obligatory. But the law forbids the unequal and cruel treatment even of wrongdoers because it *exists* to control the impulse to believe in one's own rightness, goodness, and deserts over that of others. In a democratic society, the rule of law is a tool of moral justice against power; it exists to serve this purpose. When it fails to serve it, it ceases to be law and its claim on our obedience is eroded.

Along with the abuse of legal punishment, we have seen an angry rejection of efforts to understand some of the many reasons why people commit crimes and how we might help at least some of them not to do so. But the very idea of understanding criminal behavior is now the object of automatic contempt. After 9/11, right-wingers made fun of the people whom they call "liberals" by insisting that they would try to "understand" the attackers. (Alas, all too few did. Some right-wing religious spokesmen saw the attacks as divine vengeance against fellow citizens whom they did not like, while some left-wing analysts' "understanding" seemed to excuse the murder of thousands of innocents on the grounds that the United States government had misbehaved.) People who call for compassion and mercy to criminals and wrongdoers are vehemently denounced. Sensationalist crime reporting, television crime shows, and politicians looking to make sure that the well of public outrage never runs dry constantly assure voters of a blatant falsehood: that the courts side with criminals against them. This results in passage of one ill-considered piece of legislation after another and lets corrupt legislators appear as defenders of the people.

PRIVATE VENGEANCE IN THE LAW

Encouraged by a campaign of moral miseducation carried out by unscrupulous and antimoral leaders, prosecutors, and judges, a large fraction of the public now views laws and prisons as aids to private vengeance. This attitude spawned the custom of calling on those harmed by criminal acts to speak in court after a conviction, in a ritual that is intended to allow crime victims some satisfaction of their rage and to influence sentencing. This ritual can backfire both because it is not always easy to find words to shrivel the hearts of wrongdoers and because sometimes those hearts are very hard.*

Faith in vengeance guides the thinking of the friends and relatives of victims we see on television, marching angrily down the courthouse steps and demanding the death penalty or keeping vigil outside death chambers, waiting for the satisfaction of hearing that the murderer has been killed. Or we read

---

* How many of us, for example, would know what to say to the man who murdered, cooked, and ate our relation? In a televised scene in Jeffrey Dahmer's sentencing, a young woman in that position was reduced to screaming at him, "I hate you, Jeffrey Dahmer." It was hard to believe that the experience had done anything but increase her painful sense of helpless rage.

about crime victims who claim they have *closure* because the wrongdoer has gotten what he deserves, or complain that they don't because he hasn't. For them, penalties that merely deter lawbreaking or remove dangerous criminals from society won't do. Relatives of a victim of the grotesque BTK serial killer, who is serving a number of consecutive life sentences without possibility of parole in a maximum security prison, under extremely harsh conditions, protested vehemently when he was permitted to read magazines in his cell. Even small mercies, they seemed to think, should be refused to those who have shown no mercy. These suffering people, looking for and finding no relief in the murderer's miserable imprisonment, could only conclude that he was not miserable enough. In the brave new legal world, not only protection of the innocent but torment of the guilty is what the law owes us, and *enough* torment, too—at least as much suffering and harm as the criminal caused.

The horror and rage of such bereaved people are what any of us would feel after their experience, and they elicit a grave sympathy. But we make a fundamental moral error if we offer them the criminal's suffering to comfort and satisfy them. Retaliation—or talion justice—as morality and moral religion have taught for generations, is both illogical and, emotionally and morally, self-defeating. Emotionally, it deprives the victim of the real comforts of moral responses to these evils and offers in its place an inadequate, narcissistic gratification. Morally, it involves us in a cascading series of wrongs. It requires us to act as the criminal did, which undermines the comforting confidence that causing suffering and harm is intrinsically wrong. It also makes justice turn on the psychology of the victims or their loved ones as much as or perhaps more than on the evil of the crime. The less forgiving and the more vengeful they are, it would seem, the harsher must be the punishment. In the end, it puts criminals in charge of what is morally permissible, for their acts create the yardstick by which we determine how much suffering and harm we are required to inflict. And when we subscribe to the idea that revenge is not only one's right but one's solace, we further a way of thinking that is itself a common cause of criminal behavior.*

In a variety of ways, legal revenge paradoxically dignifies crime and empowers the criminal. When the law sanctions revenge, it also implicitly grants the criminal power over our worth; his act is deemed to destroy it so effectively that only court-ordered brutality against him can restore it; and if revenge is not available, the victim suffers a second wrong, a double humiliation. Then, too, if we respond to crime by seeking revenge, and if revenge is to be measured against the crime, the worse the crime, the more paltry and ineffectual will seem our payback. He tortures a dozen innocents to death; we lock

---

* Revenge is incompatible with forgiveness, but it is not uncommon to see people who both insist that they have forgiven those who wronged them and demand that they receive severe punishment, even the death penalty. Newspapers recently reported the case of a woman who, having suffered her entire life from the aftermath of being drugged and gang raped at a college fraternity party, more than twenty years later received a letter of confession and contrition from one of the men who had done it. She took the man's letter to the prosecutor and had him charged with rape. He got an eighteen-month prison sentence (a very light one for a variety of reasons). Asked about forgiveness, she insisted that she did forgive him; but, she added, that didn't mean he shouldn't be punished. Perhaps she did not owe him forgiveness, but she was surely mistaken about the meaning of forgiveness.

him up and take away his magazines. If full revenge is the goal, then he always wins and we lose unless we are willing to become fully as barbarous as he. Thus in cases where the criminal has caused unspeakable suffering, adequate revenge might require torturing him endlessly and cruelly in ways that are unthinkable. In fact, because we refuse to torture accused criminals inquisition style (or we once did—we now sometimes do just this, when the accused are designated *terrorists*), we put ourselves in a situation in which we seem obliged to become more and more cruel yet are never quite as cruel as some people want us to be or as we need to be to "get even."

The death penalty raises these ironies and inconsistencies to an intolerable level, and not only because unavoidably it is resorted to so unfairly and ambivalently. In moral logic, too, it fails, for in the sameness, singleness, and finality of death, degrees and kinds of wrong are erased. A person who in a rage kills a faithless lover or a panicked, cornered robber who shoots a cop receives the same punishment as the methodically sadistic serial murderer of scores of victims. Deadly revenge is always too much or too little.

THE MEANING OF TASERS

The widespread equipping of police with Tasers or similar electroshock devices is another ill-understood phenomenon that reflects the deterioration of moral sense in law. Tasers cause pain so intense that it amounts to torture. Although the police and the manufacturer of Tasers maintain that they are safe, in fact they are associated with hundreds of deaths, in most cases of unarmed people.* The idea of arming police with Tasers was sold to the public initially as a means to deal with situations in which serious bodily injury or death was threatened without having to resort to guns and deadly force. Yet today, in large numbers of cases in which Tasers are used there is no threat to anyone's life and no danger of serious injury. In even fewer cases are there circumstances in which other means of coping are not readily available.

The police have begun to use Tasers as a general tool for achieving obedience and cooperation from the public. Police can now inflict terrible pain and a significant risk of death on people who simply fail to follow their orders, no matter how unreasonable, minor, or unlawful those orders. Tasers are frighteningly often used as a means to enforce police authority rather than as a last resort to avoid risk to life or prevent serious injury. Because police begin to think of Tasing as a means of controlling people's behavior and regard Tasers as less violent and dangerous than guns or billy clubs, they are tempted to use them in more and more minor circumstances—on mischief makers, drunks, the insane, the rebellious, people guilty of disorderly conduct, those who are "uncooperative," out-of-control children, the elderly, and similar targets.

News reports of such improper uses of Tasers appear with depressing frequency. Officers called in by a day care center in Indiana Tased an unruly ten-year-old, ninety-four-pound boy who was hitting and kicking caretakers. In Colorado, deputies Tased another ten-year-old who was destroying property in his

---

* There is a great debate about Tasers' safety. Amnesty International favors banning them.

foster home and justified doing so on the grounds that he threatened them with a pipe and threw a stick at them. A ten-year-old girl in Arkansas was also Tased for unruly behavior. In a famous Philadelphia case, a police officer Tased a seventeen-year-old boy who ran onto the playing field in a Phillies game. A spokesman for the police justified the action, saying, "As far as making an arrest, it's within our policy that when someone resists and attempts to elude arrest, and they are committing a crime, using the Taser to control them is something we allow." In Seattle, a woman seven months pregnant was Tased three times—in the thigh, shoulder, and neck—by three police officers, who then pulled her out of her car and laid her facedown on the ground. The woman was driving her son to school, and was to be ticketed for going thirty-two miles per hour in a school zone. When ordered to sign the ticket, under the misimpression that signing would be an admission of guilt, she had refused and then also refused to get out of her car when ordered to do so. In a 2–1 ruling, the Ninth U.S. Circuit Court of Appeals initially held that the police had done nothing wrong; in refusing to leave her car, it opined, she gave the police good reason to fear that she might escalate her disobedience in a way to create danger. A sharply divided full panel of the Court subsequently overturned this ruling and held that the officers had used excessive force, but it also held that the officers were immune from suit. In El Reno, Oklahoma, a group of police officers Tased a bedridden eighty-six-year-old grandmother twice when, according to the police report, she "took a more aggressive posture in her bed" and held up a knife. Her worried grandson had called 911 for medical assistance when he could not figure out which of her medications she had taken. There are hundreds of similar cases, and they grow more and more frequent as police become more and more confident that courts and legislatures will not restrain or correct them, more and more fond of being able to hurt and subdue the defiant, and less and less competent to deal with them by more intelligent and humane means.

The gradual relaxation of restrictions on the use of Tasers means that now citizens are Tased in situations in which nothing is threatened but an officer's ego. To suffer Tasing as the result of a quarrel with a police officer in a traffic stop, or because one spoke disrespectfully or failed to respond quickly, or at all, to some order to move or not to move by an officer who has lost his temper, is to undergo dangerous punishment and excruciating pain at the hands of the government in violation of fundamental legal and moral principle.

By invariably deciding protests and lawsuits over the use of Tasers in favor of the police, the courts have put their stamp of approval on police authority to inflict punishments that they would without question rule unconstitutional if they were imposed as penalties upon people convicted of crime. When those responsible for correcting and controlling police behavior condone or even approve of this use of Tasers, the public begins to perceive the police differently. If the police may, or must, inflict excruciating pain on members of the public for noncompliance with police authority, even in the most trivial of circumstances, the profile of young people choosing police work will change. A career in the police will become more attractive to those with sadistic and bullying impulses and less attractive to those who find this trend in police work repellent.

Tasers give police an instant, easy solution to what might

otherwise be complicated problems and, more ominously, a ready means to get instant revenge against anyone who offends them. They are dangerous tools to put in the hands of people who are more likely than average to react to disobedience or disrespect with the fury of offended authoritarian narcissism.* The ability to resort to torture to enforce authority takes away an officer's motivation to learn to negotiate, to calm himself down, and to attempt to calm others down. Using Tasers comes to seem the only thing to do. When police succumb to these temptations to use Tasers in less and less exigent circumstances, nothing can subsequently correct their misjudgments. The pain, the terrorizing, brutalizing, and demoralizing effect on the community, the imposition of a real and significant risk of death—none of this can subsequently be erased or made good.

The arming of police with a torture instrument increases fear and hatred of police. The misuse of Tasers sometimes occurs against citizens who, with good reason, have let a police officer know that they believe he is himself misbehaving. This is not conduct that we should wish to discourage. The fear of being subjected to Tasers threatens to prevent people from approaching police with the confidence and outspokenness that is utterly essential in the citizens of a well-functioning democracy. A

---

* The response to this point is often that guns are worse, but a study in California finds a 6.4–fold increase in in-custody deaths in the first year following the introduction of Tasers, followed by a return to earlier levels of such deaths in subsequent years. See Byron K. Lee, M.D., et al., "Relation of Taser (Electrical Stun Gun) Deployment to Increase in In-Custody Sudden Deaths," *American Journal of Cardiology* 103, no. 6 (2009): 877-880. The Taser does exactly what an angry, offended officer wants. It causes both humiliation and physical agony and usually does not kill or cause significant injury.

scene from the 1960s TV show *Mission Impossible* suggests how different were the relations between citizens (at least white citizens) and police fifty years ago: Foreign spies are being trained to pass as American citizens by having them live in a mock American town so as to learn American customs. One trainee has an encounter with the police in this mock town and is told by the instructor that he didn't behave like an American at all. He was too respectful and fearful. Americans, the instructor informed him, are outspoken with the police and are not afraid of them—as are people in totalitarian societies.

Perhaps more discouraging than even these consequences, however, is that police use of Tasers is quickly copied by both ordinary citizens and criminals, and the world becomes overall a crueler and more dangerous place than it used to be or would now be if these devices had been greeted with the horrified condemnation they deserve. All told, we pay a dangerously high price for the benefit of police use of Tasers in those few cases in which they are actually the sole alternative to the use of deadly force or to prevent some threat of death or serious bodily injury. That there is a muted public reaction and little hint of an outcry except among voices that tend to be regarded as illegitimate illustrates the love of punishment and comfortable sadism of an increasingly premoral public.

CRIME VS. TORT

Wedded to the modern sense that we are entitled to safety and a low-risk life, the demand for legal revenge contributes to an expansion of the boundaries of the criminal to include the careless, the stupid, the rattled, the drunken, and much behavior that a generation or two ago might have been considered regrettable or despicable, but only civilly and not criminally actionable. Negligence is moving out of civil court and across the hall into criminal court.* The law has always struggled to cope with fuzzy borders between the clueless and careless on the one hand and malevolent or criminal indifference on the other. But, as more and more readily it thinks it sees the latter, injunctions and money damages, even punitive money damages, come to seem insufficient remedy for heinous civil wrongs—even though today's torts are no more horrendous and egregious than yesterday's. In the premoral mind, the only adequate coin of recompense for outrage is the infliction of suffering and humiliation. Only criminal penalties, not money damages, will do.

Cases in which negligence is criminalized are no longer uncommon, though on their face they are often an appalling misuse of criminal sanctions.† The most familiar example is the prosecution as homicide of negligent driving that results in death. These cases often confront us with otherwise well-meaning and law-abiding people who have brought about horrifying mutilation and death unintentionally. So, for example, a

---

* The trend is also apparent in business, where more and more often legislators enforce regulatory schemes with criminal penalties.

† The argument in favor of criminalizing negligence is, of course, that it will cause people to be more careful. This is the argument of H. L. A. Hart in *Punishment and Responsibility: Essays in the Philosophy of Law* (Oxford: Oxford University Press, 1968), chapter 6, "Negligence, *Mens Rea*, and Criminal Responsibility," pp. 136–57.

Pennsylvania man pleaded guilty to involuntary manslaughter for causing the deaths of a man and two of his four-year-old triplets when a woodcutter he was hauling, which was negligently secured, came loose from his truck and crashed into the man's car; he received a prison sentence of nine to eighteen months. A tearful young man in Minnesota who rear-ended another car, causing three deaths, told the jury that he had attempted to stop his car but had been unable to. The jury did not believe him because examination of his Toyota Camry showed nothing wrong with its brakes. He received an eight-year sentence, of which he served three before his conviction was overturned. None of these cases involved drunk driving, the predictable cause of terrible, pointless, and blameworthy carnage. But even driving after drinking presents an ambiguous case for the application of criminal law and prison sentences.

The same trend is observable in other kinds of cases. A man in Massachusetts faced more than two years in prison on charges stemming from his accidentally leaving his baby in a shopping cart, thinking he had put him in the car safety seat. A Wisconsin nurse who mistakenly administered an anesthetic drug instead of penicillin, causing the death of the patient, was not simply sued, fired, or deprived of her license; vengeance required her to face felony charges and prison for "neglect of a patient causing great bodily harm." In Illinois, the death of a woman complaining of chest pains, who had waited for help for two hours in an emergency room, was determined by the coroner to be homicide and thus prosecutable. A Michigan man who put his pet boa constrictor in his mailbox as a practical joke, to frighten the mail carrier, faced a six-month prison term. Two 911 operators in Detroit who refused to send help to a five-year-old who called to say his mother had collapsed (she died and might have lived with medical aid), thinking his call a joke, were charged and faced jail time for their appalling misjudgment.

Many such attempts at criminal prosecution sputter and die, but many do not, and even failed attempts at criminal prosecution of stupidity or culpable carelessness are brutal, nightmarish, and impoverishing experiences for their targets. (Only a tiny fraction of the American public can afford to pay a defense lawyer.) These cases show an ominous willingness to criminalize departures from the average or the ideal in attention, care, intelligence, ability, or knowledge. The criminalizing of such conduct shows erosion in the fundamental principle of criminal law that only intentional wrongs may be punished by the grave criminal penalty of loss of liberty. This blurring of crime and tort is a cultural regression, a step back toward a primitive prelegalism and premoralism, to taboo and talionic justice, where any agent of harm, no matter how unwilling or unknowing, must be harmed in return, where compensation or restitution will not do because the right to vengeance demands punishment.

In the juvenile justice system, where more and more laws permit juveniles to be tried as adults for serious crimes, we see a parallel phenomenon. This movement's slogan is one so stupid as to dispirit attempts to reason with those who use it: Adult crimes should get adult punishment. Gruesome and shocking juvenile crimes lead to calls for revenge so intense that the entire civilized edifice of juvenile justice gives way, for it is built on such merciful moral concepts as juveniles' lesser capacity for understanding and impulse control and their lack of opportunity yet to have become something other than what they were raised to be. The United States is unique in the civilized world in its barbarous treatment of juvenile crime. Its harshness is almost without parallel even in the uncivilized world.

The Supreme Court abolished the death penalty for juvenile crime only in 2005, in a 5–4 decision. Until it did so, the United States was one of two countries in the entire world to permit this. The other was Somalia. In 2010, in a 6–3 decision, the Court ruled that only juveniles who have murdered may receive sentences of life without parole; for other crimes by juveniles, only life sentences with parole are permitted. The United States has still not ratified the UN Convention on the Rights of the Child, which explicitly prohibits the death penalty and a life sentence without the possibility of parole for juveniles. In 2011, in the United States there were approximately twenty-five hundred people serving sentences of life without parole for crimes committed when they were under eighteen.★ In the entire rest of the world, there were only a dozen other cases of

---

★ Eleven countries besides the United States have laws with the potential to permit the sentencing of child offenders to life without possibility of release: Antigua and Barbuda, Argentina, Australia, Belize, Brunei, Cuba (legislation pending), Dominica, Saint Vincent and the Grenadines, the Solomon Islands, and Sri Lanka (legislation pending). But as of 2011, in none of those countries was any child offender currently serving such a sentence. See "Laws of Other Nations" at the Web site of the University of San Francisco School of Law, Center for Law and Justice, accessed November 16, 2011, http://www.usfca .edu/law/jlwop/other_nations. See also "Letter from Human Rights Organizations to Committee on the Elimination of Racial Discrimination ('CERD') Regarding Juvenile Life Without Parole in the US," June 4, 2009, http://www .hrw.org/en/news/2009/06/04/letter-human-rights-organizations-cerd-re garding-juvenile-life-without-parole-us.

children imprisoned for life; all these were found in three countries, Israel, Tanzania, and South Africa, where they are eligible for parole.

CONSEQUENCES FOR DEMOCRACY

Average citizens now lack an adequate sense of the grave and destructive nature of imprisonment as a penalty or of the humility and caution that in a civilized society would make imprisonment a rare, reluctant use of an awesome authority. As a result, they also lack a full sense of the implied threat to their own dignity and freedom in the system that is evolving. They are losing the self-respecting quality necessary in citizens of a robust democracy. Many people, raised in authoritarianism and offended self-righteousness, have no qualms about the casual use of government's gargantuan powers to deprive individuals of freedom, property, and life itself, no doubts about the effects and social costs of massive levels of harsh imprisonment, no hesitation about our ability to try, convict, and cruelly imprison huge numbers of people in a manner that succeeds even in separating the guilty and the innocent—let alone any more subtle justice. If such understanding and such doubts are the cornerstone of democracy, then ours has already failed.

Political opportunism has fueled this dangerous trend of antimoralism in law, along with prosecutorial ambition and, in some jurisdictions, pressure from politicians seeking to boost their constituents' local economies with prisons and prison jobs and also from the prison industry and guards' unions, which have long thrown their considerable political weight behind broadening and lengthening criminal penalties. But a more fundamental cause is the rise of a virulent code of revenge under a sham moral flag. For centuries, wise heads pointed out the false morality and shallow psychology of revenge and armed us against its temptations. These long-established ideas, now on the verge of becoming the cranky views of a melancholy minority, were once our common heritage, and their great elaborations in our literature and art once helped to create a people who understood that these things were the basis of law.

Chapter 9

THE ACADEMY

Every despotism has a specially keen and hostile instinct for whatever keeps up human dignity and independence. And it is curious to see scientific . . . teaching used everywhere as a means of stifling all freedom of investigation as addressed to moral questions, under a dead weight of facts. . . . To crush what is spiritual, moral, human—so to speak—in man, by specializing him; to form mere wheels of the great social machine, instead of perfect individuals; to make society and not conscience the centre of life, to enslave the soul to things, to depersonalize man—this is the dominant drift of our epoch. Everywhere you may see a tendency to substitute the laws of dead matter (number, mass) for the laws of the moral nature (persuasion, adhesion, faith); . . . negative liberty, which has no law in itself, and recognizes no limit except in force, everywhere taking the place of positive liberty, which means action guided by an inner law and curbed by a moral authority.

—HENRI-FRÉDÉRIC AMIEL,
JOURNAL INTIME (1882)

Throughout their history, universities and colleges have had special responsibility for protecting moral ideals. We rely on them both to help transmit these ideals from generation to generation through education of our best young minds and to study morality—what it is, where it comes from, what it calls for. Today, the academy fails at both these tasks.

As for the first, universities have now adopted the outlook of the corporate businessmen who increasingly control them. From the corporate point of view, the academy is an institution whose primary purpose is economic. It exists to ensure the nation's competitive position in the global economy by providing business with science, technology, and employees educated to fit its needs and to prepare youth for job getting and earning. It is no longer dedicated to preparing students to approach public and private life, and all parts of the moral life, with broad knowledge, fair-minded intelligence, and humanity. The liberal arts that were once its heart and soul begin to be treated as inessentials, mere luxuries, pushed to its margins, starved, and unable to attract the talented students they need to perpetuate themselves.

As for studying morality, the academy in recent decades tends to promote and promulgate junk science on the subject. Today, for the most part, the academic voices that speak most loudly to the public about morality are no longer those of penetrating social observers—the historians, economists, anthropologists, sociologists, political scientists, philosophers, and literary scholars who once illuminated our moral lives. For enlightenment on good and evil, right and wrong, the public has lately been invited to listen instead to evolutionary scientists of all sorts—evolutionary biologists, sociobiologists, animal ethologists, psychologists, anthropologists, and neurologists.

ACADEMIC SCIENCE

The Moral Foundation of Science

Moral capacities are necessary, though not sufficient, to sustain scientific thought. They support the scientist's ability to see things as they are, to resist the temptation to let wishes, fantasies, fears, desire for money, or submissiveness to authority infiltrate factual belief. They provide the strength of mind needed to confront contradiction and face facts. The capacity to engage in a rational appraisal of reality is a core element of both the moral and the scientific mind.*

It should not surprise us, then, that the past half century has seen fraud, grandstanding,† and religious irrationality be-

---

* See chapter 1. The moral mentality has strong internal controls that give the boost to rationality that psychologists call "ego strength." This term refers not to self-esteem or pride, but to the mind's rational capacity, its ability to apprehend and accept reality.

† The self-infatuated, self-congratulatory, attention-seeking academic is a familiar figure. The evolutionary biologist Richard Dawkins has been properly and energetically outspoken about the dangers of generally declining rationality, and some of Dawkins's useful reflections on morality are taken up below on pp. 237–40. Yet he himself is something of an example of how ego infiltrates the worlds of thought and reason. Outside his own field—and he never fears to go there—his thinking, for example on atheism or religion, can be dogmatic and simplistic. Yet it is offered with the same self-delighted confidence with which he gives explanations of underwater parasites.

gin to infiltrate science in the United States and elsewhere. With the diminishing influence of morality, the scientific world—like the social world, the political world, and the academic world as a whole—comes increasingly under the influence of ideology, self-seeking, and greed.* And the measure of scientific truth by means of impartial, rational estimations of evidence begins to be undermined by reliance, instead, on the status of the scientist, his or her reputation, chair, university, and overall prestige. Of course, these tendencies have always existed, but in our times they have become stronger and harder to control and correct.

In the twentieth century, science fell almost entirely under government and corporate control. Even in universities, where

---

Dawkins, of course, is only one of many examples of an avid reach for public attention among evolutionary biologists and the tendency among that group toward striking egoism. It is a literary mystery, for example, how E. O. Wilson manages to make so many pages of his dry tomes, such as *Sociobiology* (1975) and *Consilience* (1998), drip with ego.

* For example, scientists sign their names to articles that they have not written; or they conceal conflicts of interest that arise when their research is paid for with corporate money. Psychiatry is so grossly dominated by big pharma that psychiatrists today often receive minimal education aimed at psychological insight and understanding of social and psychological dimensions of mental maladies. But ideology and other irrational influences may be most obvious in the case of economics, which has been justly accused of abandoning its already tenuous status as science to spend decades promoting free-market capitalism on slender or absent rational grounds. "Conservative" economists' response to the economic crises that began in 2007 have been the subject of bitter complaints on these grounds. Such influences creep into harder science, too, particularly when it makes human behavior and the human mind its object of study.

scientists might seem to enjoy greater independence, they became dependent on grants and other support from government
and corporations. This dependency permits ideology and profit
to determine the directions of research, and this, in turn, affects
the kind of people who choose to become scientists.

Every scientist today must work within some massive
bureaucracy—governmental, corporate, or academic—and this,
too, has a large effect on the kinds of people who choose this
work and the kinds who succeed in it. In the hierarchical structures of bureaucracies, an underling whose work challenges
that of superiors or the security of the bureaucracy or fails to
forward the purposes dictated at the top of the hierarchy is less
likely than others to win advancement. The safest, fastest road
to success (and funding) is to avoid offending or surprising, to
advance the interests of those in charge of one's advancement,
and to support the preselected purposes of the bureaucracy. Yet
brave new scientific thinkers must inevitably do the opposite.
There is an obvious conflict, well understood by the people
who cope with it daily, between the type of character who is
most successful in climbing bureaucratic ladders (to some degree ruthless and highly attentive and skilled socially) and the
type of character who is likely to come up with new ideas and
follow through on proving them. Good scientists often have
moral qualities that enable them to tolerate seeing things in
ways that others disdain; they are also more likely to have the
patience and strength to stick with what seems to others an un-
promising avenue of research and to soldier on despite opposition, without encouragement and rewards. But all too often
these qualities will not win them tenure or secure employment
or get their ideas accepted even when proved. Such is their de-

votion and strength that, despite the obstacles, many survive even in the contemporary world of hard science.*

When scientists' personal ambition outweighs their scientific curiosity, they are likely to gravitate toward studies that provide

---

* It is an open question whether the staggering amounts of money and manpower devoted to scientific research today are matched by a proportionate rise in major scientific advances and whether our rationalized bureaucracy is a suitable mechanism for fostering scientific progress. Occasionally, someone argues that in our era science gives us completions or elaborations of long-ago revolutions but no revolutions of its own, and some suggest that this is true perhaps simply because we are reaching the end of the major discoveries that are possible—a suspiciously comfortable opinion in the age of corporatized science, although it crops up in every era. See, for example, Russell Stannard, *The End of Discovery: Are We Approaching the Bounds of the Knowable?* (Oxford: Oxford University Press, 2010); and John Horgan, *The End of Science: Facing the Limits of Knowledge in the Twilight of the Scientific Age* (New York: Broadway Books, 1996). See also George Dvorsky, "The 'End of Science' My Ass," Institute for Ethics & Emerging Technologies blog, July 7, 2009, http://ieet.org/index.php/ IEET/more/dvorsky20090707; Ehsan Masood, "Are We Witnessing the End of Science?" Guardian.co.uk science blog, June 22, 2009, http://www.guardian .co.uk/science/blog/2009/jun/22/end-science-unified-theory-mavericks.

See also the conversation between John Horgan and George Musser entitled "The End of Science," http://video.nytimes.com/video/2011/08/01/ opinion/100000000977216/the-end-of-science.html?ref=opinion. Musser thinks that we are near a "convergence of fundamental physics" that will indeed be the final word.

There are even those who insist, triumphantly, that the scientific method itself, with its reliance on models and theories, is obsolete. See, for example, the megalomaniac effusions and abject Google worship in Chris Anderson, "The End of Theory: The Data Deluge Makes the Scientific Method Obsolete," June 23, 2008, *Wired* magazine 16, no. 7 (2008), http://www.wired.com/ science/discoveries/magazine/16-07/pb_theory.

career success and admiring attention. All too often, this produces results that are useful in making profits, in social manipulation and control, or in military strength. Such scientists are likely to be among the increasing numbers of those who turn out pseudoscience, unreliable work that tends to be done in fields outside or at the margins of "hard" science. Some of this pseudoscience is research into the nature of morality itself. (See chapter 10.)

PHILOSOPHERS AND MORALITY

Historically, in the academy, morality belonged to philosophers, who taught that the study of ethics was the highest and most important. Moral philosophy today makes no such claim, and it has been no more immune to the rise of antimoral thinking than have those subdisciplines that study morality from scientific perspectives.

Until the twentieth century, there was no such thing as a specialized discipline, let alone a department, called "philosophy." "Philosophy" was often synonymous with much or all of a college's curriculum, including natural sciences, mathematics, psychology, religion, and political science—as well as the metaphysics, ethics, and logic that philosophy departments now claim. Philosophers were merely those learned and serious scholars, no matter what their specialty, who cared about the large questions and knew what earlier thinkers had said about them. René Descartes was also a scientist and mathematician. Immanuel Kant made discoveries about the earth's rotational speed. David Hume wrote history. William James was a groundbreaking psychologist. The modern university gives philosophy departments responsibility for ethics, but as philosophy has become narrow and insignificant, so has its moral theorizing.

In the eighteenth and nineteenth centuries, the capstone of a student's education was often a college-wide course in moral philosophy taught by a grand, respected figure—the president or provost of the college or some renowned scholar. The students were typically expected to learn what the ancients had said and to become familiar with the Scottish, English, or German moral philosophy of their own day. But after Darwin's revolution, skepticism grew about the moral philosophies that had preceded Darwin.

In nineteenth-century America, the school of philosophical thought that took the challenge of evolution most seriously was called, misleadingly, pragmatism.* The pragmatists took the central task of philosophy in their day to be the reconciliation of philosophical theories of all sorts with the facts of evolution. Human behavior and thought, including morality, they believed, had to be reconceived as part of the natural world. This meant rejecting pre-Darwinian ways of thinking that, obviously or subtly, were based either on the old dualisms of mind and body or on one of the old-style forms of rebellion against dualism—idealism

---

* Charles Sanders Peirce gave this school of thought its name, which was not intended to suggest anything related to practicality or expediency. He took the term from Kant, who referred to empirical beliefs (that is, those based on sense experience), as *pragmatisch*. See "What Pragmatism Is," *The Essential Peirce*, vol. 2: *Selected Philosophical Writings, 1893–1913* (Bloomington: Indiana University Press, 1998), pp. 332–33.

(nothing exists but minds and ideas) or materialism (nothing exists but matter). The pragmatists called for empirical investigations into human institutions, human minds, and human conduct, but being antimaterialist and fiercely nonreductionist, they also believed that history, sociology, economics, psychology, and comparative studies of culture and religion would be key sources of the relevant empirical knowledge. History and culture, including moral culture, existed on a continuum with physical and biological reality, not in some separate realm of the spirit, yet they were neither reducible to that physical reality nor entirely determined by it.

After World War II, pragmatism, now grown elderly, together with all other schools of American philosophical thought, was pushed aside by analytic philosophy imported from England. Today most American philosophers are analytic philosophers, although they now may reject the name because they carry their work into ambitious arenas rejected by the first generation of analytic philosophers. They are, nonetheless, their obvious intellectual descendants. Those earlier analytic philosophers were heavily influenced by logical positivism, a school of thought that arose in Vienna in the period between the world wars and subsequently moved to England and the United States. Logical positivism taught that by and large science should or would replace much of philosophy and that philosophers' job was merely to carry out narrow analyses that would resolve logical snafus arising in science or other disciplines. Positivism took a highly constricted view of ethics and had little interest in the psychology, history, or sociology of morals. Moral judgments, it claimed, were not empirically verifiable—verifiable, that is, through the evidence of our senses—and therefore were not meaningful or rational. They were merely arbitrary imperatives or expressions of emotion, neither true nor false, and ultimately there was no way to show that one moral judgment was superior to another. This was a thoroughly skeptical attitude toward the ideas of moral truth and knowledge and an affirmation of moral relativism.

While it may seem obvious that skeptical theories of moral knowledge would tend to undermine moral life and moral commitment, this was not obvious to analytic philosophers. Even those who understood the effects of their work took no moral responsibility for helping to shore up what their theories— tragically, they occasionally admitted—tore down. While a David Hume or Immanuel Kant might have believed that the chief goal of moral philosophy was to help people achieve virtue and to provide an account of moral life that served that purpose, analytic moral philosophy in its early days had little interest in that responsibility.

In both its disregard of the historical, cultural roots of the moral mentality and its overall skepticism, analytic philosophy took an approach that dovetailed with that of evolutionary scientists. The scientists tried to understand morality through the lens of relatively fixed biological characteristics, whose evolutionary preconditions would shed light on their nature and function. Thus they, too, approached moral life in a way that ignored its moorings in history and culture. This underlying affinity of the biological and analytic approaches to morality eventually led, at their margins, to a joining of forces. Today, there are evolutionary scientists who study morality by drawing on concepts that they learned from analytic moral philosophers, and there are philosophers whose moral theorizing adopts an evolutionary framework provided by scientists. Together, intentionally or not, they often promote what are in effect anti-moral theories of the moral.★

Normative Ethical Theories

Eventually, a reaction set in against the views that dominated the thinking of analytic philosophers in the 1950s and 1960s. By the late 1960s and early 1970s, a new generation of analytic moral philosophers attempted to counter this skepticism and its denial of the existence of moral truth or moral knowledge in any full-blooded sense with what amounted to a philosophical end run: They would produce *normative ethical theories*—theories that could be applied to facts to tell us what acts were right and wrong under specific circumstances.

Appealing to neopragmatist accounts of the nature of theories, the new thinking relied on moral "intuition" to play the role in ethics that observation played in science. Moral intuitions were said to provide evidence against which general theories of right and wrong could be tested in a manner analogous to the way in which observations in science provided evidence against which scientific theories could be tested. The fact that

---

★ Now, as always, there is a philosopher or two who explicitly rejects morality. See, for example, Joel Marx describing his complete rejection of morality and all its attitudes and concepts on a *New York Times* blog and the debates with commenters that followed. Joel Marx, "Confessions of an Ex-Moralist," August 21, 2011, and "Atheism, Amorality and Animals: A Response," September 2, 2011, in The Opinionator, the *New York Times,* http://opinionator.blogs.nytimes.com/2011/08/21/confessions-of-an-ex-moralist/ and http://opinionator.blogs.nytimes.com/2011/09/02/atheism-amorality-and-animals-a-response/.

moral intuitions seemed to be unreliable, culture-bound, and not confirmable by others, while scientific observations were reliable, uniform across cultures, and confirmable by others, did not dampen their enthusiasm. Sweeping skeptical objections aside, they argued that if they actually came up with a theory that succeeded in accounting for our moral intuitions (on a parallel with scientific hypotheses accounting for our observations), that would establish moral truths in accordance with a scientific model of truth. The truths that would be established would be general principles—*normative theories**—of right that could be applied to life's dilemmas to produce right answers. This rationale was most fully articulated by John Rawls in support of his theory of justice,† which was an attempt not only to refute theoretical sources of skepticism, but also to upend utilitarian theories of right that critics for more than a century had regarded as inadequate and even immoral.

With the new interest in normative ethical theories in the 1960s and 1970s came a renewal of the nineteenth-century battle between utilitarianism and what contemporaries call "deontological" theories, a catch-all term for nonutilitarian theories,

---

* The term *normative* is used to describe anything related to norms or standards, but I can find no reference to normative *theories* earlier than the 1960s. One finds earlier references to "normative science," but this phrase refers simply to disciplines that address one or another type of norm—such as logic and perhaps grammar as well as ethics. The very phrase has an oxymoronic ring. The meaning of the term *deontology* has also drifted. In the nineteenth century, it meant the study of ethics generally, not one type of normative ethical theory.

† John Rawls, *A Theory of Justice* (Cambridge, Mass.: Harvard University Press, 1971).

especially those that emphasize conformity to rules.* Utilitarian theories like Jeremy Bentham's and John Stuart Mill's held that right actions were those whose consequences produced the most utility, or human welfare, or good, measured in terms of pleasure. Deontological theories like Rawls's reached back to Kant, the British intuitionists, and natural law for explanations of what makes right acts right, and they claimed that certain actions or moral rules were intrinsically or inherently right or that right actions were those dictated by reason or known through moral sense or rational intuitions. Deontologists argued that no utilitarian theory could explain ordinary right and wrong: why, for example, it would be wrong to kill a man for his organs to save five people who needed transplants. Clearly, killing the man would produce more good, more human welfare, yet we all know—intuitively, or so the argument goes—that this is wrong. In fact, however, it is hard to find a utilitarian who disagrees. Utilitarians generally manage to find a way to interpret their theory so as to rule out such actions. Indeed, vagueness in both kinds of theories makes it hard to see how, on any practical question, either could be forced into one position or another.

Professional Philosophers and Applied Ethics
The enormous enthusiasm that greeted Rawls's work gave rise in the 1970s to the new field of "applied ethics." Believing that Rawls had proven the rational legitimacy of normative theo-

---

* A few years later, "virtue theory" attracted interest. This was an attempt to return to an Aristotelian emphasis on excellence in character as the center of ethics.

ries, some philosophers began to claim the right to train experts to act as practical ethicists, people qualified to give professional moral counsel in medical schools, businesses, governments, and schools. This trend was fueled in large part by a need for philosophy departments to find jobs for their graduate students when academic jobs began to dry up; the rise of normative theorizing provided a rationale for offering those graduates to the world as professional moralists. At last, we had proven theories of right and wrong, and those theories were taught and properly understood only in philosophy departments.

Although philosophers claimed a kind of moral expertise, they did not claim superior wisdom and goodness.* Their confidence stemmed from faith in their analytic skills and in their knowledge of the new normative theories that seemed to them so convincing. They argued that training in normative theory, in logic and conceptual clarity, and in the analysis of moral arguments made their graduates better at evaluating moral claims than other people. This is doubtful.

Even among philosophers, there is no consensus about which normative theory we should turn to and grave reason to doubt their justifications and their usefulness. Philosophers' alleged logical and conceptual skills—even if these were truly superior to those of people educated in other fields—are consistent with perverse ideas and gravely deficient character. Academic achievement and bad character go together in philosophy at least as

---

* I have occasionally had the private experience of hearing philosophers argue for the superior virtue of philosophers and attribute this superiority to their training in moral philosophy, but I have not encountered such claims in print.

often as they do in other disciplines; and people of weak or poor or bad or narrow character, with perverse ideas, are unlikely to be the source of sound moral advice no matter how analytically skilled. One might even suspect that representatives of other disciplines have far more to offer than philosophical ethicists. Often enough, what matters in moral judgment is a grasp of psychology or history or the long engagement in the relevant arena—business, say, or medical practice—that in receptive minds so often breeds sound and humane judgment.

The best moral advisers are people who are in relevant ways good or what we would once have called "virtuous,"* who also have large and deep experience in the matters calling for judgment and serious concern about them, and who have education and intelligence adequate to the complications involved. There are no moral experts—not in science, not in philosophy, not in any field. There are at best people worth listening to and learning from. Such people are hard to identify—and sometimes hardest to believe precisely when they are right.

"Morals" as a field for experts, separated from ordinary, human-sized capacities and individuals' experience and situations, is a contradiction in terms. Morality addresses reality from the point of view of whole human beings who live in it; the

---

* Readers will recognize, I hope, that I understand, as they do, that there is not one single form that human goodness takes and that everyone's character is to some extent compartmentalized. People may be good in this respect and not in that and, often enough, not overall. A doctor who is a superb moral judge of certain aspects of medical practice may behave badly as a spouse or neighbor or sportsman. Likewise, people sometimes understand more than they can do.

impersonality and objectivity relevant to moral judgment is that of individuals thinking and acting conscientiously, who achieve it out of their suffering, affections, memories, temptations, compassion, and experience. Attempts to rely on expert or professional "humanness" will inevitably fail and will only hasten the trends that have bred a nation of people who every year become less and less capable of self-government and more and more indifferent to wrongs done in their name.

Chapter 10

SCIENCE AND MORALITY

Moral philosophy has, indeed, this peculiar disadvantage, which is not found in natural [science], that in collecting its experiments, it cannot make them purposely, with premeditation, and after such a manner as to satisfy itself concerning every particular difficulty which may be. When I am at a loss to know the effects of one body upon another in any situation, I need only put them in that situation, and observe what results from it. But should I endeavour to clear up after the same manner any doubt in moral philosophy, by placing myself in the same case with that which I consider, 'tis evident this reflection and premeditation would so disturb the operation of my natural principles, as must render it impossible to form any just conclusion from the phenomenon. We must therefore glean up our experiments in this science [of human nature] from a cautious observation of human life, and take them as they appear in the common course of the world, by men's behaviour in company, in affairs, and in their pleasures. Where experiments of this kind are

judiciously collected and compared, we may hope to
establish on them a science which will not be inferior in
certainty, and will be much superior in utility to any
other of human comprehension.

—DAVID HUME, INTRODUCTION TO *A*
TREATISE OF HUMAN NATURE: BEING AN
ATTEMPT TO INTRODUCE THE EXPERIMENTAL
METHOD OF REASONING INTO
MORAL SUBJECTS (1739–1740)

DOES SCIENCE PROVIDE the insight into the moral life that philosophers lack? Many people think so, and research into morality has become a center of attention in several scientific subdisciplines. Unfortunately, influential scientific studies of morality are often unfriendly to the moral enterprise, sometimes intentionally and sometimes unintentionally.

Morality, like all realms of human behavior, is a proper subject of empirical study. Until recently, much of that study took place in university departments of history, economics, anthropology, and sociology, and its goal was both to understand the nature and causes of morality and to deepen moral understanding. This moral purpose was clear even in books and lectures that avoided explicit moral language—when, for example, historians analyzed the causes of the Civil War, when sociologists described the lonely crowd or the "organization man" or when anthropologists compared marriage customs. In fact, however, the most explicit empirical studies of the moral mind occurred outside the university and were carried out by psychoanalysts, and psychoanalytic ideas of moral autonomy and strength influenced historical and social scientific research.* From its beginnings, psychoanalysis focused major attention on the mental structures that favor moral character and on the workings of the moral emotions—shame, guilt, remorse, pride, love—and their function and dysfunction in self-governance. It also placed unusual emphasis on the psychoanalysts' capacity for self-examination and self-awareness during the analytic process as a means of ensuring objectivity and neutrality. Psychoanalysis thus has a natural alliance with the moral mentality, in that both its subject matter and its methods are highly concerned with it, and it should not surprise us that moral and psychoanalytical influence declined in tandem.

In the last decades of the twentieth century, scientists in subdisciplines of evolutionary biology, neurology, and psychology became the most prominent investigators of moral phenomena. These scientists tend to fall into one of three main types. One

---

* In the United States, though not everywhere, psychoanalytic research lies outside mainstream science, which is housed in universities or in government or corporate laboratories, and is the sole serious, influential intellectual endeavor carried on outside those powerful institutions. (Think tanks do not house whole disciplines or sciences or certify student training and accomplishment.) A few universities—Columbia, New York, Emory, and the University of Colorado—have psychoanalytic institutes that function within departments of psychiatry. In a number of places (Yale, the University of Chicago, the University of California at Los Angeles, and others) there are psychoanalytic programs, shared faculty, or cooperative projects. The Menninger Clinic is now part of Baylor College of Medicine's department of psychiatry, but it no longer has a psychoanalytic institute. Some psychoanalysts would like to see their discipline absorbed into the university. See, for example, Robert S. Wallerstein, "Psychoanalysis in the University: A Full-Time Vision," *International Journal of Psychoanalysis* 90, no. 5 (2009): 1107–21.

type tends toward hard-nosed skepticism about moral goodness, especially in the form of altruism—for example, Richard
Dawkins, E. O. Wilson in 1975,* or David Barash—and is dominated by scientists whose background is in evolutionary biology,

---

* This skepticism was true of Wilson in 1975 but not in 2010. In 1975, in
Sociobiology, he recognized only the altruism of individuals toward kin,
those who share genes with them, and he believed that kin selection, not
group selection, explained cooperative behavior. Wilson now rejects these
ideas. He believes that altruism in favor of unrelated group members is significant in some mammalian behavior, that it becomes dramatically important in
human beings, and that it depends on forms of group selection. E. O. Wilson,
public remarks as panel member, June 12, 2009, World Science Festival at
New York University, New York, New York; Martin A. Nowak, Corina
E. Tarnita, and Edward O. Wilson, "The Evolution of Eusociality," *Nature*
466 (2010): 1057–62; Edward O. Wilson and Bert Holldobler, "Eusociality:
Origin and Consequences," *Proceedings of the National Academy of Sciences* 102
(September 20, 2005): 13367–71. See also Danielle Fanelli, "Kinship Doesn't
Matter—How Insects Are Altruistic," *New Scientist*, January 12, 2008,
pp. 6–7; and Richard Conniff, "Interview: E. O. Wilson," *Discover*, June
2006, p. 58.

Richard Dawkins continues to reject the hypothesis that group selection
occurs. See Richard Dawkins, "The Evolution of Altruism—What Matters
Is Gene Selection," *New Scientist*, January 12, 2008, p. 17. See also Richard
Dawkins, "The Group Delusion," January 10, 2008, http://richarddawkins
.net/articles/2121?page=3. For Dawkins, the ultimate unit upon which natural selection operates is the gene (and, in important ways, the individual organism, or "survival machine," that carries the gene). See Richard Dawkins,
The Selfish Gene (1976) (Oxford: Oxford University Press, 2006), pp. 19, 24,
46–47. Dawkins has never denied that altruistic behavior in humans is possible; he merely argues that it has to struggle against a strong biological predisposition in favor of self-interest. He also argues that the question of
altruism should be separated from that of group selection.

animal ethology, and sociobiology. The tone of this group is at times cynical, snide, debunking, and occasionally aggressively sarcastic toward those unenlightened people who, they believe, cherish myths about our moral capacity. They have studied the respective roles of altruism and self-interested motives in animal behavior and conclude that natural selection holds few rewards for altruism.* They also have studied the prevalence of deceit, manipulativeness, infidelity, and other "vices" throughout the animal kingdom and find that they occur as a relatively predictable percentage of all animal behavior, including human behavior, and that they are genetically determined. These scientists are contemporary representatives of the underlying philosophical attitude that William James long ago, with a mixture of admiration and deprecation, called "tough-minded."†

---

* Evolutionary biologists sometimes (not always) talk as though altruism is all there is to morality. But altruism, so far from being nearly coextensive with morality, is often absolutely opposed to it. Political and religious fanatics are often terrifyingly selfless. There are powerful psychological mechanisms that can lead individuals to act with ferocious altruism against their own interest for the sake of cruel, irrational, and destructive social purposes. The struggle between selfishness and altruism is one of many struggles in the moral life, and one that tends to dominate the moral mind only relatively early in life. There are deeper, more perilous moral struggles having to do with love, with self-knowledge, with courage, with honesty, and with things that lack these simple, familiar names.

† These tough-minded scientists of morality tend to disdain those theorists of the past whom they regard, rightly or wrongly, as having taken the "nurture" side in the "old nature versus nurture" debates. Thus they tend to fasten on Margaret Mead as a target, pointing a finger at alleged imperfections in her impressive work as a twenty-four-year-old. See, for example, Richard Dawkins, *Unweaving the Rainbow: Science, Delusion, and the Appetite*

A second type tends to be what James, somewhat conde-scendingly, called "tender-minded." It tends to be earnest, sin-cere, and often brotherly and informal in addressing its readers; it wants to believe in goodness. Those in this group—Marc Hauser, Jonathan Haidt, and Steven Pinker are well-known examples—are protective of what its members regard as "moral" thought and behavior. These men usually have backgrounds in psychology and work at the junctions of more traditionally defined disciplines. Marc Hauser's Harvard title, for example,

---

for Wonder (New York: Houghton Mifflin Harcourt, 1998), p. 211, where he classes Mead with those who sentimentally deny that nature is red in tooth and claw, boosts his point with a footnote that attributes to Mead a "rose-tinted environmentalist theory of human nature," and bluntly affirms Derek Freeman's questionable criticisms of Mead's work. See Derek Freeman, *Margaret Mead and Samoa: The Making and Unmaking of an Anthropological Myth* (Cambridge, Mass.: Harvard University Press, 1983), and *The Fateful Hoaxing of Margaret Mead: A Historical Analysis of Her Samoan Research* (New York: Basic Books, 1999). A recent book by Paul Shankman, *The Trashing of Margaret Mead: Anatomy of an Anthropological Controversy* (Madison: University of Wisconsin Press, 2009), gives a convincing rebuttal of Freeman's claims and an important analysis of why Freeman's flawed attack was far more effective than the rational defenses of Mead's work that several competent people in the field offered.

Shankman points out that the Mead-Freeman controversy was an early battle in the culture wars: "Conservatives felt that things had gone too far. . . . The Moral Majority was ascendant, and Mead became vulnerable as a public intellectual and a feminist, embodying the alleged evils of liberalism and per-missiveness for this audience. In these ways conservatives and evolutionary psychologists found common cause against Mead. Although these groups dis-liked and disparaged Mead for different reasons, they were able to use Free-man's critique to advance their own agendas" (*Trashing of Margaret Mead*, p. 210.)

was Professor of Psychology, Organismic & Evolutionary Biology, and Biological Anthropology.*

Then there is a third, miscellaneous group whose approach is more neutral. It attempts to provide empirical answers to philosophical questions and sometimes to provide empirical refutation or proof of philosophical theories. It includes philosophers who rely on scientific experiments to back up their ideas as well as neurologists who carry out brain studies, often designed by cross-disciplinary teams, intended to shed light on philosophical questions.

Both the tender-minded and this third group tend to adopt

(*continued from previous page*) Of course, Mead had no quarrel with evolutionary theory, evolutionary explanations of human behavior, or the general claim that biology would teach us important things about human behavior, and she had more than enough respect for man's capacity for evil and nature's bloody indifference. Indeed, she was an enthusiastic promoter of all these ideas. Mead, like many others, did mistrust E. O. Wilson's personal efforts to plow this ground and took them to mark the dawning of an intellectual dark age. Nonetheless, when the occasion arose, at the 1976 meeting of the American Anthropological Association, she came to Wilson's defense and spoke up angrily against a resolution to ban discussion of *Sociobiology*. "Book burning," the elderly Mead called it with fierce disapproval, and followed up with a rousing defense of free speech. (The resolution was defeated.) See Helen Fisher, "Introduction to the Perennial Edition: A Way of Seeing," in Margaret Mead, *Male and Female* (New York: HarperCollins, 2001, 1949), p. xxiii.

* In 2010, Harvard University announced that Marc Hauser had committed acts of scientific misconduct, and in 2011, he resigned his post. The remarks on Hauser later in this chapter are addressed only to his theories, not to these allegations.

the framework of understanding provided by contemporary moral philosophy and often delve explicitly into philosophers' questions, using philosophers' jargon. How do we resolve moral quandaries? Is moral knowledge innate or acquired? What are the roles in moral judgment of reason and emotion or reason as opposed to moral intuition or moral sense? Is utilitarianism or some deontological theory (see pages 221–22) the truer account of moral judgment? To the extent that moral philosophy has gotten lost, whether by misconceiving the nature of morality, moral deliberation, or the goals of moral philosophy, empirical work based upon it runs the risk of falling into the same errors.

The investigations of all three types are considered academically respectable, and their authors, who seek to offer a scientifically valid account of our moral nature, are widely granted authority to speak as experts on the subject of morality both within the academy and to a remarkable extent in the mass media. All have large numbers of co-workers and supporters. (Indeed, they are so numerous, the nature of their task is so well understood among them, and the battle lines so clear that one of them speaks in print of the need to promote harmony and mutual respect among "the community of morality researchers.")*

---

* Jonathan Haidt and Craig Joseph, "The Moral Mind: How Five Sets of Innate Intuitions Guide the Development of Many Culture-Specific Virtues, and Perhaps Even Modules [sic]," in *Foundations and Future*, vol. 3 of *The Innate Mind*, ed. Peter Carruthers, Stephen Laurence, and Stephen Stich (Oxford: Oxford University Press, 2007), pp. 367–92.

The diversity of these scientists' work and the many obscurities of the portions of their conceptual apparatus that they borrow from philosophers present daunting obstacles to efforts at describing them. The best I can do here is to suggest the flavor and direction of the three types through a glance at an example or two of each, with no attempt to do anything like justice to the fields as a whole or to the whole oeuvre of individuals. There are many more than the half dozen I describe, as well as many who fit none of these types,★ and the debates are fine-tuned and hairsplitting beyond the tolerance of those with no professional stake in them. All of them, reaching for the nearest word, tend to refer to value systems that have little to do with Western moral culture as "morality"—a defensible English usage, but one that seems to contribute to a disregard of the peculiar characteristics of the one "morality" that has mostly inspired and shaped their questions.

★ Examples of those many scientists who fit easily into none of these types are Michael S. Gazzaniga, who defends free will and moral responsibility against determinism in *Who's in Charge? Free Will and the Science of the Brain* (New York: Ecco Press, 2011); Frans de Waal, who, in *Primates and Philosophers: How Morality Evolved*, ed. Stephen Macedo and Josiah Ober (Princeton, N.J.: Princeton University Press, 2006) and elsewhere, offers evidence of primate altruism and interesting distinctions between human and primate capacities; Elliott Sober, a philosopher, and David Sloan Wilson, a biologist, in *Unto Others: The Evolution and Psychology of Unselfish Behavior* (Cambridge, Mass.: Harvard University Press, 1998), who erect a conceptual framework in which key questions about selfishness and altruism can be asked, and support the possibility of disinterested motives.

I. THE TOUGH-MINDED SCIENCE OF MORALITY

WILSON'S SOCIOBIOLOGY (1975)

The tough-minded masters of sociobiology and evolutionary biology are well-known in the academy and to the public. It is less well-known that thirty-five years ago, the field of ethics was a primary target of E. O. Wilson, the father of sociobiology. The first chapter of Wilson's *Sociobiology*, which appeared in 1975, is titled "The Morality of the Gene"; the first word in the first chapter is "Camus," and its first sentences announce that biology trumps ethics:

> Camus said that the only serious philosophical question is suicide. That is wrong even in the strict sense intended. The biologist, who is concerned with questions of physiology and evolutionary history, realizes that self-knowledge is constrained and shaped by the emotional control centers in the hypothalamus and limbic system of the brain. These centers flood our consciousness with all the emotions— hate, love, guilt, fear, and others—that are consulted by ethical philosophers who wish to intuit the standards of good and evil. What, we are then compelled to ask, made the hypothalamus and limbic system? They evolved by natural selection. That simple biological statement must be pursued to explain ethics and ethical philosophers, if not epistemology and epistemologists, at all depths. Self-existence, or the suicide that terminates it, is not the central question of philosophy. The hypothalamic–limbic complex automatically

denies such logical reduction by countering it with feelings of guilt and altruism. In this one way, the philosopher's own emotional control centers are wiser than his solipsist consciousness, "knowing" that in evolutionary time the individual organism counts for almost nothing. . . . [T]he organism is only DNA's way of making more DNA. More to the point, the hypothalamus and limbic system are engineered to perpetuate DNA.*

It is hard to understand why Wilson thinks that the hypothalamus and limbic system do not let us put the question of suicide at the center of moral philosophy, given that they let us actually kill ourselves if we want to. But if Wilson's remarks about suicide and logical reduction are somewhat obscure,† it is at least clear that he means that biology must explain ethical philosophers and ethics (and maybe other subdisciplines of philosophy, too), because they are "constrained and shaped" by the hypothalamus and limbic system of the brain, which are products of natural selection. The hypothalamus and limbic system serve the survival of our genes; therefore ethics does, too. Wilson ends his book on the same note. "Scientists and humanists

---

* Edward O. Wilson, *Sociobiology* (1975) (Cambridge, Mass.: Harvard University Press, 2000), p. 3.

† In this passage and elsewhere in the book (see *Sociobiology*, p. 562), Wilson tends to focus his critique of philosophical ethics on Rawlsian and similar forms of intuitionism, in which moral intuitions are thought to provide evidence for general theories of right and wrong in the same way that observations in science provide evidence for scientific theories. It was the vogue then, and even now, but Rawlsian intuitionism is only one theory of ethics, which many find unsatisfactory.

should consider together the possibility," he states in his final chapter, "that the time has come for ethics to be removed temporarily from the hands of philosophers and biologicized."[*] In 1978, he sounds more sure of his ground than ever. Human behavior, he asserts, "is the circuitous technique by which human genetic material has been and will be kept intact. Morality has no other demonstrable ultimate function."[†]

DAWKINS'S SELFISH GENES (1976)

Richard Dawkins, an evolutionary biologist and ethologist, has said far less about morality in print than Wilson has, and he does not share Wilson's grandiose concerns with the architectonic of all knowledge and with academic turf, but he may have had far more influence on how people think about the moral life. His deservedly popular book, *The Selfish Gene* (1976), was uniquely successful in conveying sophisticated science in a readable, entertaining style. The overt lesson about morality in that book is presented as an aside, and it is short. He argues that natural selection ultimately selects not the species or the group but the gene, whose evolutionary success he describes as "ruthless selfishness"—a metaphor, he carefully explains, for objective effects on survival, not subjective motives. Selfish behavior on the part of the *individual* organism, as the genes' "survival machine," will often be necessary to increase

---

[*] Wilson, *Sociobiology*, p. 562.

[†] E. O. Wilson, *On Human Nature* (Cambridge, Mass.: Harvard University Press, 1978), p. 167.

the survival odds of its selfish genes. As a result, we should expect individual animals, generally speaking, to be genetically predisposed to selfishness and ruthlessness, and to display altruism primarily toward those who share their genes. Human beings are no exception. Like other animals, "we are born selfish."* But our actions are uniquely affected by culture and our capacity for foresight. Generosity and altruism are humanly possible, but difficult, and they are not natural, instinctive human characteristics—any more than the choreography of *Swan Lake*, the calculus, or the harmonic minor scale—but must be carefully *taught*.

This explicit theory of morality in relation to genetic predisposition is, to my mind, largely true. Yet it is hard to imagine that Dawkins's book leaves an intelligent reader with anything but increased moral doubts and diminished moral motivation. Dawkins offers us the fairly empty possibility that we are able to override predispositions to behave selfishly or countermorally. But he provides us with little evidence that we ever actually do so, and properly points out that explanations of how it is that we have this ability, or what it might amount to, lie outside his province as a biologist. At the same time, he overwhelms us with dazzling, delicious evidence of selfish and ruthless behavior throughout the animal kingdom; he insistently points out ways in which human behavior fits animal patterns, readily mixing discussions of animals and humans; he habitually refers to kinship relations among animals with words that the layperson reserves for humankind—insects, birds, and seals, in this book, have children, sons, daughters,

---

* Dawkins, *The Selfish Gene*, p. 3.

brothers, sisters, and parents—with the result that the reader is tempted to think of the book's ideas as descriptions of people even when they are not. The overall effect is that the book de-livers a covert, deeply skeptical message, a kind of message that for obvious reasons always tends to undermine moral commit-ment. In this way, his book is effectually, though not intellectu-ally, antimoral.

MORALITY BIOLOGICALLY EXPLAINED? WILSON REDUX (1998)

In Dawkins's account, morality—like the calculus and the harmonic minor scale—is rooted in biology but, presumably, is not for that reason biologically inevitable in any individual or people. After all, he argues, correctly as I believe, that being moral requires education and struggle. His view also seems to allow proper room in ethics for the facts of culture and history.

Wilson, however, offers a much more heavily "biologicized" (to use his own term) account of ethics. For example, he seems to believe that fairly specific moral dispositions such as self-respect, empathy, and moral outrage are an evolved biological inheri-tance. But even if very specific dispositions to moral action are heritable and inevitable, it does not follow that biologists are best able to study them. Are biologists good observers of cultural and historical overlays on evolved traits, of complex social interac-tions, motives, and multiply conditioned values and their histori-cal preconditions, of economics, or of the complexities of guilt and conscience, or how these have interacted with religion, poli-tics, power, and danger? If they are, that should surprise us, for biologists can no more claim professional competence in doing those things than geologists or quarterbacks.

Likewise, even though all animal behavior, including thinking and explaining things, has a biological and genetic basis, it does not follow that biologists can best explain that behavior or, more important, that evolutionary explanation sheds much light on most subjects outside biology. In important ways, morality is rooted in biology, but that does not mean that the study of morality belongs to biologists—any more than the study of mathematics, which is equally rooted in biology, should be given over to biologists, or that our mathematical progress would be particularly advanced by evolutionary accounts of how biology makes the calculus possible.

Wilson's claims fell into a conceptual bog—a swamp in which even what we meant by "cause," "explanation," and "theory" was muddy. Dawkins sidestepped this bog for the most part, but Wilson waded in. Wilson and others of his ilk, like all thinkers ambitious not just for truth but for turf, claimed more than he was entitled to—possibly because he overlooked the effect of the hypothalamus and limbic system on his own thinking and his own discipline. If philosophers' intuitions of good and evil are biologically shaped and constrained, then surely so are sociobiologists' reasonings concerning the turfs and priority of scholarly disciplines. Those reasonings may well be saturated with ruthless, blinding ambition.

Twenty-three years after he published *Sociobiology*, Wilson spoke in some ways more circumspectly, acknowledging the contributions to his project that a few other disciplines must make. But he continued to regard biology as the key to ethics. In *Consilience*, published in 1998, he wrote that we must put right and wrong on

an empirical footing and claimed that weakness in our understanding of the biology of "the moral sentiments" is the *main*
obstacle to doing so,* and he explained the moral sentiments
in terms of epigenetic rules, evolutionary products of an interplay
between biology and culture, or "hereditary biases of mental development" that generate moral sentiments.[†] "[I]f we explore the
biological roots of moral behavior and explain their material origins and biases," he maintained in an article drawn from the
book, "we should be able to fashion a wise and enduring ethical
consensus."[‡] We must try to create such an empirically derived
consensus, moreover, because modern societies' moral reasoning is "a mess," full of contradictions, unstable, and volatile—
because it is dominated by tribalistic and Paleolithic egalitarian
instincts, dysfunctional remnants of our evolutionary past.[§]

---

* Edward O. Wilson, *Consilience* (New York: Alfred A. Knopf, 1998), p. 255.

[†] Ibid., pp. 246–47, 255.

[‡] Edward O. Wilson, "The Biological Basis of Morality," the *Atlantic*, April
1998. This *Atlantic* essay is extracted from *Consilience*, where (pp. 240 and 254)
he makes the same claims about ethical consensus and Paleolithic egalitarian
and tribalistic instincts.

[§] Wilson, "The Biological Basis of Morality," and *Consilience*, p. 254. There
are hints in this essay and in *Consilience* that Wilson expects future human
evolution to make corrections in this problematic heritage and to endow us
with an improved genetic makeup, one that better reflects our cultural reality: "Above the fundamental instincts rise superstructures of arguments and
rules that accommodate the novel institutions created by cultural evolution.
These accommodations, which reflect the attempt to maintain order and
further tribal interests, have been too volatile to track by genetic evolution;
they are not yet in the genes" (*Consilience*, pp. 254–55). *Not yet, but someday?*
Nonbiologists may be mystified as to what evidence exists that evolution
might or will take such a turn. How can Wilson be so certain that it would be

A science of ethics—indeed, a scientific ethic—is the only cure for these ills.

How can we forge this necessary new scientifically grounded moral consensus? Wilson says that the new consensus must be based on good biological, genetic, and neurological accounts of the "moral sentiments," one that will at last discover the "innate epigenetic rules of moral reasoning."* To accomplish this, we will need a complete evolutionary history that tells how those sentiments aided survival and reproductive success, plus an understanding from anthropology and psychology of how they have been affected by cultural evolution.† When at last we

---

biologically favorable to have cultural superstructures "accommodated" genetically? Wilson's grandiose comments on the future direction of evolution have the same attraction as religious prophecies, and the same logical status.

Wilson leaves us with the same doubts when, in *Consilience*, he maintains that "indoctrinability" in religious and moral precepts is an evolved characteristic that supports cultural evolution (pp. 246–47). In *Sociobiology*, in fact, he says: "Human beings are absurdly easy to indoctrinate—they *seek* it" (p. 562). Even assuming that people are absurdly indoctrinable, in the absence of conceptual analysis of indoctrinability (especially how it differs from the ability to *learn*), of empirical study of resistance to indoctrination, or of comparative historical studies of indoctrinability and its conditions and consequences, it is hard to imagine how anyone could look to this idea as any significant part of an explanation of history or, for that matter, of reproductive success. And, of course, we always question whether reproductive success is the ultimate test of human interest.

* Wilson, *Consilience*, p. 254.

† Although Wilson thinks we will need "histories of ethical systems as part of the emergence of different cultures" (*Consilience*, p. 255), he does not mention a need to consult any historians or sociologists about them, and in the *Atlantic* essay he does not list history—or sociology, economics, philosophy, literary arts, or political science—as a discipline with a contribution to make.

achieve this fully adequate grasp of the moral, we will be able to find "the most effective means for reaching consensus." Of course, we cannot know in advance what we will agree on in that consensus, but how we will reach it "can be predicted with assurance":

> It will be democratic, weakening the clash of rival religions and ideologies. History is moving decisively in that direction, and people are by nature too bright and too contentious to abide anything else. And the pace can be confidently predicted: change will come slowly, across generations, because old beliefs die hard, even when demonstrably false.*

Only a few years later, unfortunately, history looked as though it had headed off in quite the opposite direction from the one Wilson predicted, shedding old beliefs at breakneck speed, and perhaps not the ones Wilson objected to.

Wilson proposed, in effect, to supplant present-day values with a new ethic based on an understanding of the evolutionary biology of the moral instincts or sentiments:†

> [G]enes predisposing people to cooperative behavior would have come to predominate in the human population as a whole.
>
> Such a process . . . gave birth to the moral instincts. . . . [T]hese instincts are experienced by every person as conscience, self-respect, remorse, empathy, shame, humility,

---

* Wilson, *Consilience*, p. 256.

† Ibid., pp. 254–55.

and moral outrage. They bias cultural evolution toward
the conventions that express the universal moral codes of
honor, patriotism, altruism, justice, compassion, mercy, and
redemption.*

These are surprising ideas coming from a man whose bid for
credence rests on his claim to be a thoroughgoing empiricist, for
few historians could concur in his judgment that honor, patriotism, and the rest are universal codes, and self-respect, remorse,
empathy, and humility do not seem to qualify as biological "instincts," given that there are times and places in which they seem
to be widely absent and that they seem to require specific types
of cultural environment to flower. The capacities for remorse
and empathy, for example, are highly dependent on childhood
experience, therefore on child-rearing methods and thus on cultural habits. Perhaps shame, of all the items on his list, comes
closest to qualifying as instinctive; psychologists say that infants
first experience shame at around eighteen months. Humility
(unlike *humiliation*) is surely far distant from instinctive roots, as it
is a complex, highly self-conscious attitude, and many, perhaps
most, people never develop any at all. And perhaps here I may
digress long enough to point out that humility is truly a virtue,
and one that all scientists need a large dose of, especially when
they study morality, which is psychologically, and even logically,
prior to science in several ways.† The scientific imperative to seek

----

* Ibid., p. 253.

† In the same *Atlantic* essay cited earlier, Wilson also offers a surprising opinion on what behavioral scientists *from another planet* would think about us. He
is confident that they would think precisely what he himself thinks:

truth above all else is a moral imperative; the logical conditions on what can count as truth are dependent on this moral imperative; and the mental qualities that enable people to find and respect truth include enough humility to resist exaggerating and minimizing evidence or claiming knowledge or competence when those logical preconditions have not been met.

Wilson seems to think it obvious that we would be better off with a *stable, consensus-based* ethic, but stability is not an obvious or ultimate moral value; and change, reform and progress, may well be permanent moral necessities or desirable characteristics of societies. Nor is consensus an ultimate or even a very important moral value. We cannot know a priori that we need or

---

[They] would notice immediately the parallels between animal dominance behavior on the one hand and human obeisance to religious and civil authority on the other. They would point out that the most elaborate rites of obeisance are directed at the gods, the hyperdominant if invisible members of the human group. And they would conclude, correctly, that in baseline social behavior, not just in anatomy, *Homo sapiens* has only recently diverged in evolution from a nonhuman primate stock.

(A similar passage occurs in *Consilience*, p. 259.) Richard Dawkins, too, expects that aliens would think the way he does. If superior creatures from space came to earth, he says on the first page of *The Selfish Gene*, the first thing about us that they would want to know, so as to assess the level of our civilization, is whether we had discovered evolution yet. Aliens, that is, just like earth's late-twentieth-century biologists, would regard the state of *biological* knowledge as definitive of our species' state of cultural advance. Wilson's and Dawkins's move from what their science teaches to their own opinions on their science's cultural and moral significance is easy to see and harmless. Sometimes, their inferences are harder to see and less innocent.

want or should strive for either a stable value system or an ethic based on consensus. It is highly questionable whether we ought to aim at moral reform that is consciously devised to serve these or any other goals that will make societies "work better."

Moral systems do not function like, nor do they serve as, constitutions and political systems or governmental structures. Besides, there is no possible understanding, prior to and independent of moral understanding, of what "working better" might amount to. An empirically grounded ethic that revised those of our values that depended on our unfortunate tribal and Paleolithic egalitarian instincts, one that enabled us to experience less quarreling and discord, more order and less chaos, might conceivably be evil or otherwise morally objectionable. But, even more important, we should ask Wilson why it is such a good idea, morally speaking, to seek this new ethic, for Wilson offers no critique of moral values that makes us want new ones. Yet he talks as though it is obviously our morality itself that is the problem, not our failure to abide by it. But perhaps other biologists are better ethicists than Wilson.

BARASH AS MORALIST

David Barash is an evolutionary biologist who is also professor of psychology at the University of Washington. He is one of those to whom the media turn for scientific comment on moral and social matters, and his efforts illustrate just how well evolutionary biology prepares a man to reason morally. In an op-ed essay in the *Los Angeles Times* (March 12, 2008) about the fall of New York's governor Eliot Spitzer, Barash begins: "As an evolutionary biologist, I look at New York Gov. Spitzer's now-public sexual indiscretions and feel justified in saying, 'I told you so.'" Pointing to the behavior of "a wide array of species" and "overwhelming" biological evidence that "maleness plus money plus political power isn't likely to add up to sexual restraint," he advises the disgruntled voters of New York: "You want monogamy? Elect a swan."

Barash seems to be offering moral advice based on expert knowledge of our species that he has gained in his study of evolutionary biology. He seems to be suggesting that the citizens of New York sigh, shrug, and forgo outrage; biological necessity, he reminds us, cannot be judged but only bemoaned. But no biological evidence exists that would support Barash's conclusion. From the fact, cited by Barash, that "before the homogenization of cultures that resulted from Western colonialism, more than 85% of human societies unabashedly favored polygamy," we cannot infer that polygamy is good or better than monogamy or that it is so inevitable as to make it useless to struggle against it or as to make outrage or distaste pointless. (Very often, the best is also the rarest and hardest to achieve, and what occurs in 15 percent of all societies cannot really be considered rare anyway.) The same goes for the sexual behavior of alpha males and their female worshippers. Professor Barash, by the way, in this op-ed makes no distinction between biological evidence about the aphrodisiac effect of power and evidence about the ability of powerful men to get sex through coercive or economic exercise of that power. What relevance to the case has the aphrodisiac effect of power if the prostitutes didn't find the governor attractive?

Whatever one's opinions of Spitzer's true deserts and despite all that Barash says, wouldn't the voters of New York be nothing but rational to insist that their governor strive to belong to a civilized minority, to be better than average, and to be contemptuous when he failed to be? Difficult as it may be to mold the psyche and society so as to conform to higher than average standards, what is difficult is not impossible and may be so obviously worthwhile as to make Barash's cynical musings beside the point. Nonetheless, they were published in a prominent journal, and their author's juvenile opinions gained undeserved influence on account of his status as an evolutionary scientist, a scholar and expert whose view it is that we ought not to expect too much from people, even if they are governor.

II. THE TENDER-MINDED SCIENCE OF MORALITY

In every system of morality, which I have hitherto met with, I have always remarked, that the author proceeds for some time in the ordinary ways of reasoning, and establishes the being of a God, or makes observations concerning human affairs; when all of a sudden I am surprised to find, that instead of the usual copulations of propositions, is, and is not, I meet with no proposition that is not connected with an ought, or an ought not. This change is imperceptible; but is however, of the last consequence. For as this ought, or ought not, expresses some new relation or affirmation, 'tis necessary that it should be observed and explained; and at the same time that a reason should be given; for what seems altogether inconceivable, how this new relation

can be a deduction from others, which are entirely dif-
ferent from it.

—DAVID HUME, *A TREATISE*

OF HUMAN NATURE (1739)

The tender-minded investigators of the science of morality look for, and find, universal morality in fundamental, biological human capacities. Despite their good intentions, their approach ignores the distinctive characteristics of the moral and results in antimoral and immoral conceptions of right and wrong. The moral theory developed by Marc Hauser, an interdisciplinist with background in evolutionary psychology, biology, and anthropology, provides a clear example of how this happens.

A UNIVERSAL GRAMMAR OF MORALITY

In Hauser's words, we must understand "our moral psychology as an instinct—an evolved capacity of all human minds that unconsciously and automatically generates judgments of right and wrong. . . ."[*] He thinks not only that there is a universal moral instinct, but that "we are equipped with a moral faculty—an organ of the mind that carries a universal grammar of action."[†] This faculty he likens to the human faculty for acquiring language: Both, he claims, operate on principles that are

[*] Marc Hauser, *Moral Minds: How Nature Designed Our Universal Sense of Right and Wrong* (New York: Ecco Press, 2006), p. 2.

[†] Ibid., p. 11.

unconscious and accommodate enormous cultural variation; the different languages of different cultures are analogous to the value systems of different historical cultures. The values of other cultures, he points out, may be as incomprehensible to us as Mandarin, yet just as Mandarin is built on an underlying universal grammar, those foreign values are built on the same evolved, biologically determined, unconscious grammar of action as our own.

It would be hard to find anyone who disagrees with the idea that morality, like all other human thought and behavior, somehow depends on evolved, unconscious, universal abilities, on genetics and biology and neurology. But it does not follow that those abilities themselves are helpfully named "moral" or that morality is genuinely instinctual. We use the term *instinctual* to describe, for example, sexual feelings, hunger, and certain kinds of fears and hatreds. Morality appears to consist, at least in part, in the effort to establish a higher level of judgment and control over instinctual behavior and thus to be quintessentially *not* instinctual, even though it relies heavily on our capacity for emotion. While Hauser is certainly right that morality depends on innate abilities and that we often have immediate moral or intuitive reactions to complicated situations, this is still not good enough reason to call it an instinct. To show that certain judgments are automatic and rest on unconscious processes does not prove it, either. The unconscious obviously learns; what was once not even part of the psychic apparatus can, for good or ill, become an automatic, seemingly instinctive part of it—racist reactions, for example, or reactions to music in major and minor keys—and what is sometimes conscious can at other times be unconscious.

Hauser often speaks of a *faculty* of moral judgment or moral *organ* of the mind,★ but this, too, is a questionable idea. Several areas of the brain seem to be involved in moral judgments, and not all moral judgments appear to activate the same kind of brain activity. In fact, we might ask whether the same judgment—say, a passionate decision in favor of pacifism or a guilty reflection on lies one has told to a potential lover—might not correlate with different brain activity at different times of life or on different occasions or in different contexts or in different kinds of people. And wouldn't the answer depend heavily on what we mean by a "moral judgment" and even "the same moral judgment"? There seems little reason to believe in the existence of a faculty or organ uniquely dedicated to moral judgment or moral reaction—unlike other things we call faculties, like sight or hearing.

Hauser's views would make it senseless to judge that some appalling value system is *morally* wrong or inferior. If Hauser is right, we could no more sensibly question or condemn a value system—that of the ancient Assyrians or the Mundugumor, say—than we could sensibly judge that Chinese violated English grammar. It would make sense to say that some value system violated morality only if it violated the deep grammar of morality—which, presumably, no value system can, any more than any real language could violate Noam Chomsky's deep grammar. Hauser's universal "grammar of action" is offered to us as an underlying universal morality, but using his own Chomskyan analogy, it would seem more fair to say, and it is certainly true, that in the human brain there are innate capaci-

---

★ Hauser, *Moral Minds,* pp. 36, 85, 425, and elsewhere ("faculty") and 163ff ("organ").

ties that make morality possible for all normal human beings, but that these capacities themselves are not moral. The deep grammar of languages is not a language; likewise the deep grammar of action, if it exists, is not a kind of morality.

In Hauser's account of "moralities," the one that preaches equality, freedom, the value of individuals, mercy, and universal compassion is not better than one that condones slavery, torture, revenge, and hierarchy and grants the powerful cruel rights over the weak. It is thus an implicit demotion of the specific values of morality. In this way, his theory is effectively, though not intentionally, antimoral.

THE UNIVERSAL EVOLUTIONARY PSYCHOLOGY OF MORALITY; CONSENSUS TRUMPS REASON

Jonathan Haidt's theories lead to the same result. Haidt, a social psychologist,* is another academic whom journalists call on for commentary on a variety of moral questions, from attitudes toward fundamentalism and homosexuality to the morality of rejoicing in the streets in celebration of the killing of Osama bin Laden.

---

* Jonathan Haidt is professor of social psychology at the University of Virginia. In addition to his moral research, he is a proponent of positive psychology, the study of what makes people happy and the therapeutic use of the results of such study to help them attain happiness. This school of thought is promoted at the Center for Positive Psychology at the University of Pennsylvania, where Haidt studied. He is the author of the popular *The Happiness Hypothesis: Finding Modern Truth in Ancient Wisdom* (New York: Basic Books, 2006), which happens to be Chris Anderson's favorite book. See chapter 9, footnote p. 215.

Haidt is unusual in his overt attention to social relations among "morality researchers." In a somewhat smarmy conclusion to an essay about the moral mind, he appears to equate scientific disputes with power struggles, and he seems to call for consensus on a matter of scientific truth by vote rather than by the usual scientific criteria. After describing how chimpanzees and humans alike share a desire for peace and harmony in their groups and celebrate when power struggles are resolved, he (and his coauthor, Craig Joseph) go on to confess:

> We find this desire in ourselves: We are a part of the community of morality researchers that has long been divided on the question of moral innateness. This makes us uncomfortable, for we truly like and value the many members of our community, and we have tried . . . to show how all are right about something, all have something to contribute. We propose that some degree of harmony and synergy can be restored if most morality researchers are willing to endorse this statement: *The first draft of the moral mind has diverse moral content that was specified in advance of experience, but this innately given content gets revised and greatly extended during the course of development as children actively construct their moral knowledge within a cultural context that uses narrative to shape and guide the development of specific virtues.* Is anyone ready to celebrate with us—or to propose an alternative consensus statement?★

★ Jonathan Haidt and Craig Joseph, "The Moral Mind: How Five Sets of Innate Intuitions Guide the Development of Many Culture-Specific Virtues and Perhaps Even Modules [sic]," in *Foundations and Future*, vol. 3 of *The*

Haidt and Joseph's wheedling flattery of their colleagues here, and their invitation to "celebrate," following immediately on their allusion to the celebratory peacemaking social behavior of chimpanzees, seems obviously offered as the human version of whatever chimps do to celebrate the end of intragroup struggles—grooming, say, or submissive posturing.

The same concern for harmony and consensus crops up in Haidt's description of the moral mind. Like Hauser, Haidt derives morality from a set of universal innate capacities. He divides these into five categories—care, fairness, loyalty, purity, and respect—which he describes as "modules,"* or as "an evolutionary preparedness . . . to link certain patterns of social appraisal to specific emotions and motivational reactions."† Haidt argues that these five categories, or "innate intuitions," are shaped into the historically specific "moralities" of many cultures. The view that morality is the product of interplay between innate, evolved, universal capacities and culture is unobjectionable and widely recognized, but, like Wilson, Haidt has a program of moral reform in mind, in which his five innate intuitions play an important, and questionable, role.

Analyzing contemporary American politics in terms of this theory, Haidt suggests that those Americans whom he calls

---

Innate Mind, ed. Peter Carruthers, Stephen Laurence, and Stephen Stich (Oxford: Oxford University Press, 2007), pp. 367–91, 390–91.

* Haidt's view that these five categories are "modules" is tentative. Modules, roughly speaking, are innate, evolved structures or subsystems of mind that are addressed to specific domains of experience. Their existence and nature are controversial.

† Haidt and Joseph, "The Moral Mind," p. 381.

"conservative" hold values from all five categories, while liberals seem not to understand the values based on loyalty, respect, and purity, but only those that express caring and fairness. He suggests that those who make theories about morality are typically liberals, who, out of ideological blindness, wrongly exclude any values based on loyalty, purity, and respect. Their moral theories, therefore, are always concerned solely with rights and limits on harm. If liberals would only learn to be more sensitive to these other values as well, we could reconcile the estranged political camps, red and blue, of the United States—and build a moral majority that would support Barack Obama.* Thus, Haidt is proposing a program of moral and political reform.

But Haidt's conservatives, whose moral thinking includes strong elements of disgust (the reaction to impurity), respect for authority, and loyalty, surely include many whose mentality is the authoritarian premoralism described earlier in this book.† The values that they espouse, and that Haidt depicts as having been wrongly excluded from theories of morality, are better understood as nonmoral and antimoral values, values that are

---

* See Jonathan Haidt, "Obama's Moral Majority," *Prospect*, February 28, 2009, accessed November 17, 2011, http://www.prospectmagazine.co.uk/2009/02/obamasmoralmajority/.

† According to the Moral Foundations Web site, run by Jonathan Haidt and his colleagues, disgust is aroused by contamination or a failure to treat the body as a temple by contaminating it in immoral activities; to value purity is to treat a less carnal life as more noble. Loyalty is loyalty to the group, arising out of our long tribal history. And respect for authority and tradition hark back to our primate roots in hierarchical social interactions. Accessed November 17, 2011, http://faculty.virginia.edu/haidtlab/mft/index.php.

specifically superseded and condemned in the historical era of moral dominance. Presumably, Haidt regards the three values that liberals supposedly exclude as the equals of the others because he thinks they have the same origins in the structure of the mind and finds it hard to see how one set of such values *could* be held superior to others. If this is his thinking, he does not defend it; nor does he see how it implicitly attacks the *moral* sense of value.

Consider the respect for authority that Haidt wishes liberals to learn. Morality is wary of all authority except moral authority. It has always put itself above kings, popes, priests, patriarchs, masters, senators, lords, dictators, and professors; it has repeatedly counseled rebellion, and its antiauthoritarianism has made possible the explosion of science as well as the spread of democracy. Moral minds understand this and correctly regard the authoritarian spirit as inherently opposed to important moral values.* Respect for power and, as the Quakers say, "respect of persons" are wrong, and this is true even though people *do* seem to have a natural tendency to respect power and wealth and to set up social hierarchies, which inevitably imbue people—often unworthy ones—with authority. Morality exists to moderate and when necessary to oppose such natural tendencies. Morality also limits our loyalty to the group and respect for its leader, and it often insists on its right to trump what one owes to a tribe, government, or clan.

---

* Scientists, especially, should be mindful that rebellion against religious and political authority is science's birthright. Scientific truth respects only evidence, never ideology, superstition, or expedience, and has at times defied authorities who stood for all three.

From a moral vantage point, disgust, too, the response to dirtiness or contamination, the absence of purity, is a poor guide to right. (See the earlier discussion of this point in chapter 6, page 157.) While morality makes what use it can of disgust to reinforce its directives, it also undertakes to educate and correct and sometimes to override our feelings of disgust toward impurity. Some innocent sexual acts once struck many people as disgusting and impure; their attitudes were misguided, the result of miseducation and a deep-seated irrationality that took generations of education to overcome. Abortion arouses a sense of disgust in most of us but is nonetheless, in proper cases, morally permissible. It also disgusts some people to hear of discarding fertilized human eggs or to imagine homosexual acts, but these acts, too, are innocent. Disgust is prerational and primitive; the moral mind exists to impose a rational override on it, as it does on many other instinctive responses. Haidt, who knows perfectly well that homosexuality is innocent, nevertheless chides liberals for being "tone-deaf" to values derived from disgust—and respect and purity.* But all moral minds, including liberal ones, hear them loud and clear; they hear them and, when morally necessary, struggle against the temptation to give in to them. Morally speaking, what Haidt proposes is regressive—immoral and antimoral. He implicitly rejects both the substance of moral judgment (by sometimes favoring premoral over moral

---

* It does not follow that we should *always* strive to avoid feelings of disgust, nor is it true that we may always override them. As a tool of the moral, disgust at the idea of abortion serves to remind us that we are dealing with potentials for human life and helps us avoid crossing moral lines. But we should also not rely on disgust to provide more than a signal to stop and think.

values) and the authority of morality (over premoral inclination and over other authorities).

Haidt's ideas show how easy it is to slip from an attempt at scientific description of what morality *is* into questionable programs of political and moral reform. Of course, scientists have the same rights and obligations to moralize as anyone else. But, as we can never remind ourselves too often, they must always take off their white coats to do so because no science exists that qualifies them to claim that scientific expertise backs their moral opinions. Haidt's recommendation that liberals learn some conservative values appears to rest on his belief that our chief moral goal must be to build consensus and agreement. Although it should go without saying, the prevalence of views on consensus like Haidt's—notably among liberal politicians—makes it necessary to point out that consensus is worth having only when it is in favor of something good or something true. A consensus in favor of what is wrong or false, such as slavery or denials of evolution or genocide, is evil or dangerous. Moral consensus inevitably comes to seem the foremost moral goal, however, to those who rule out the possibility of moral truth. If moral beliefs have no truth, if they are arbitrary cultural habits or merely personal wishes, attitudes, and likes and dislikes, then we should abandon them and compromise them when necessary for the sake of group solidarity and peace and can be called on to do so.

Haidt's resort to consensus is unavoidable because he is, in fact, skeptical of the role of reason and truth in morality. In his view, emotion drives moral judgment, and the reasons we offer in support of judgment are usually not our real reasons, which we may not even know, but are, for the most part (though not always), ex post facto rationalizations of attitudes determined by largely unconscious processes.* In moral judgment, he claims, people are likely to search for justifications and arguments that support their intuited opinions in a process of "motivated" reasoning in which the "reasoning process is more like a lawyer defending a client than a judge or scientist seeking truth."† In other words, we attribute our moral attitudes to reasoning that does not in fact give rise to them, falling for, and helping to create, an illusion of objectivity, and doing this is an evolved characteristic of the moral mind.

Why does natural selection rig our moral minds so awkwardly? According to Haidt, it is because moral reasoning is a "process used to influence the intuitions (and hence judgment) of *other* people" [emphasis added].‡ Misattributed moral arguments are able to influence others' judgments, and this favors group cohesion and group survival.§

---

* This view is subscribed to by other tender-minded moral researchers, including Marc Hauser and Joshua D. Greene, cited in footnotes pp. 249 and 275.

† Jonathan Haidt, "The Emotional Dog and Its Rational Tail: A Social Intuitionist Approach to Moral Judgment," *Psychological Review* 108 (2002): 814–34.

‡ Ibid., p. 820. Haidt implies that Hume, like Haidt himself, maintains that "reason's main job is to formulate arguments that support one's intuitive conclusions." But the meaning of Hume's famous dictum that reason must be the "slave of the passions" is not that reason rationalizes what the sentiments want, but that only the sentiments can motivate us to action: "reason alone can never produce any action, or give rise to volition. . . ." David Hume, *A Treatise of Human Nature* (1739–1740), ed. David Fate and Mary J. Norton (Oxford: Oxford University Press, 2000), p. 266. Reason's job is to provide the sentiments with truths about the world so that they can respond to the world as it really is.

§ Haidt, "The Emotional Dog," p. 822. Haidt claims that his views on misattribution find support in studies of split-brain patients, hypnosis, and,

When people think that they are reasoning their way to moral conclusions, what they are actually doing, Haidt says, is drawing from "a pool of culturally supplied norms" that provide "acceptable reasons for praise and blame." Thus "the enormous literature on moral reasoning can be reinterpreted as a kind of ethnography of the a priori moral theories held by various communities and age groups."★ In fact, Haidt attributes the heat and bitterness of the culture wars to people's regrettable illusions that their own moral views are based on reasoning: Each person decides that since he or she has been rational, those who disagree must be close-minded, insincere, and not truly morally motivated.†

Haidt thinks that we should not be surprised to learn that moral judgment is heavily influenced by what he calls "relatedness" motives, desires for harmony or agreement, or bias in favor of one's own group. "From an evolutionary perspective," he argues, "it would be strange if our moral judgment was designed principally for accuracy, with no concern for the disastrous effects of periodically siding with our enemies and against our friends."‡ Morality evolved to "bind people together into teams

---

especially, a group of experiments from the 1960s and 1970s in which people misattribute causes of their bodily sensations, including a well-known experiment conducted by Richard E. Nisbett and Stanley Schacter. Richard E. Nisbett and Stanley Schacter, "Cognitive Manipulation of Pain," *Journal of Experimental Social Psychology* 2 (1966): 227–36; and Richard E. Nisbett and Timothy DeCamp Wilson, "Telling More Than We Can Know: Verbal Reports on Mental Processes," *Psychological Review* 84 (May 1977): 231–59.

★ Haidt, "The Emotional Dog," p. 822.

† Ibid., p. 823.

‡ Ibid., p. 821. Haidt seems to take it for granted both that morality is heavily instinctive and evolutionarily determined and that a scientific and evolu-

that seek victory, not truth."* Here again, Haidt claims that morality *is* something that morality, in fact, condemns, and identifies morality with innate tendencies that morality, in fact, comes into being to control and guide.† The whole concept of the moral evades him at every turn.

Bias in judgment in favor of one's own is something that morality specifically rejects. Morality often opposes consensus and sometimes takes sides against one's own group; this was precisely the moral position of southern abolitionists prior to the Civil War and antifascists in Germany in 1939 and of many others on the brink of other wars. Morality demands conflict and division when dissent is morally obligatory.‡ The moral ideal of truth is also an ideal of how consensus ought to be achieved and when it is to be valued.

---

tionarily satisfactory account of morality would have to show that it favors our survival.

* Jonathan Haidt's Web page, accessed October 1, 2011, http://people.virginia .edu/~jdh6n/.

† Likewise, natural selection may fit us with an ability to understand and seek truth because this favors our survival and propagation, but this does not imply that *truth* is merely what serves the survival of the fittest.

‡ See Luke 12:51–53: "Suppose ye that I am come to give peace on earth? I tell you, Nay; but rather division: For from henceforth there shall be five in one house divided, three against two, and two against three. The father shall be divided against the son, and the son against the father; the mother against the daughter, and the daughter against the mother; the mother in law against her daughter in law, and the daughter in law against her mother in law." Christians might recall, too, that Jesus also defied authorities, overrode the otherwise universal disgust at touching the diseased and unclean, and repeatedly refused to condemn the impure.

Haidt, like so many others, confuses the "purposes" of natural selection with those of the phenomena that are selected. Even if it is true that morality is naturally selected because its existence furthers group survival and cohesion, that does not mean that moral judgment is biased so as to favor friends over enemies, us over them. Would not clear-sighted and objective judgers be the best aids to survival? I myself have no idea whether morality—or even the natural capacities out of which it is molded—is advantageous to our survival, but it is certainly possible that it is neutral or even negative in its effect on survival; and if it favors survival, that might well be just because it *restrains* us from bias in favor of our own.

But who knows? When the argument reaches this point, we have arrived in fantasyland, the site of so much sociobiological and evolutionary psychological debate, where evidence is scant and the loudest or coolest or most flattering or most intriguing argument wins. It is a place where neither scientific rigor nor moral good sense restrains thought. I am not the first to complain that evolutionary psychology deals in vague, bendable, untested, and untestable ideas that fall short of anything that deserves to be called science. That it does so gives enormous room for exactly the kind of lawyerly rationalizing about the moral mind that Haidt says the moral mind itself characteristically engages in. In fact, Haidt makes his case about morality and moral reasoning in a style so much more like a lawyer's than a scientist's that a reader must wonder if he has not drawn a more accurate picture of his own mind than the moral mind.

III. THE MARRIAGE OF SCIENCE AND PHILOSOPHY

Just as scientists have at times gone wrong by borrowing from philosophers a weak framework for moral theorizing, so philosophers have sometimes turned to inapposite science to shore up their views.* An essay by Gilbert Harman, a Princeton University philosopher, is an example of the latter phenomenon.† Harman, like Haidt, is impressed with the social psychologists' idea of misattribution, which he describes as the error of attributing patterns of behavior to people's character traits rather than to situational factors. "[I]n fact," Harman says, "there is no evidence that people differ in character traits. They differ in their situations and in their perceptions of their situations. They differ in their goals, strategies, neuroses, optimism, etc. But character traits do not explain what differences there are."‡ Harman means not that people are unpredictable or that we should stop behaving well, but that we should understand predictability and good behavior differently from the way we have. And he, like Wilson and Haidt, calls for moral reform based on his ideas. While his view is not the predominant one

---

* Clearer heads in either science or philosophy too rarely step forward to sort out the resulting confusions. Two praiseworthy exceptions among philosophers are Philip Kitcher, *Vaulting Ambition: Sociobiology and the Quest for Human Nature* (Cambridge, Mass.: MIT Press, 1987), and Kwame Anthony Appiah, *Experiments in Ethics* (Cambridge, Mass.: Harvard University Press, 2008).

† Gilbert Harman, "Moral Philosophy Meets Social Psychology: Virtue Ethics and the Fundamental Attribution Error," *Proceedings of the Aristotelian Society* (1999): 315–31.

‡ Ibid., p. 329.

among philosophers, it is a much-discussed, mainstream hypothesis with influential adherents in philosophy and social psychology.

SCIENCE RULES OUT VIRTUE?

Harman's attack on the idea of character traits requires that we reject the concepts of virtue and vice, which are moral character traits. They are terms fading from use. With its present-day connotations of absurd sexual purity and more generally of fusty, outmoded moralism, the word *virtue* has become all but unutterable. Still, though we may be embarrassed by the word, we continue to recognize the idea when we praise people as courageous, generous, selfless, honest, or kind. The idea of character traits is tied naturally to our ideas about character, identity, moral autonomy, and moral responsibility, all of which lie at the heart of morality.

According to Harman, scientific evidence shows that whether people behave morally is almost entirely a matter of the situation in which morality is tested and has little to do with their character traits. His view flies in the face of "folk psychology." In the commonsense world, we do not hesitate to conclude that some people are kind or scrupulously honest or that others are selfish or grouchy or sleazy. Although everyone's moods and conduct vary with circumstance, we still feel confident that we know what some people "are like." We are even confident that dogs and four-year-olds do, too; and what we and they know, when we know this, is one or more of their character traits.

Harman supports his conclusion, in part, with some of the same misattribution studies that Haidt relies on. But he also appeals to a different line of experiments that includes the famous Milgram experiment at Yale in 1963 and the well-known Good Samaritan study done at Princeton Theological Seminary ten years later.★

In Milgram's central study, subjects were told to obey scientists' directions to administer increasingly painful shocks to other people, starting at 15 volts and increasing in 15-volt intervals up to 450 volts. The shocks at various levels were labeled "slight," "moderate," "strong," "very strong," "intense," "extremely intense," "Danger: severe shock," and, finally, "XXX." In reality, the apparent victims were not being shocked at all and faked their agony, but the test subjects believed that they suffered terribly and dangerously. Thus the experimenters expected few subjects to be willing to administer shocks in excess of "very strong," but in fact all forty of them did. Five balked at 300 volts, right before the extremely intense level. Four more stopped at 315, two at 330 (when the shockee had gone ominously silent), one at 345, and one at 360. Twenty-six people, or 65 percent of the total, administered the maximum shock when directed to do so by an authority.

The Milgram experiment did not aim at proving or disproving a theory about character traits, and it seems to take them for

---

★ Stanley Milgram, "Behavioral Study of Obedience," *Journal of Abnormal and Social Psychology* 67 (1963): 371–78; and John M. Darley and C. Daniel Batson, "'From Jerusalem to Jericho': A Study of Situational and Dispositional Variables in Helping Behavior," *Journal of Personality and Social Psychology* 27 (1973): 100–108.

granted. Milgram himself used frankly moral language in talking of his results—results that are difficult even to describe without referring to qualities of character—and concluded that few people have the "resources" needed to resist authority.★ But Harman argues that when 65 percent of subjects administer the maximum shock, it is a mistake to regard the experiment as indicating "character defect," and we should not conclude that "'extreme personal dispositions are at fault.'"†

He buttresses this conclusion with the results of the Good Samaritan study, which explicitly aimed to show that situational factors, not "helping norms and their salience," best predict the subjects' behavior. This study examined the willingness to stop and help a stranger in need. The subjects were students at the Princeton Theological Seminary. Each was told to give a talk in another building; half were assigned the topic of the Good Samaritan, and half got other assignments. Some were told they were late, some were told they had just enough time to reach the other building, and some were told they would be early. Then, en route, each encountered a "victim" slumping in a doorway—an actor, of course, planted by the experimenters. The majority of students gave no aid, and the only variable that predicted their behavior was whether or not they were in a hurry. Those who were presumably thinking about their Good Samari-

---

★ Stanley Milgram, "The Perils of Obedience," *Harper's*, December 1973, pp. 62–77.

† Harman, "Moral Philosophy Meets Social Psychology," pp. 322 and 323, quoting Lee Ross and Richard E. Nisbett, *The Person and the Situation: Perspectives of Social Psychology* (New York: McGraw-Hill, 1991).

tan talks did not behave differently from those thinking about other subjects. Sixty-three percent of those not in a hurry stopped to help, 45 percent of those in the group with just enough time, and only 10 percent of those told they were late. Harman, again, concludes that this shows that character traits could not explain the students' behavior; only situational differences mattered.

Neither experiment supports Harman's conclusions. In the first place, 10 percent of the seminarians in the Good Samaritan study were not deterred by their lateness from rendering aid; and 12.5 percent of the Milgram subjects balked before they reached the "extremely intense" shock level (and more did so at higher levels short of the maximum). Thus it seems to be precisely something about these individuals—their characters—that explains why they, and not others, behaved as they did.

In the second place, both experiments deal with many individuals, each one of whom faces the same situation. But surely, if we hoped to learn whether it was character or situation that determined moral reaction, we would have to show, among other things, how single individuals faced with different situations posing similar moral demands would act; we would have to show how the *individual* did or did not *characteristically* behave— and neither of these experiments does anything of the kind. Harman draws conclusions about the behavior of a single individual in many different situations from evidence about the behavior of a *group* of many individuals in a single situation. This is strikingly question-begging reasoning.

In the third place, the existence of character traits does not mean that behavior does *not* vary with situations. At most it suggests something about the *way* it varies with situation. When we describe a person as kind, we are making a complicated judgment. One person may be kind in quite a different pattern from another, perhaps in a manner more attentive to emotional than material injuries. When we describe two people as courageous, we are not committing ourselves to the idea that they behave alike: There are many kinds of courage. To determine the existence of a trait in some individual would require knowing that person well, studying his or her behavior over time and a variety of situations. We would need to attend to the fact that traits have different degrees of strength and that different individuals display them under different circumstances; for example, a woman might be generous to her friends and colleagues but grasping when dealing with her sisters or after quarreling with her husband. Some people will misbehave in small things but "come through" when it really matters. Under certain circumstances, even the kindest person will cause hurt, but not all kind persons will fail to be unkind under the same circumstances or in the same ways. Kind persons are simply those whose concern for others' suffering is a prominent and habitual feature of their actions—one that reliably predominates over specific angry and sadistic impulses under certain kinds of circumstances.★ Given

---

★ Mood, circumstance, and degree of seriousness affect how traits are displayed, and we are all skilled in learning the fine points of these interactions in our family and friends. Even strong character traits can be muted in certain circumstances. One's reliably even-tempered, calm friend may burst out in anger over trivia in the weeks following an illness, a fright, or the death of an intimate; or a normally easygoing acquaintance may under severe stress become angry and controlling. We then say that he or she acted "out of character."

Changeability itself, moreover, does not indicate the falseness of the idea of character traits. Mr. Micawber may sob in despair one minute and in the all this, Harman's reading of these experiments as evidence against the existence of virtues or character traits seems mystifying.

The explanation for Harman's peculiar reasoning may be found in his odd assumption that morally virtuous behavior would be average, normal behavior and that vicious behavior would be abnormal or extreme.

> But can we really attribute a 2 to 1 majority response to a character defect? And what about the fact that *all* subjects were willing to go at least to the 300 volt level? Does *everyone* have this character defect? Is that really the right way to explain Milgram's results?★

In fact, we would need much more knowledge of the test subjects before going so far as to judge their character, rather than their behavior in the experiment. But there is nothing at all hard to swallow in the idea that a majority of people, or all of the subjects in a small experiment, lack some virtue or, in owning or lacking some specific character trait, have what

---

next call for ale and burst into song. This does not show that he has no character traits; rather, it shows that he has the traits of volatility and lability. Persons with "as if" personalities, who simply absorb and reflect the ideas and characteristics of whomever they happen to attach themselves to, might well be said to lack real character traits of their own.

Of course, we also use "character" in a different sense when we remark that someone "has character." Then we mean not simply that the person has settled habits of feeling and action, but that the person is strong or good or, sometimes, unusual.

★ Harman, "Moral Philosophy Meets Social Psychology," p. 322.

amounts to a flaw.* On the contrary, it is exactly what we should expect. Average behavior is, rather obviously, not what we mean by virtuous behavior, and in equating flaws with "extremes," Harman creates a straw man; flaws, defects, and vices are, alas, anything but "extreme" or uncommon. No matter how hard it is to achieve some kinds of virtue and no matter that only a minority succeed, we may regard their absence as a flaw. In doing so, we follow a moral tradition testified to in a vast, ancient literature on human imperfection: "There is none that doeth good, no, not one" (Psalms 14:3).

In the Good Samaritan study, the trait studied is a form of altruism, a sacrifice of one's own interests and priorities for the sake of serving a stranger's, in a situation in which one has no special responsibility for that stranger (and, perhaps, in which many other people are equally capable of rendering that aid). It is not surprising that most of the seminarians did not display this kind of altruistic behavior. There is no reason to think seminarians are more altruistic or virtuous than other people, and in any random group of people, only a very few will be genuine Good Samaritans, which is not only what the experiment shows but also partly the point of the biblical story of the Good Samaritan. (Of three passersby, only one stops to render aid.) That none of Milgram's subjects showed great strength and independence is just what one expects after fascist Germany

---

* Harman plays on the difference between saying that the subjects *lacked* the virtue of strength of mind and that they *had* the corresponding vice or flaw of weak-mindedness. But the absence of a virtue does not necessarily imply the presence of a corresponding vice, though it sometimes does.

and My Lai.* Few people indeed have these qualities; they are virtues or excellences, and as such, they are uncommon. Their absence, not their presence, is predictable. Morality nonetheless considers their absence as a flaw even if most people have the flaw.

Harman, like Wilson and Haidt, wants us to reform, to give up thinking in this old-fashioned moral way. "If there is no such thing as character," he concludes, "then there is no such thing as character building."† Thus, if we want to get people to behave better, or to behave better ourselves, we should stop trying to improve ourselves or others; instead we should try to change the situations that people encounter. Our habit of attributing character traits to people "has deplorable results, leading to massive misunderstanding of other people, promoting unnecessary hostility between individuals and groups, distorting discussions of law and public policy."‡ And it prevents "implementation of situational changes that could have useful results."§

---

* Milgram conducted several trials. In the central one, his subjects were forty males between the ages of twenty and fifty from New Haven and its environs, with different occupations and education levels. He also studied Yale students, with the same results. As he points out, most people regard obedience to authority, in at least some circumstances, as itself virtuous. But moral education could probably make the ability to resist improper authority more common. Perhaps even familiarity with the Milgram and Good Samaritan studies would help some people to behave better in situations resembling those of the experiments.

† Harman, "Moral Philosophy Meets Social Psychology," p. 328.

‡ Ibid., p. 330.

§ Ibid. Harman's overall argument includes many subparts that cannot be addressed here.

Harman offers little to no evidence that these evils either exist* or that they do really flow from belief in virtues and character traits. His conclusions could not be more distant from those of Milgram, who stresses the need for individuals to take responsibility, not the need "to implement situational change":

> For a person to feel responsible for his actions, he must sense that the behavior has flowed from "the self." In the situation we have studied, subjects have precisely the opposite view of their actions—namely, they see them as originating in the motives of some other person. Subjects in the experiment frequently said, "If it were up to me, I would not have administered shocks to the learner."†

Harman's awkward use of the Milgram and Good Samaritan experiments makes one wonder whether what motivates him is really concern over allegedly grave social problems or whether

---

* Harman suggests (p. 329) that the recent "terrible events in Yugoslavia," which are "often attributed to historical 'ethnic hatreds,'" can be explained "in rational terms" involving limited resources and coalitions that exclude certain people, without any appeal to the idea of ethnic hatred. He also suggests that belief in character leads to blaming others and that we would be more tolerant of others' failures if we had greater understanding of their situations—a bit of threadbare morality that no one until now has believed inconsistent with the idea of moral character.

† Milgram, "The Perils of Obedience," p. 77. Milgram conducted an experiment to determine whether it was true that subjects "left to themselves" would not have administered the shocks, and he found that it was.

it is simply a dislike of the expectations, the habits of judgment, and the characteristic goals of the moral.

THE MORAL BRAIN: TROLLEYS AND CRYING BABIES

Psychologists and neurologists who do research into brain function in moral judgment frequently turn to philosophers for guidance. They have sometimes taken on philosophy's classic questions and investigated their hypotheses—that moral judgment is or is not like an intuition or that we have something like a moral sense, that reason or emotion dominates moral judgment or that moral judgments are "deontological" or "utilitarian."* Scientists have even borrowed hypothetical moral quandaries or dilemmas from philosophical texts.

The most famous of these quandaries is known as the "trolley example," and it has a number of variations.† In one

---

* A utilitarian theory claims that moral right is determined by actions' utility or the value of the consequences of actions (or classes of actions or rules about actions). Thus the classic utilitarian principle is that right is what produces the greatest utility, or good (in pleasure or happiness or welfare), for the greatest number of people. Deontological theories have nothing in common except that they all deny that an act's moral rightness depends on its utility. They might say, for example, that right actions are those that conform to rules or principles known through reason or rational intuition or those commanded by God or those established by an innate moral sense.

† It was invented by the British philosopher Philippa Foot. See Philippa Foot, "The Problem of Abortion and the Doctrine of the Double Effect," *Virtues and Vices* (Berkeley: University of California Press, 1978). The literature

standard version, the subject is asked to react to the following situation:

> You are near a point on the trolley tracks where the track splits in two. You can see that a single man is working on one of the tracks and that five people are working on the other. At the same time, you see that a trolley is barreling down the tracks and will strike the five and kill them all. At your hand is a switch that will divert the trolley to the track with one man. Throwing the switch will result in that man's death but will save the five. Should you throw the switch?

In a variation known as the "footbridge example," you again see the trolley barreling toward the five people, but this time:

> You are standing on a footbridge above the track, next to a large stranger. (You are a slight, not a large, person.) You quickly perceive that if you push the large person off the

---

on the trolley example is huge. Indeed, the literature on every aspect of the philosophical and scientific issues arising in the study of morality is now so enormous—and the debates are so hairsplitting and so often dubiously reasoned—that only those who devote their professional lives to them can be confident that they have a fine-tuned grasp of them. Unfortunately, the more that is written in a field, the less it is possible for a single person to know, and the more room there is for extrarational factors to influence which ideas succeed and become widely disseminated. It is perhaps why someone like Haidt openly resorts to coaxing his readers toward consensus. He knows how thoroughly politicized the process of fixing belief has become in the academy.

footbridge into the path of the trolley, you will stop it and save the lives of the five workmen in its path, although you will kill the large stranger.

A similar, famous example is the "crying baby" dilemma:

You and a number of others are hiding from the secret police. Your baby begins to cry, and if it continues, the secret police will hear it, discover your hiding place, and kill everyone, baby included. Should you smother the baby to silence it and save everyone else?★

Studies of people's responses to dilemmas like the trolley, footbridge, and crying baby cases have led experimenters to draw connections between emotion and deontology, on the one hand, and lack of emotion and utilitarian thinking on the other.† This connection between utilitarianism and coldhearted thinking is old and familiar. John Stuart Mill recalls in his *Autobiography* that for a short period in his youth he himself fit "the

---

★ Philosophers and scientists ask this question not because they want to know the right answer, but because they want to know which theory of moral judgment is true or how the brain works in moral deliberation. We should ask ourselves whether this motivation would not be likely to defeat actually understanding the moral question and how to address and answer it, and thus whether the use of hypothetical quandaries to test moral thought and moral brainwork is not a wrongheaded, or at least extremely limited, approach.

† See, for example, Joshua D. Greene, "The Secret Joke of Kant's Soul," in *The Neuroscience of Morality: Emotion, Brain Disorders, and Development*, vol. 3 of *Moral Psychology*, ed. Walter Sinnott-Armstrong (Cambridge, Mass.: MIT Press, 2007), pp. 39–91.

description so often given of a Benthamite as a mere reasoning machine," and he discusses at some length the accusations of coldness and hard-heartedness made against utilitarians, with their mistrust of feeling and dislike of sentimentality.*

Recently, a well-known and illuminating study tried to provide hard evidence that "normal moral judgment" in fact depends on emotion. The study compared the judgments of people with normal brains with those of people with lesions to the ventromedial prefrontal cortex (VMPC) that damaged their ability to experience emotion. If emotion plays no causal role in moral judgment, the experimenters hypothesized, VMPC patients' judgments would "show a normal pattern." If emotion did not play a causal role in moral judgment, they would show a more "utilitarian" pattern of judgment.[†]

The experiment tested twelve subjects with normal brains, twelve with brain damage that left their emotional capacities intact, and six with VMPC lesions that were believed to result in defective ability to experience emotion. All were given many scenarios to read, without time limits, but they were allowed only twenty-five seconds after reading the material to respond. The scenarios described hypothetical moral situations designed to inspire higher and lower levels of emotion. The footbridge, crying baby, and similar dilemmas were used to evoke higher emotions; the trolley and similar cases were used to evoke lower

---

* John Stuart Mill, *Autobiography* (1873) (Indianapolis: Bobbs-Merrill, 1957), pp. 71–72.

† Michael Koenigs, Liane Young, Ralph Adolphs, et al., "Damage to the Prefrontal Cortex Increases Utilitarian Moral Judgments," *Nature* 446 (2007): 908–11.

emotions. The subjects' responses were characterized as "utilitarian" when they favored the sacrifice of a single life to save
several lives.

The results were what John Stuart Mill would have predicted:
In the personal, high-emotion scenarios, about 45 percent of the
responses of the people with VMPC lesions affecting the capacity
for emotion, but only 20 percent of the responses of those with
normal brains, favored pushing the large stranger, smothering
the crying baby, or similar actions so as to save a group of people.
Those with brain damage that did not affect the emotions voted
much as the normal subjects did. The subjects with VMPC lesions
gave more "utilitarian" responses to high-emotion scenarios;*
but in lower-emotion scenarios, their responses were roughly the
same as the responses of those with normal brains: Half or slightly
more favored the "utilitarian" option.

The researchers concluded that "for a selective set of moral
dilemmas, the VMPC is critical for normal judgments of right
and wrong. The findings support a necessary role for emotion in
the generation of those judgments."† Normal people's judgments

---

* This conclusion is sometimes described as the claim that VMPC patients
were "more utilitarian" in their judgments, but that is misleading. A greater
percentage of VMPC patients' total responses than normal subjects' responses
were utilitarian in the high-emotion scenarios, but even then, slightly more
than half were not utilitarian. When a group makes many utilitarian responses, that is different from any or each individual in the group making
"more utilitarian judgments." The title of the study ("Damage to the Prefrontal Cortex Increases Utilitarian Moral Judgments") promotes the same
ambiguity.
† Koenigs et al., "Damage to the Prefrontal Cortex Increases Utilitarian
Moral Judgments," p. 908.

were less "utilitarian," and that fact was attributable to the influence of emotion on judgment. The experiment gives strong support to the views of those who, like myself, both reject utilitarianism and believe that emotion and affective states play a crucial role in morality.

But, though its outcome is welcome, and easy for people like myself to believe, we must not exaggerate what it can and cannot teach us. To begin with, the experimenters claim to have shown that in the relevant cases, emotion plays a causal role in the generation of *normal judgments of right and wrong*. In fact, they showed nothing about normal moral judgment; they showed only that emotion affected the reactions of people with normal brains.

Even the greatest proponent of the view that moral judgment must be based on reason alone, Immanuel Kant, believed that emotion usually dictates people's attempts to make moral judgments. But he, like *Star Trek*'s Mr. Spock, thought that it shouldn't, that moral judgment should be based on reason. Many wise and well-informed people agree with Kant and Mr. Spock: Good moral judgment should appeal only to reason, not to emotion, even though this is difficult and requires maturity and discipline. If they are right, then it is possible that many, or even most, normal-brained people often do not make good moral judgments because they let their feelings, or perhaps the wrong feelings, sway them. And if so, normal subjects' responses in the study are not unequivocal examples of *normal* moral judgment— unless, that is, we are willing to regard *poor* moral judgment as normal. But that would be an uncomfortable way of thinking about it; for to describe judgment as normal suggests that there is nothing wrong with it—something the experiment did not and could not show. Perhaps the lesson to be learned here is that the concept of a "normal" moral judgment is not of much use. At a minimum, we should avoid equating normal moral judgment with what people with normal brains, on average, judge, and recognize that if "normal moral judgment" means "good and acceptable judgment," then the experiment does not show that it is emotion-dependent. The experiment cannot tell us whose judgments were better; and its results are consistent with the hypothesis that in high-emotion scenarios a number of the normal subjects had their good judgment *overthrown* by emotion.

The studies' conclusions are questionable on an even more basic ground. There are several weighty reasons to doubt that the study actually succeeded in inducing subjects to make any moral judgments at all. The first reason is the twenty-five-second time limit for responding. To call quick responses "moral judgment" is to treat first reactions as judgment. Conceivably, however, when we have more time, we deliberate in morally crucial ways that this experiment does not address. Certainly, what we think after twenty-five seconds is very often not what we think on reflection, and we are very likely to reject and modify or overthrow our first, often emotional, reactions when we think them over. In unimportant circumstances we may try to think no further, but in important situations quick, initial takes may initiate a long process of judgment, and typically, when we face serious moral problems, we have plenty of time for pondering, investigating, and debating.

Moral emergencies, in which we are forced to act on our first "take" on a situation, are rare; and in such situations we are likely to say that we had no time to judge. It is not uncommon for people to puzzle for hours, days, months, or years to reach important decisions. Sometimes the time is needed to understand complicated realities, including other people. The moral mind also often needs time to educate itself about itself. If it finds that under certain circumstances its reactions are distorted, unreliable, or weak, it compensates in complicated ways; it temporizes and seeks counterbalances. Moral judgment in a self-observant and conscientious person may rely on many such delicate adjustments. Seat-of-the-pants reactions are also part of the moral life, but they are not at its core, and they do not really amount to an exercise of judgment.

Yet another reason to doubt that this and similar experiments induce any moral judgment is the fact that the moral problems used in the experiment are merely hypothetical. On this point, there is everything to be said for Hume's view that while moral science is necessary, possible, and desirable, it cannot make use of purposeful experimentation in the way that the natural sciences do.* In the nature of the case, real moral judgment can happen only when someone actually must make a moral decision, that is, one in which self-worth and identity are at stake and in which guilt, self-approval, anxiety, and similar feelings are aroused by aspects of the situation calling for

---

* David Hume, Introduction to *A Treatise of Human Nature: Being an Attempt to Introduce the Experimental Method of Reasoning into Moral Subjects* (1739–1740), ed. David Fate Norton and Mary J. Norton (Oxford: Oxford University Press, 2007), p. 6. Hume speaks generally—correctly, in my view—of the likelihood that arranged, formal experiments on moral behavior would derange the natural principles that one wishes to learn about. Thus there can be no experimental moral science on the model of the physical sciences, and the disciplines that must teach us about ourselves are those whose "experiments" look only at the way people behave "in the common course of the world, by men's behaviour in company, in affairs, and in their pleasures."

judgment—as they would be for Macbeth contemplating murder or Lincoln contemplating the Emancipation Proclamation.
None of this happens when subjects respond to hypothetical
dilemmas faced by a fictional other, in which they themselves
have no direct or indirect stake. The reactions examined by this
experiment may tap capacities relevant to morality, but what
real people would think, feel, and do in real life-and-death situations will be very different from what research subjects think
and feel in fake ones. Furthermore, the more obviously unrealistic or strikingly improbable the scenarios, the less likely they
are to arouse authentic or significant moral emotion and moral
thought. It does not take a brain scientist to know that armchair
moralizing is unlike what one does when one is actually in the
hot seat.

Experimental studies like this one, which rely on moral quandaries to examine moral judgment, are also limited by their failure to investigate the thinking of the test subjects. What questions
did they *take* themselves to be answering? What was the meaning
of their answers? What was their reasoning? What personal history lay behind a response? This knowledge would be necessary
even to give an accurate description of a response as utilitarian, at
least in philosophers' terms. A subject who concludes that one
ought not push the large stranger off the footbridge may nonetheless be reasoning as a utilitarian—one who assigns very high
disutility to that action or to a rule prescribing it.

Finally, the unanswerable nature of some of the test questions is also a reason for doubting that they induce real moral
judgment for study. The unanswerable problems require us to
choose between equal evils or incommensurate evils, evils we
cannot choose between or compare, and often require us to

contemplate action in circumstances where we are ignorant of key facts. Any choice we make inspires some degree of uncertainty and a restless, ineffectual mental search for an escape from the dilemma. We continue to scour our brains for a solution that, given the nature of the problem, is impossible. But in these cases what we experience is not real moral doubt because there is no real moral question in our minds.

Moral dilemmas of the type illustrated by the trolley example can be constructed out of any two distinct and important moral values. One need only have enough imagination to construct a factual scenario in which it is not possible to serve two values simultaneously. As any competent writer of fiction will confirm, it is always possible to do this. In fact, all of morality is always potentially open to the kind of inauthentic doubt that the trolley example creates, doubt that does not demand an answer. For real moral judgment to occur, real doubt and a real moral question must arise, and in the absence of any reality that placed the experiment's subjects, morally speaking, on the line, they do not experience it. For the same reason, they do not really make a moral judgment. The study tells us things, but it does not tell us about moral judgment and the moral life.

MUCH EMPIRICAL STUDY of moral thinking, in particular that portion of it oriented toward evolutionary biology, is compromised by bias, ill-formed hypotheses, and conceptual confusion. Some is sheer speculation unsupported by evidence. Those who carry out such research too often seem to be poorly equipped to cope with the culture-laden, history-bound, and multiply ambiguous concepts involved in the subjects they investigate. Sometimes, too, they appear to lack any internal understanding of the moral life—the understanding of someone who lives it and is part of it. That deficiency leads them to adopt gratuitously cynical, skeptical, and skewed views about morality, which they sometimes approach with hostile intent, and to offer naive proposals for fundamental reform of the highest human capacities. Their investigations into the moral mind and the moral life, their antimoral theories of the moral, are a sad illustration of how today's university participates in the deterioration around it. Those of us who are looking for understanding of the moral mind and the moral life can no longer turn to the academy to find it.

Afterword

MORAL DISAGREEMENT
AND MORAL TRUTH

DISAGREEMENTS ABOUT MORALS are of two types. One arises among people with the moral psychology. The other arises between those who have the moral psychology and those who do not. They are very different kinds of disagreements. The disagreements of the culture wars were mostly of the second sort. Among people with the moral psychology, there was substantial consensus on much of what got debated in the culture wars. Within the moral point of view and among moral minds, disagreements are often resolvable, and debate proceeds under the premise that moral truth exists and can be found if we search hard enough and have enough patience.

Although many people have become convinced that to believe in the existence of moral truth is to subscribe to moral dogmatism, rigidity, arrogance, and intolerance, the ideal of truth is what actually saves us from such errors. Once we give up the ideal of truth, as moral relativism does, we have little motive for scouring our beliefs and commitments to discover whether and where we may have gone wrong. But we need not abandon this ideal. A straightforward idea of moral truth will allow us to approach moral inquiry with the confidence we need to let us devote ourselves to the search for shared understanding and a common ground.

If by "moral people," we mean people with the mentality described in this book, whose various moral traits exist along a spectrum of weak to strong, and if by "morality" we mean the values that the thinking of such people converges on, then we might fruitfully define moral truth as the opinion that moral people exercising their moral capacity would *eventually agree on*,★ whether soon or in a long distant future, provided that their characters and judgments were mature, balanced, and consistent and provided that they were thoroughly, deeply knowledgeable about the matter being judged. This is a definition of moral truth that easily accommodates the realities of moral life, including the evolution of moral ideas, moral uncertainty and fallibility, moral progress and regress, and the multivalenced complexity of moral truth. It avoids relativism, on the one hand, and, on the other, dogmatism and the fanatical certainties of those whose ideas of right and wrong rest on absolutes dictated by religious and other authorities. It recognizes how getting things right morally depends on understanding one another and the world we live in factually and empirically. It harks back to natural law theories in pinning moral truth to something that could be called human nature. It differs from older theories of this type in insisting that the human nature involved is a second nature, a cultural type or a historical psychological type, not a universal nature shared by

---

★ This is a paraphrase of Charles Sanders Peirce's "fallibilist" definition of scientific truth as what the community of rational inquirers would ultimately come to agree upon, in the infinitely distant future.

all human beings, while retaining the truth that moral values govern us all.

Much moral disagreement—and here I mean only conflicts of moral value, not conflicts between moral and nonmoral value systems—stems from minor causes; it irons itself out over time as we understand one another better and allow for emphases that reflect proximity, perspective, poor information, personal prejudice, differences in training, education, and culture, and similar factors. All of us, for example, occasionally subscribe to some view only because most people or our families or neighbors do, without having looked closely at the reasons for it or even the motives of those whose opinions we borrow. Moral disagreement also derives from failures in rationality, as when we are tempted to believe what flatters our ego or serves our desire for revenge. Differences in religious belief, knowledge, understanding, intelligence, and education produce considerable moral disagreement. There are often disagreements between those who do and do not have personal or professional experiences relevant to reaching a sound decision, and sometimes personal experience, personal flaws, or high emotion may blind us. Most of us have limited moral imagination in some respect or other—an inability to put ourselves into certain shoes or to adjust to some startling idea; few people can imagine the experience of those who are very different from themselves. And time alone has a large effect on moral opinion.

Certain characteristics of moral questions and answers, as compared with those of mathematics or science, contribute to the error of thinking that real moral truth does not exist. Of course, in many everyday situations there is a single "right thing to do," just as there is a single right answer to scientific and mathematical questions. But in ordinary moral situations, there are often several ways to do right as well as several ways to do wrong, and some of the right or permissible actions may be better or worse than others, and some ways of doing wrong, likewise, may be better or worse than others. Or, we might say, in many cases, that there are ranges of permissible and impermissible action and thought, and thus room for broad agreement alongside disagreements. In such cases, we may make the error of thinking that the range and variety of choices mean that there is no truth, or that a worse choice is wrong when it is only not quite as good as another, or that a wrong choice is right when it is only not as bad as another; or we fail to see how our differences are ripples in a sea of agreement. In situations with heroic dimensions, these confusions are particularly likely to arise, and we are prone to confuse ideals with duties or "musts." There are also situations in which it is impossible not to sacrifice one or another grave moral principle.

Finally, there are certain good decisions that are right only for the people who make them. Although moral values are universal, some of these universal values concern our obligations to ourselves, and these in turn may vary according to our characters, histories, and life situations. There are also obligations that turn on our individual capacities, qualities, social debts, or other factors. Thus, individuals may rightly know that they must take steps that seem unnecessary, foolish, or plain wrong to others because they rest on inner, invisible factors. These situations, too, can become the subject of intense moral quarreling, especially in intimate relationships.

Then there is the simple fact that sometimes we disagree because of the ways in which we are not equally good. Although no one is perfect, some people, in this or that respect or from time to time, under different circumstances, may have more insight, more kindness, more self-control, or more courage than the rest of us. To make the same point from the opposite direction, at times all of us are stubborn, blind, or cranky or have other dispositions that impede our ability to reach and accept good judgments. And there are people who see more clearly than most others even when their behavior falls short of what they know. Virtue is admired and honored because it is hard. Moral inequality is particularly difficult for Americans to accept, even when the superior character is modest and unassuming. Americans do not like to think that some people are better than others in any way, even morally. This makes them want to see moral virtue as average and expectable, but morality is not normality. To think so confuses the equal right to moral respect with equality of moral character, and the equal right to have an opinion—and to vote it—with having equally right opinions. Morality itself underlies this error because egalitarianism is an important moral value. This fact can easily disguise the error, for it allows it to be seen as a form of virtue instead of the offended narcissism that it really is.

In cases where moral-minded, sincere, and hard-thinking people continue to disagree, even after long deliberation and careful weighing of factors of individual psychology, we acknowledge the others' right to their opinion, but unless there is some specific reason to think so, we do not conclude that this is one of those cases in which individual considerations create personal answers. Nor do we decide that this is one of those cases in which the alternatives are roughly equal in moral quality unless we have figured out, objectively, that this is true. On the contrary, what we say is, "We'll wait and see." In the mean-time, we respect the difference and grant one another as much freedom as possible to think and act according to conscience. This waiting for time, events, experience, or intelligence to shed light on a moral question can be a long process. It may be our descendants, not we ourselves, who finally reach the truth. What we must not do is conclude that because at present we do not have the answer, no answer exists. Since we look back on a history of moral progress, in which we can see that answers were slowly carved out of confusion, we also look forward to a future in which new truths are uncovered, new solutions devised.

The idea of moral truth is partly what makes possible an idea of "us" over against self (an "us" that disregards race, religion, sex, political affiliations, and other morally irrelevant groupings of human beings) in a way that feels not alienating or oppres-sive, but reassuring and strengthening. Confidence in the ideal of moral truth provides the common ground that lets us feel this way and allows us to turn to one another for help when we cannot find answers.

The search for moral truth is strongly social. Although moral autonomy requires that ultimately we each judge moral matters for ourselves, this does not mean that we ignore what others think or that our moral education occurs in isolation. On the way to making up our individual minds, we draw on traditions and we seek others' opinions, insights, and knowl-edge. We watch one another's faces and strain to sense shared and conflicting emotions in order to test our own and to be alert to what we may have missed. We check in with one another, not so as to avoid the responsibility of autonomous judgment, but so as to refine and check judgment against a shared reality. This process not only helps us to locate moral truth and avoid error, by letting us learn what others see from their vantage points, but it helps us to avoid dogmatism. It also lets us sometimes laugh at the same things, feel grateful together, share indignation, and work for common goals. It is one of life's reliable sources of pleasure, fellow feeling, and confidence. It is what allays the feeling that the center cannot hold, that I am alone in the midst of turmoil, confusion, cruelty, and danger. For moral individuals trying to find their way in a chaotic antimoral world, understanding these dimensions of the search for moral truth is utterly essential to perseverance, hope, and strength.

The kinds of public debates about values that have marked the past few decades, splitting families, states, and the nation, are virulent and dangerous in part because they are moderated by no idea of shared truth, of common ground, or of "us." Because they are quarrels among people with mentalities that are not only different but inherently at odds with one another, they are often genuinely irresolvable from the point of view of logic and truth. Once the differences are clearly and thoroughly laid out, these debates must always come down to the question of what sort of person it is better to be: a person with the moral shape of mind or some other sort of person. And who but a Tiresias of morality could know the answer?

Tiresias, of course, was the seer in Greek myth whom Hera punished by turning him into a woman for seven years. One day, after Hera had changed him back into a man, she and Zeus called him in to settle a quarrel. Who had more pleasure in sex, they asked him, men or women? Hera thought men, but Zeus thought women. Only Tiresias could tell them.★ Likewise, the only person who could tell us whether it would be better to have the moral psychology or some premoral psychology would be someone who had experience of both.

Happily, each of us is to some extent a moral Tiresias. We begin life as a nonmoral creature and for several years have only the rudiments of conscience. We can all remember something of what that was like. It is also true that we never lose our premoral character. The moral mind builds over and around it and governs it, but it stays with us. All of us have tried life both ways, moral and nonmoral, and we can all give ourselves fairly good answers to the question as to which is better. If we strain our memories, our imaginations, and our empathic perceptions of our own early life and the premoral parts of our own psyche, we will conclude that the moral life is far preferable. We will do so despite its genuine costs and strenuous demands on us, despite the suppression of self-interest and pleasure that morality so often calls for and the ease with which it sometimes misfires

---

★ Tiresias answered that of ten parts pleasure in sex, men got one, in other words that women had nine times more pleasure in sex than men—a surprising answer from our contemporary point of view. It made Hera so angry that she struck Tiresias blind. But it is unclear whether she was angry simply because he had told her that she had lost the argument or because of what his answer implied about women. Perhaps his answer reflected the idea that men were less physical, more rational, less animal, and hence superior; women were more physical and animal, and though that meant they experienced more animal pleasure, it also meant that they were inferior. Today, when we are more accepting of our animal, physical nature, the common prejudice, probably equally false, is that men experience greater sexual pleasure than women.

and causes useless suffering. The same conclusion follows from observation of the built-in pain and frustration of premoral thinking in others. Morality is that lovely invention that makes happiness the consequence of goodness. No one who understood would choose anything else.

ACKNOWLEDGMENTS

Many generous friends and colleagues reviewed all or part of this book and saved it from error and oversight. Nancy Miller, my editor at Bloomsbury USA, is the book's godmother. She offered it a home, then protected and improved it, poring over each manuscript page, penciling in scores of hard questions, insights, corrections, and encouragements with a gentle and generous hand. I am deeply grateful to her and the other wonderfully talented people at Bloomsbury with whom I have had the honor and pleasure of working.

Sarah Flynn's well-tempered insight, advice, and moral sense were truly invaluable; her moral sense and her calm, kindhearted intelligence enabled me to find the style and tone I wanted to write with. It was a great privilege to be able to avail myself of Geri Thoma's brainpower, wit, knowledge, and sound guidance, but you might have to know her to believe just how wonderful and unusual she is.

Several other people read all or part of the manuscript at various stages and made crucial contributions to its ultimate shape. Edward Mendelson read and responded to every draft with an unmatched moral intelligence and a scholar's watchful eye. What I have learned from him and owe him is more than I can describe. James Mendelson, our son, debated the ideas of the book with me through high school and three years of college. He read and commented most helpfully on a late draft. His clear, cogent thinking and talent for discovering examples have benefited many passages in this book.

David Bromwich offered a number of shrewd, eye-opening comments which I have gratefully incorporated.

Anne and Terry Vance showed great skill in shredding arguments with one-liners at breakfast, after having read themselves to sleep with the book's first drafts, pieces of which they found strewn around the house. As a result of their influence, several sections of the book have been saved from murk. Anne also talked through countless issues addressed in the book with me over countless lunches, and for whatever clarity I achieved on these I am greatly indebted to her.

Paula Holm read and offered invaluable comments on chapter 5 with her usual combination of kindness, sane perspective, and intelligence.

I am also glad to acknowledge people from my past whose influence goes far to explain why I wrote this book. These include, notably, Robert L. Holmes, who taught me moral philosophy and clear thinking, and Lewis White Beck, from whom I learned the history of thought and the difference between substance and fluff. Both were equally moral models and scholars whose ultimate loyalty was to truth—qualities even more rare today than they were in my graduate student days. Rick Werner was an invaluable comrade in learning in those days, always ready to talk it through, always thinking, always asking the right questions, and always generous.

I am especially grateful to Christopher Lasch, who first suggested I write on these subjects and guided my earliest thinking and reading aimed at finding a way of doing so. I am among many who know that they might have done better had he been here to offer his wisdom and moral clarity.

INDEX

pseudoscience, 216
psychoanalytic study of morality,
    77–78, 114–17, 140*n*, 227–28,
    228*n*
purity and disgust, 254–58, 255*n*

Qaeda, al-, 178–79
Quincy, Samuel, 41*n*

rage. *See* narcissism
rationality, 24–25, 56–57
    and morality, 24–25, 27, 30, 38,
        56–57, 83, 111
    narcissism, flawed in 79–80
    disgust, overriding, 157, 257
    and science, 56, 212–13
rationalization, 95–96, 96*n*,
    258–59
Rawls, John, 221, 222, 236*n*
Red Cross, International Com-
    mittee of, 149
redemption and atonement, 16
regulatory czar of White House,
    95–96
Rehnquist, William, 162–63
relativism. *See* moral relativism;
    universal governance of
    morality
religion
    and abortion, 160–61
    antiabortion movement,
        160–62
    Christianity, 29, 74*n*, 81–82,
        100, 104–5
    and cool, 175
    fundamentalism, 74*n*, 75, 97, 100,
        106, 157, 159, 164, 175, 252.
    and moral culture, 40
    Mormon, 105–6, 106–108*n*
    torture, approval of 154
respect, 255–56, 255*n*

retaliation, refusal of, 73*n*
revenge. *See* vengeance; ven-
    geance in law; authoritarian
    antimoralism, revenge and
    punishment
reversal fantasies, 167. *See also*
    cool
right-to-life movement, 160–62
Right wing and conservatives
    anomic antimoralism, 88–90
    antimoralism, 11, 31–33, 96–98,
        146, 148
    authoritarian antimoralism,
        100–9, 255–56
    cool conservatives, 177–79
    family as battlefield, 112–13
    historical conservatism vs.
        contemporary Right, 89–90,
        103, 145–46
    "moral majority", 31, 150–51
    opposition to legal reform,
        189–91
    spirit of murderousness, 102
    See also antimoralism, authori-
        tarian antimoralism,
        premoral psychology
Roe v. Wade, 162–63
rule of law, 186, 188. *See* law;
    vengeance in law

sadism
    of authoritarian antimoralism,
        100, 102, 104
    of Bush administration,
        154–55
    and cool, 175, 179, 183
    and police bullying, 201–2
    in prisons, 189–90
    sympathy and empathy vs.,
        55–56
    See also cruelty; torture

ABOUT THE AUTHOR

CHERYL MENDELSON teaches philosophy at Barnard College. She has also taught at Columbia and Purdue Universities and has practiced law in New York City. Her eclectic writings range from philosophy to housekeeping to fiction. She is the author of *Home Comforts* and a trilogy of novels set in Manhattan's Morningside Heights. She lives in New York City with her husband and son.